A BEGINNI[I0016049]
GUIDE TO
INTERNET
OF THINGS
F U N D A M E N T A L S

A V L N SUJITH
T.S. SANDEEP
G SUNIL KUMAR

INDIA · SINGAPORE · MALAYSIA

Notion Press

Old No. 38, New No. 6
McNichols Road, Chetpet
Chennai - 600 031

First Published by Notion Press 2019
Copyright © AVLN Sujith T.S. Sandeep G Sunil Kumar 2019
All Rights Reserved.

ISBN 978-1-64678-731-9

CONTENTS

UNIT - I 5

UNIT - II 47

UNIT - III 107

UNIT - IV 157

UNIT - V 265

UNIT - I

1. Introduction to Internet of Things

IOT refers to an Internet of Things (IOT). Connecting any device (including everything from cell phones, vehicles, home appliances and other wearable embedded with sensors and actuators) with Internet so that these objects can exchange data with each other on a network. The IOT devices can create information about individual's behaviors, analyze it, and take action (IOT is smarter than Internet).

Life is Easier with IOT

The IoT gadgets can make data about individual's practices, dissect it, and make a move. IoT an inquiry would emerge in your mind that why we are worried about IoT? Here is the appropriate response that we say for instance you are headed to a gathering; your vehicle could approach your timetable and as of now realize the best course to take. On the off chance that the activity is overwhelming your vehicle may send content to the next gathering advising them that you will be late. Imagine a scenario in which you wake up timer awakens you at 6 a.m. and afterward informs your espresso producer to begin making espresso for you? Having the capacity to turn the lights on in your home or warming before getting back home utilizing your Smartphone? Truly, every one of these things is conceivable due to IOT.

Smart System and the Internet of the Things are driven by a mix for:

1. Sensors and Actuators
2. Connectivity
3. People and Process

1. **Sensors and Actuators:** we are giving our world a digital nervous system. Location data using GPS sensors. Eyes and ears using cameras and microphones, along with sensory organs that can measure everything from temperature to pressure changes.

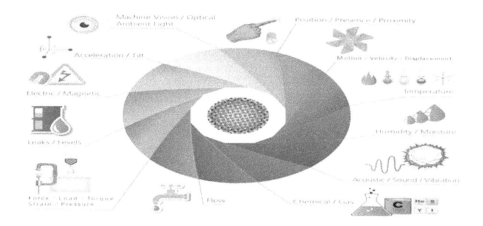

2. **Connectivity:** These inputs are digitized and placed onto networks.

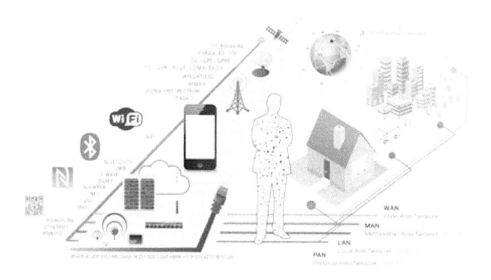

3. **People and Process:** These networked inputs can then be combined into bio-directional systems that integrate data, people, process and systems for better decision making.

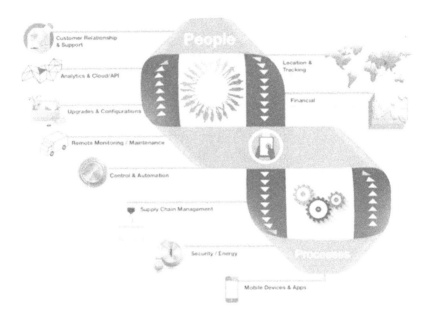

IOT frameworks enable clients to accomplish further mechanization, investigation, and reconciliation inside a framework. They enhance the scope of these territories and their precision. IOT uses existing and rising innovation for detecting, systems administration, and mechanical autonomy. IOT abuses ongoing advances in programming, falling equipment costs, and current mentalities towards innovation. Its new and propelled components bring significant change in the conveyance of items, merchandise, and benefits; and the social, financial, and political effect of those changes. The most essential highlights of IoT incorporate man-made brainpower, availability, sensors, dynamic commitment, and little gadget utilize. They key features of IoT are given underneath:

- **AI** –IOT basically makes for all intents and purposes anything smart, which means it improves each part of existence with the intensity of information gathering, man-made brainpower calculations, and systems. This can mean something as basic as improving your fridge and cupboards to recognize when drain and your most loved grain run low, and to then put in a request with your favored food merchant

- **Connectivity** – New empowering advances for systems administration, and explicitly IOT organizing, mean systems are not any more solely attached to significant suppliers. Systems can exist on an a lot littler and less expensive scale while as yet being functional. IOT makes these little systems between its framework gadgets.

- **Sensors** – IOT loses its qualification without sensors. They go about as characterizing instruments which change IOT from a standard latent system of gadgets into a functioning framework prepared to do true incorporation.

- **Active Engagement** –Much of the present association with associated innovation occurs through latent commitment. IOT presents another worldview for dynamic substance, item, or administration commitment.

- **Small Devices** –Devices, as anticipated, have turned out to be littler, less expensive, and all the more amazing after some time. IOT abuses reason fabricated little gadgets to convey its exactness, adaptability, and flexibility.

1.1 Advantages

The benefits of IOT range over each region of way of life and business.

- **Improved Customer Engagement** – Current investigation experience the ill effects of vulnerable sides and noteworthy blemishes in precision; and as noted, commitment stays aloof. IOT totally changes this to accomplish more extravagant and more successful commitment with gatherings of people.

- **Technology Optimization** – similar advances and information which enhance the client encounter additionally enhance gadget utilize, and help in more intense upgrades to innovation. IOT opens a universe of basic useful and field information.

- **Reduced Waste** – IOT makes territories of enhancement clear. Current investigation give us shallow knowledge, however IOT gives certifiable data prompting more powerful administration of assets.

- **Enhanced Data Collection** – Modern information accumulation experiences its confinements and its plan for uninvolved utilize. IOT breaks it out of those spaces, and places it precisely where people truly need to go to examine our reality. It permits a precise picture of everything.

1.2 Disadvantages

Though IOT conveys a noteworthy arrangement of advantages, it additionally shows a critical arrangement of difficulties. Here is a rundown of a few its significant issues:

- **Security** – IOT makes a biological system of always associated gadgets imparting over systems. The framework offers little control regardless of any safety efforts. This leaves clients presented to different sorts of assailants.

- **Privacy** – The modernity of IOT gives considerable individual information in extraordinary detail without the client's dynamic investment.

- **Complexity** – Some discover IOT frameworks convoluted as far as structure, organization, and upkeep given their utilization of various innovations and a substantial arrangement of new empowering advances.

- **Flexibility** –Many are worried about the adaptability of an IOT framework to coordinate effectively with another. They stress over winding up with a few clashing or bolted frameworks.

- **Compliance** – IOT, similar to some other innovation in the domain of business, must consent to directions. Its intricacy influences the issue of consistence to appear to be unbelievably testing when many consider standard programming consistence a fight.

1.3 Application Areas for the Internet of Things

1. Smart Home

The idea of Smart Home is raised to spare time, vitality and cash. With the presentation of Smart Homes, we would have the capacity to switch on cooling before achieving home or turn off lights even in the wake of leaving home or open the ways to companions for brief access notwithstanding when you are not at home.

2. Smart Cities

Smart urban communities' Smart reconnaissance, robotized transportation, more astute vitality the board frameworks, water conveyance, urban security and natural checking all are instances of web of things applications for keen urban communities.

IOT will tackle real issues looked by the general population living in urban areas like contamination, movement blockage and lack of vitality supplies and so forth. By introducing sensors and utilizing web applications, subjects can discover free accessible stopping openings over the city. Additionally, the sensors can recognize meter altering issues, general breakdowns and any establishment issues in the power framework.

3. Wearables

Wearable gadgets are introduced with sensors and virtual products which gather information and data about the clients. This information is later pre-prepared to extricate basic experiences about client. These gadgets comprehensively cover wellness, wellbeing and amusement prerequisites. The pre-essential from web of things innovation for wearable applications is to be exceptionally vitality productive or ultra-low power and little measured.

4. Healthcare

IOT in social insurance is gone for engaging individuals to live more beneficial life and standard checkup by wearing associated gadgets. The gathered information will help in customized investigation of an individuals wellbeing and give customized procedures to battle sickness.

1.4 Challenges to IOT

In the period of IOT, everything is associated, connected up? much more than we see in and around us. IOT is absolutely opening way to a considerable measure of chances yet additionally to numerous difficulties.

- **Security Challenges—IOT can be hacked**

IOT can be hacked Security is a major issue with IOT gadgets. With billions of gadgets being associated together over Internet, by what means can individuals make sure that their data is secure? These security issues can be of the accompanying

- **Data Encryption**

IOT applications gather huge amounts of information. Information recovery and handling is vital piece of the entire IOT condition. The majority of this information is close to home and should be secured through encryption. Encryption is broadly utilized on the web to secure client data being sent between a program and a server, including passwords, installment data and other individual data that ought to be viewed as private. Associations and people utilize encryption to secure delicate information put away on PCs, servers and cell phones like telephones or tablets.

- **Data Authentication**

After effective encryption of information odds of gadget itself being hacked still exist. On the off chance that there is no real way to build up the realness of the information being conveyed to and from an IOT gadget, security is imperiled. For example, say you constructed a temperature sensor for savvy homes. Despite the fact that you scramble the information it exchanges is there is no real way to confirm the wellspring of information then anybody can make up phony information and send it to

- **Side-channel Attacks**

Encryption and validation both set up still leave scope for side channel assaults. Such assaults center less around the data and more on how that data is being exhibited. For example on the off chance that somebody can get to information like planning data, control utilization or electromagnetic release, the majority of this data can be utilized for side channel assaults

1.5 Physical Design of IOT

Devices and Local Networks

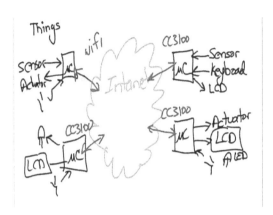

Many individuals have endeavored to characterize the Internet of Things. Here are a few definitions: Making a portion of the things that we are utilizing has the capacity of Internet get to (keen things). Anything that can be joined to it preparing unit (microcontroller) and associated with the Internet is viewed as a thing in the realm of IOT.

CC3100 is Wi-Fi and Internet-of-Things answer for MCU Applications. The CC3100 gadget is the industry first Wi-Fi CERTIFIED chip utilized in the remote systems administration arrangement. It is stick good with TM4C123GXL ARM Launch pad. Microcontrollers can be Arduino, TM4C123G ARM processor, and so on. In IOT, we think how to fabricate interconnected items. IOT equipment ought to dependably be ease, so we can surge the planet with IOT gadgets. IOT frameworks are not confounded, but rather structuring and constructing them can be a perplexing undertaking. We as of now have every one of the apparatuses we require today to begin making the IOT a reality. The initial phase in building an IOT gadget is to make sense of how it will speak with whatever remains of the world.

Your decision of correspondence innovation straightforwardly influences your devices equipment necessities and expenses. So which organizing innovation is the best decision? For instance: a manufacturing plant as a run of the mill case for an IOT framework. A production line would require countless sensors and actuators scattered over a wide region. A remote innovation would be the best fit. This is a remote sensor organize. Information from every sensor goes through the system hub to-hub. The hubs in a remote sensor organize are minimal effort gadgets, so they can be sent in high volume. They likewise work at low power with the goal that they can keep running on battery, or even utilize advances, for example, vitality reaping.

An edge hub goes about as a portal between the remote sensor organize and the Internet. It can likewise perform neighborhood handling, give nearby capacity, and can have a UI. The main clear systems administration contender for an IOT gadget is Wi-Fi, in light of the fact that it's all over. There are more up to date organizing advances that take into account the improvement of ease, low-control arrangements. One of the real bits of low-control remote is the IEEE 802.15.4 radio standard. It was discharged in 2003. 6LoWPAN has been received by organizations, for example, ARM and Cisco. 6LoWPAN gives embodiment and header pressure systems that take into account briefer transmission times. 6LoWPAN will be the decision for remote sensor systems and for other IOT frameworks that require IP-based conventions. On the off chance that IOT arrange is neighborhood and machine-to-machine, the remote conventions are great hopefuls. In any case, if the objective is to remotely control gadgets or generally transmit information over the Internet, we'll require IPv6.

Its essential that IOT arranges all make utilization of the suite of Internet conventions. That's UDP, TCP, SSL, HTTP, etc and must help IPv6. Why? Since the current IPv4 standard faces a worldwide tending to lack, and in addition restricted help for multicast, and poor worldwide portability. With IPv6, it is a lot less difficult for an IOT gadget to acquire a worldwide IP address (open IP), which empowers effective distributed correspondence. The significance of IP to the Internet of Things doesn't naturally imply that non-IP systems are pointless. It just implies that non-IP systems will require a passage to achieve the Internet.

Logical Design of IOT

This subject advises how to structure an information warehousing condition, and incorporates the accompanying themes:

- Logical versus Physical
- Create a Logical Design
- Data Warehousing Schemas

1. Logical vs. Physical

If you are perusing this guide, almost certainly, your association has officially chosen to manufacture an information distribution center. Additionally, all things considered, the business prerequisites are as of now characterized, the extent of your application has been settled upon, and you have a calculated plan. So now you have to make an interpretation of your necessities into a framework deliverable. In this progression, you make the legitimate and physical plan for the information distribution center and, simultaneously, characterize the explicit information content, connections inside and between gatherings of information, the framework condition supporting your information product house and, simultaneously, characterize the explicit information content, connections inside and between gatherings of information, the framework condition supporting is invigorated. The intelligent structure is more reasonable and conceptual than the physical plan. In the logical Design, you take a gander at the coherent connections among the articles. In the physical design, you take a gander at the best way your information distribution center, the information changes required, and the recurrence with which information of putting away and recovering the articles. Your plan ought to be situated toward the requirements of the end clients. End clients regularly need to perform examination and take a gander at accumulated information, as opposed to at individual exchanges. Your plan is driven basically by end-client utility; however the end clients may not recognize what they require until the point when they see it. An all around arranged plan considers development and changes as the requirements of clients change and advance. By starting with the coherent plan, you center on the data necessities without getting hindered promptly with quickly with execution detail.

2. Create a Logical Design

An intelligent plan is a theoretical, unique structure. You don't manage the physical execution points of interest yet; you bargain just with characterizing the kinds of data that you require. The procedure of intelligent plan includes organizing information into a progression of sensible connections called substances and properties. An entity represents a lump of data. In social databases, an element regularly maps to a table. An attribute is a part of an element and characterizes the uniqueness of the element. In social databases, a credit maps to a segment. You can make the sensible structure utilizing a pen and paper, or you can utilize a plan instrument, for example, Oracle Warehouse Builder or Oracle Designer. While substance relationship charting has customarily been related with profoundly standardized models, for example, online exchange handling (OLTP) applications, the method is as yet helpful in dimensional demonstrating. You simply approach it in an unexpected way. In dimensional demonstrating, rather than trying to find nuclear units of data and the majority of the connections between them, you attempt to recognize which data has a place with a focal actuality table(s) and which data has a place with its related measurement tables. One yield of the coherent structure is an arrangement of substances and ascribes comparing to certainty tables and measurement tables. Another yield of mapping is operational information from your source into subject-arranged data in your objective information distribution center blueprint. You recognize business subjects or fields of information, characterize connections between business subjects, and name the characteristics for each subject. The components that assistance you to decide the information distribution center blueprint are the model of your source information and your client prerequisites. Here and there, you can get the source show from your organization's endeavor information model and figure out the consistent information display for the information distribution center from this. The physical usage of the intelligent information stockroom model may require a few changes because of your framework parameters- - size of machine, number of clients, stockpiling limit, sort of system, and programming.

3. Data Warehousing Schemas

A mapping is a gathering of database objects, including tables, sees, files, and equivalent words. There are an assortment of methods for masterminding mapping objects in the pattern models intended for information warehousing. Most information distribution centers utilize a dimensional model.

- **Star Schemas**

The star mapping is the least complex information stockroom composition. It is known as a star blueprint in light of the fact that the chart of a star pattern takes after a star, with focuses transmitting from an inside. The focal point of the star comprises of at least one actuality tables and the purposes of the star are the measurement tables demonstrated inFigure2-1:

Unlike other database structures, in a star pattern, the measurements are de-normalized. That is, the measurement tables have repetition which kills the requirement for different joins on measurement tables. In a star pattern, just a single join is expected to set up the connection between the reality table and any of the measurement tables. The primary preferred standpoint to a star blueprint is streamlined execution. A star pattern keeps inquiries basic and gives quick reaction time since all the data about each dimension is put away in one column. See Chapter16, "Mappings", for additional data with respect to blueprints. Note: Oracle prescribes you pick a star mapping except if you have an unmistakable reason not to.

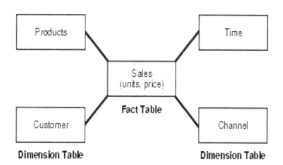

Figure 2.1 Star Schema

- **Other Schemas**

Some compositions utilize third ordinary frame as opposed to star mappings or the dimensional model.

Data Warehousing Objects

The accompanying sorts of items are usually utilized in information distribution centers: Fact tables are the focal tables in your stockroom pattern. Truth tables commonly contain realities and outside keys to the measurement tables. Certainty tables speak to information typically numeric and added substance that can be investigated and analyzed. Models incorporate Sales, Cost, and Profit. Measurement tables, otherwise called query or reference tables, contain the generally static information in the stockroom. Precedents are stores or items.

Fact Tables

A reality table is a table in a star pattern that contains actualities. A reality table commonly has two sorts of segments: those that contain actualities, and those that are outside keys to measurement tables. A reality table may contain either detail-level actualities or certainties that have been totaled. Reality tables that contain accumulated certainties are frequently called rundown tables. A reality table generally contains certainties with a similar dimension of total. Qualities for certainties or measures are typically not known ahead of time; they are watched and put away. Actuality tables are the reason for the information questioned by OLAP apparatuses.

Creating a New Fact Table

You should characterize a reality table for each star diagram. A reality table ordinarily has two sorts of segments: those that contain certainties, and those that are remote keys to measurement tables. From a demonstrating point of view, the essential key of the reality table is normally a composite key that is comprised of the majority of its outside keys; in the physical information distribution center, the information stockroom head might make this essential key unequivocally. Actualities bolster numerical computations used to provide details regarding and examine the business. Some numeric information are measurements in mask, regardless of whether they appear to be realities. On the off chance that you are not keen on a rundown of a specific thing, the thing may really be a measurement. Database size and by and large execution enhance in the event that you classify marginal fields as measurements.

Dimensions

A measurement is a structure, frequently made out of at least one orders, that orders information. A few particular measurements, joined with measures, empower you to answer business questions. Usually utilized measurements are Customer, Product, and Time. Figure 2.2 shows somewhere in the range of a run of the mill measurement chain of command.

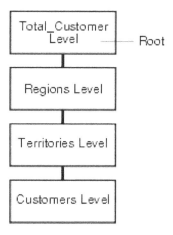

Figure 2.2 Typical Levels in a Dimension Hierarchy

Dimension information is regularly gathered at the most minimal dimension of detail and afterward accumulated into more elevated amount sums, which is more valuable for investigation. For instance, in the Total Customer measurement, there are four dimensions: Total Customer, Regions, Territories, and Customers. Information gathered at the Customers level is accumulated to the Territories level. For the Regions measurement, information gathered for a few districts, for example, Western Europe or Eastern Europe may be amassed as a reality in the reality table into aggregates for a bigger zone, for example, Europe

1.5.1 Hierarchies

Hierarchies are consistent structures that utilization requested dimensions as a methods for sorting out information. A chain of importance can be utilized to characterize information accumulation. For instance, in a Time measurement, a pecking order may be utilized to total information from the Month level to the Quarter level to the Year level. A chain of importance can likewise be utilized to characterize a navigational penetrate way and set up a family structure. Inside an order, each dimension is consistently associated with the dimensions above and underneath it; information esteems at lower levels total into the information esteems at larger amounts. For instance, in the Product measurement, there may be two chains of command - one for item distinguishing proof and one for item response.

Measurement chains of importance likewise assemble levels from extremely broad to exceptionally granular. Chains of importance are used by question devices, enabling you to penetrate down into your information to see diverse dimensions of granularity- - one of the key advantages of an information distribution center. When structuring your chains of importance, you should consider the connections characterized in your source information. For instance, a progression configuration must respect the outside key connections between the source tables with the end goal to legitimately total information. Pecking orders forces a family structure on measurement esteems. For a specific dimension esteem, an incentive at the following more elevated amount is its parent, and qualities at the following lower level are its youngsters. These familial connections enable investigators to get to information rapidly.

Levels

Levels speak to a situation in a chain of command. For instance, a Time measurement may have a chain of importance that speaks to information at the Month, Quarter, and Year levels. Levels go from general to unmistakable, with the root level as the most elevated, or most broad dimension. The dimensions in a measurement are sorted out into at least one chains of importance.

Level Relationships

Level connections indicate start to finish requesting of levels from most broad (the root) to most explicit data and characterize the parent-youngster connection between the dimensions in a progression. You can characterize chains of importance where each dimension moves up to the past dimension in the measurement or you can characterize progressive systems that skirt one or different dimensions.

IOT Enabling Technologies

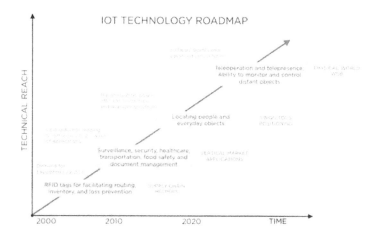

As referenced to a limited extent one What is the Internet of Things this series is not planned to be a designing reading material on the IOT and its empowering innovations. Be that as it may, the IOT's innovation guide is appeared in Figure and we will show some broad foundation on the IOT's specialized scene to educate our IP procedure discourse (approaching).

1. Big Data

As more things (or smart objects) are associated with the IOT, more information is gathered from them with the end goal to perform examination to decide patterns and affiliations that prompt bits of knowledge. For instance, an oil very much outfitted with 20-30 sensors can create 500,000 information focuses each 15 seconds20, a jetliner with 6,000 sensors produces 2.5 terabytes of data every day [21], and the in excess of 46 million savvy utility meters introduced in the U.S. produce in excess of 1 billion information focuses every day. [22] Thus, the term big data alludes to these vast informational collections that should be gathered, put away, questioned, broke down and by and large oversaw with the end goal to convey on the guarantee of the IOT knowledge! Further aggravating the specialized difficulties of huge information is the way that IOT frameworks must manage the information gathered from savvy objects, as well as subordinate information that is expected to legitimately perform such investigation (e.g., open and private informational collections identified with climate, GIS, monetary, seismic, outline, wrongdoing, and so forth.).

Along these lines, as more keen articles come on the web, something like three measurements (the three V's) are regularly utilized by IOT administrators to depict the enormous information they handle: volume (i.e., the sum.information they gather from their IOT sensors estimated in gigabytes, terabytes and peta bytes); speed (i.e., the speed at which information is gathered from the sensors); and assortment (i.e., the diering sorts of organized and unstructured information gathered, particularly when contrasted with video and picture documents as is ordinary inside the customer Internet).

2. Digital Twin

Another outcome of the developing and advancing IOT is the idea of a digital twin, introduced in 2003 by John Vickers, supervisor of NASA's National Center for Advanced Manufacturing.[23] The idea alludes to a computerized duplicate of a physical resource (i.e., a keen protest inside the IOT), that lives and develops in a virtual situation over the physical assets lifetime. That is, as the sensors inside the protest gather continuous information, an arrangement of models shaping the advanced twin is refreshed with the majority of a similar data.

In this manner, a review of the advanced twin would uncover indistinguishable data from a physical examination of the keen protest itself albeit remotely. The advanced twin of the brilliant question would then be able to be concentrated to not just advance tasks of the shrewd protest through lessened support expenses and downtime, yet to enhance the up and coming age of its structure.

3. Cloud Computing

As the word cloud is regularly utilized as an allegory for the Internet, cloud computing alludes to having the capacity to get to figuring assets by means of the Internet as opposed to conventional frameworks where processing equipment is physically situated on the premises of the client and any product applications are introduced on such nearby equipment.. All the more formally, cloud computing is characterized as: [A] show for empowering pervasive, advantageous, on-request organize access to a mutual pool of configurable processing assets (e.g., systems, servers, stockpiling, applications, and administrations) that can be quickly provisioned and discharged with insignificant administration e ort or specialist organization interaction. [24] Cloud registering and its three administration models of Software as a Service (SaaS), Platform as a Service what's more, Infrastructure as a Service (IaaS) are critical to the IOT in light of the fact that it permits any client with a program and an Internet association with change keen protest information into noteworthy insight. That is, distributed computing gives the virtual foundation to utility processing coordinating applications, observing gadgets, stockpiling gadgets, examination instruments, perception stages, and customer delivery [to] empower organizations and clients to get to [IOT-enabled] applications on interest whenever, wherever and anywhere.

4. Sensors

Central to the usefulness and utility of the IOT are sensors installed in savvy objects. Such sensors are equipped for distinguishing occasions or changes in an explicit amount (e.g., weight), imparting the occasion or change information to the cloud (specifically or by means of a door) and, in a few conditions, getting information once more from the cloud (e.g., a control direction) or speaking with other shrewd articles. Since 2012, sensors have for the most part contracted in physical size and along these lines have caused the IOT market to develop quickly. All the more explicitly: Technological enhancements made minuscule scale sensors, prompting the utilization of innovations like Micro electromechanical frameworks (MEMS). This implied sensors were currently little enough to be installed into one of a kind spots like dress or other [smart objects].

5. Communications

Regarding sending and accepting information, wired and remote correspondence advancements have additionally enhanced with the end goal that about every type of electronic gear can give information network. This has permitted the consistently contracting sensors installed in keen items to send and get information over the cloud for accumulation, stockpiling and inevitable investigation. The conventions for permitting IOT sensors to transfer information incorporate remote advances, for example, RFID, NFC, Wi-Fi, Bluetooth, Bluetooth Low Energy (BLE), XBee, ZigBee, Z-Wave, Wireless M-Bus, SIGFOX and Nuel NET, and satellite associations and portable systems utilizing GSM, GPRS, 3G, LTE, or Wi MAX. [27] Wired conventions, useable by stationary shrewd items, incorporate Ethernet, Home Plug, Home PNA, Home Grid/G.hn and Lon Works, and in addition traditional phone lines.

6. Analytics Software

Within the IOT biological community, Application Service Providers (ASPs) which could conceivably dier from the organizations who move and administration the brilliant items give programming to organizations that can change raw machine (enormous) information gathered from savvy objects into significant knowledge (or understanding). As a rule, such programming performs information mining and utilizes numerical models and factual systems to give understanding to clients. That is, occasions, patterns and examples are removed from huge informational indexes with the end goal to display the software's end-clients with understanding as portfolio investigation, forecasts, hazard examination, robotizations and restorative, support and streamlining proposals. By and large, the

ASPs may give general expository programming or programming focusing on explicit businesses or sorts of shrewd items.

7. Edge Devices

Not appeared in our oversimplified IOT ecosystem of Figure 1 is actually how the savvy objects installed with sensors interface through the Internet to the different specialist organization frameworks. The appropriate response is by means of edge devices any gadget, for example, a switch, directing switch, incorporated access gadget (IAD), multiplexer, or metropolitan zone arrange (MAN) and wide territory organize (WAN) get to gadget which gives a passage point from the worldwide, open Internet into an ASPs or different enterprises private system. [29] In Industry 4.0, these edge gadgets are getting to be more brilliant at handling information before such information even achieves an endeavor networks spine (i.e., its center gadgets and cloud server farms). For instance, edge gadgets may decipher between different arrange conventions, and give first-jump security, starting nature of administration and access/conveyance strategy functionality.

Privacy in IOT

Privacy is an extremely close to home thing. This basic truth gets intricate extremely quick. Consider it: We regularly share more with the general population we trust. My possess chance resilience for offering individual data to someone up close and personal might be totally not quite the same as yours, and my resistance level may change after some time. This user- characterized limit to information sharing revealing individual data, history, musings, and feelings is generally dependent on ones trust in a framework (or individual) and its protection settings (or probability to chatter). Protection and Trust in the applications and gadgets we utilize likewise changes after some time. At the point when Face book let us ensure our information utilizing security settings, we characterized new cutoff points for showing that information and believed Face book to secure it going ahead.

The Evolution of Privacy & Trust

Privacy and Trust both factor into our laws and societal standards. During the 1980s, we lived more mysterious lives. Despite the fact that the police could get to a persons name, address, telephone number and permit, our own data was not normally accessible to general society. Today our data can turn into a product for advertisers, a reasonable vote in favor of legislators, or a measurement for information researchers. Our security laws ensure our by and by recognizable data (PII) in light of current circumstances; our own information may open the way to our personality, funds, and then some. Nowadays PII is regularly distributed online alongside photographs, life occasions, bank adjusts, property records, financial record, continue wellbeing status, family tree, companions, schools, side interests and governmental issues. Our resistance for believing destinations with our information has changed after some time. In an open society like our own, online Trust is remunerated. Craigslist and web based dating bring outsiders into our lives. Airbnb and Couch surfing locales bring outsiders into our homes.

Opening up to outsiders continuously progresses toward becoming standardized conduct, particularly for our childhood. All things being equal, regardless of what our necessities are, we should always gauge the advantages of confiding in others with the dangers of uncovering our private information. James Robinson offers a unique Mapping of Cyber Attacks to Maslows Hierarchy of Needs.

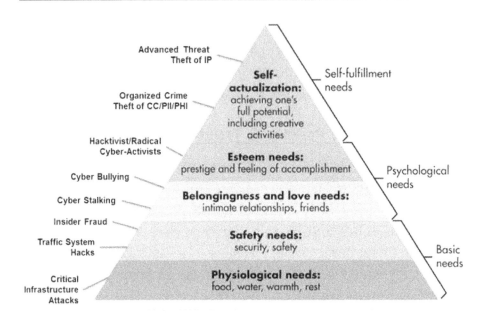

Connecting Privacy to IOT

Similar to individual connections, Trust administers how we control Privacy in our IOT surroundings. As IOT gadgets turn out to be more associated, more information is shared between individuals, organizations, governments and environments. Sensors, gadgets, information, machines and cloud associations depend vigorously on built up trust connections. Associating more sorts of IOT gadgets (i.e., including interruption focuses) builds the danger surface of a given framework, along these lines expanding the general security hazard. Without the capacity to constrain security settings, its hard to set up trust with an IOT framework or gadget.

Security is generally a challenge for numerous gadget makers speeding toward early reception of their IOT items. Without programmed security refreshes, 2-factor verification, or laws advancing security assurance, numerous IOT gadgets will keep on present security dangers.

The Internet of Things Needs Privacy and Security

Imagine an existence where everything is associated on the web, as well as in the physical universe of remote and wearable gadgets, for example, Fit bits, Nymi groups, Google Glass and Apple Watch with a connecting to associated autos, planes, prepares and puts. On the off chance that one adds to that the following of exercises from ones checked home by method for computerized indoor regulators, light apparatuses, brilliant TVs, shrewd meters and the savvy framework, it will prompt the depiction of the quantified self, finish with the individual points of interest of way of life, propensities and exercises all followed and recorded. Furthermore, ones whole way of life, containing a point by point set of exercises and inclinations, would possibly be open for all to see and, through the intensity of machine learning, to examine and make expectations about ones future conduct.Welcome to the Internet of Things, or maybe more relevantly, the Internet of Everything.

Is this what we truly need? Will the future world we live in be without any security, whereupon our individual opportunities are manufactured? Since that is correctly what we need to consider all that connectedness will make ready for the reconnaissance of our lives, at an inconceivable scale. A scale that was suitably depicted by the chief of U.S. national knowledge, Mr. James Clapper, when he showed that knowledge administrations would before long utilize the IOT for recognizable proof, reconnaissance, checking, following, focusing on and getting to systems. Be that as it may, it doesn't must be that way. On the off chance that we insert protection into the structure of these interconnected gadgets and projects, we can have the best of the two universes: security and the IOT. Reconnaissance is the direct opposite of security, and as needs be, the absolute opposite of opportunity. Yet, fortunately neither security nor the advantages inborn in the rising IOT must be relinquished.

We require just relinquish the constraining either/or, zero-aggregate reasoning that sets you can just have some intrigue. It will be troublesome. This defective line of reasoning is so profoundly engrained in our points of view that attempting to surrender it represents a genuine test. Be that as it may, by supplanting the restricting versus with the intensity of and, the two interests security and the IOT may coincide at the same time in a win/win situation, instead of the win/lose model to which we have turned out to be so acclimated. This can be practiced by installing or coding security inclinations into the innovation itself, with the end goal to keep the protection hurts from emerging. This is famously inside our range, as the designing and tech networks have over and again let me know. Presumably, it will require development and creativity, yet in the event that we are to proceed with existing innovative advancement in an undeniably associated world, it will be basic to keep up our future security and opportunities. It will likewise require foreknowledge and authority, with an end goal to dismiss pointless tradeoffs and false divisions.

Security by Design is a system I made for anticipating security hurts by installing the essential protection defensive measures into the plan of data innovation, arranged foundation and business rehearses. It was collectively passed as a global system for security and information insurance in 2010. From that point forward, it has been converted into 37 dialects, giving it a genuine worldwide nearness. Be that as it may, no place is it required more than in the developing universe of the IOT.

On the off chance that we are to save any similarity to security in such a world, we should guarantee that it is incorporated with the specific frameworks that are being produced. Something else, the interconnected idea of for all intents and purposes all that we do may lead us down a way of observation that will be excessively extraordinary, making it impossible to vanquish sometime later. In any case, it doesn't need to play out that way. We can have security and the Internet of Things. In any case, just in the event that we talk up and dismiss the zero-total business as usual. As the Internet of Things warms up, we should bolster the developing number of incredible associations that work to ensure our entitlement to security including the Canadian Privacy Commissioners at all dimensions of government, the U.S. Government Trade Commission, UKs Information Commissioners Office, European Parliament, Online Trust Alliance, Deloitte and the Knowledge Flow Cyber safety Foundation. I welcome you to find the Privacy by Design for the Internet of Things structure and urge you to implant your innovation with the Principles and ideas displayed here.

I trust you investigate the fantastic capability of mind full plan and receive the rewards security driven innovations. This article, by Dr. Ann Cavoukian, official executive of the Privacy and Big Data Institute at Ryerson University, and previous data and protection magistrate of Ontario, initially showed up in the Globe and Mail. http://www.ryerson.ca/pbdi/

The 7 Foundational Principles of
Privacy by Design

1. Proactive not reactive; Preventative not remedial
2. Privacy as the default setting
3. Privacy embedded into design
4. Full functionality – positive-sum, not zero-sum
5. End-to-end security – full lifecycle protection
6. Visibility and transparency – keep it open
7. Respect for user privacy – keep it user-centric

DO THE PBD PRINCIPLES APPLY IN THE IOT AGE? YOU BET!

THE 7 FOUNDATIONAL PRINCIPLES: AN INTEGRATED FRAMEWORK FOR PRIVACY AND THE INTERNET OF THINGS

Principle #1: Proactive not Responsive; Preventative not Medicinal IOT Privacy Concept: Anticipate and Eliminate Opportunities for

Abuse The trap of gadgets effectively associated and interconnected today is just a fragmentary piece of the universe of innovations that will shape the Internet of Things in the coming years. These gadgets will before long dwarf individuals, strain2 the land-based Internet's ability and take to the skies to move data progressively. For all its future advantages, the Internet of Things must utilize today as a gauge. This existence where reason assembled gadgets needn't bother with data sharing to work must be the gauge for data sharing into what's to come. We should utilize proactive measures to envision protection challenges. That implies the esteem we get today from a toaster with zero insight and limit with respect to information accumulation should dependably be weighed against future apparatuses that offer included comfort with the proviso of expanded data sharing. Envisioning such advances might be simple, however developments should dependably cease from expecting what general society needs from innovation and power themselves to just inquire. Assent will be the best test to security maltreatment later on Internet of Things.

Principle #2: Privacy as the Default Setting IOT Privacy Concept: Configure Privacy by Default

Building protections into inventive innovation arrangements, instructive projects and interpersonal interaction must not be viewed as an unmistakably extraordinary advancement life cycle process. Characteristically planning protection into all developments previously data the board capacities are added is the most ideal approach to cultivate trust and support full utilization of the assets made accessible by tomorrow's associated items. At the point when shoppers can depend on the information that their wellbeing is secured, that level of affirmation is the simple component that will open the guarantee of tomorrow's innovation environments. In-constructed trustworthiness must rub off from the planner into the item to breed the certainty to reinforce marks and make the positive attitude essential for appropriation. Energetic customers will dependably bolster the advancements that help their goals. Default security and trustworthiness in the Internet of Things don't simply include layers of information insurance, they make dynamic associations look great... also, all things considered. Those associations will profit by an undeniable open recognition hole that will dependably support reliable advancements over voracious information gathering rehearses.

Principle #3: Privacy Embedded into Design IOT Privacy Concept: Embed Integrity into Design

Consistently embedded privacy into IOT technologies means seriously treating the obligation to secure client data at all dimensions. A real commitment to privacy means integrity, not manufactured demand and market influence, drive product design and engineering. The Internet of Things will include increasingly intelligent devices competing for bandwidth, data and attention. If the repeatable, reliable and consistent application of information management brings about increased sentience, responsible design will necessarily include privacy and integrity to form the strong fabric of tomorrow's society, in which intelligent devices will seamlessly interface with, augment and enhance human existence. Instead, layering and inserting privacy into layers of IOT is of paramount importance to preventing abuses and anchoring protection early on. Those early layers represent bottom-up functionality that make sense to good designers, will thrill developers and create a sense of security among customers.

Principle #4: Full Functionality – Positive-Sum, not Zero-Sum

IOT Privacy Concept: Fuse Optimized Experiences to Full Functionality

Fostering consumer interactions and experiences that infuse trust into relationships begins with the end goal. A world where users must choose between privacy and security, or accept surveillance in exchange for safety is not a positive sum solution to the social problems of the day. To create a win-win scenario, thinking bigger, introducing innovations that maximize user experiences while protecting user interests represents a solid, principled approach.

Functionally effective safeguards are unobtrusively designed to provide the comfort to take in value offered by legitimate programs, systems and networks. Embracing public interest means delivering solutions that are not limited by the natural need for safety and security, nor curtailed by the human right to privacy. Reducing the richness of feature sets reduces user experiences and ultimately limits the potential to effectively reach greater communities and satisfy more audiences.

Principle #5: End-to-End Security – Full Lifecycle Protection IOT Privacy Concept: Clarify & Simplify for Protective Design

Complexity is the enemy of usability. The online world's dependence on a reactive model where transparency reports, terms of service, privacy and security policies have become the norm, the clear goal needs to remain the provisioning of effective solutions that mitigate the risk of abuse. Privacy by Design for Internet of Things begins with a simple message clearly articulated and easily accessible throughout the entire design and user experience. User awareness and security assurance are the building blocks of the most comprehensive solutions but it is that full lifecycle protection that ensures privacy. The scalability of approaches for safe use of technology in family settings, for complete user-centricity in systems development and for responsible engineering in discrete environments are the keys to effective consumer protection. Organizations, industrials and developers that adopt privacy best practices can therefore ensure the consistent, end-to-end application of simple but overlapping security measures that effectively represent the foundation of tomorrow's trusted Internet of Things. The alternative is not an option.

Principle #6: Visibility and Transparency – Keep it Open IOT Privacy Concept: Control Monitoring and Awareness

The Internet of Things was borne of open design. By design, privacy principles embrace an overlapping but transparent mesh of privacy protective measures intended to eliminate opportunities for abuse. As a layered approach, Privacy by Design's inclusive model ensures awareness, encourages responsible use and enhances the relationship between innovator and consumer.

To do so, technologists must know where the line is between protective monitoring and opportunistic surveillance. Treating audiences as stakeholders whose needs for security and safety must be respected above all else is a fundamental approach. Effective controls must be tempered with responsible monitoring. Collected information must be shared with the people it was collected from. Practices must be compatible with independent verification to generate trust. Without these concepts, even the most innovative initiative will squander the traction, value and trust it was originally created to garner. Flexibility, visibility and transparency are some of the key notions used to combat Fear, Uncertainty and Doubt (FUD), and it is critical that they be in-built at this beginning time all the while.

Principle #7: Respect for User privacy – keep it user-centric IOT Concept: Include Users as Stakeholders, not Victims

Data collection is about respecting users and consumers. In the evolving Internet of Things, every individual is a content generating node. Such notions can lead innovators and engineers on a path away from privacy protection. Responsible Internet of Things solutions must necessarily address a problem, but beyond that, they must demonstrate respect for the public in their collection and handling of information. Secret securing of insight has no place in capable plan. If we are to leverage public trust as a quantifiable asset then users must be stakeholders, not victims. For that, engineers must leverage Privacy Principles as a springboard to good implementation that shares, not obscures its activity. This approach is the glue used to build the bonds of confidence and create trust-based ecosystems. By architecting non-invasive technology platforms that encourage the responsible use of information, builders can scale individual user relationships into vast networks for information exchange, knowledge transfer and personal growth... on a vast scale. The notions of users as stakeholders – not unwitting victims – are intrinsic to privacy protection. These once abstract ideas are today very real, with damaging consequences that can only be alleviated by the systematic, assiduous application of controls that protect not only the most vulnerable, but every single, valuable member of each user base, every citizen of our online society and every element in our growing ecosystem of interconnected people & devices - the Internet of things.

Design Methodology

The design of products and solutions within the greater Internet of Things space must necessarily be innovative, useful and effective, but to buy in to standards of good structure it should likewise be careful and definite, unpretentious and tasteful, socially dependable and legit.

This approach meshes well with Privacy by Design, where user-centricity, openness and design integrity are valuable principles that need to be fundamentally adopted to ensure protection and trust.

In broad strokes, systematic design for IOT depends on the application of Privacy by Design using tools, techniques and processes that may not yet be in existence. Yet the principles upon which all such products and solutions will base their operational integrity has existed for decades and it is only a matter of ensuring their fit from an engineering perspective.

The authors encourage organizations, associations, groups and individuals in all sectors to use the PBD Principles for IOT Design framework in building, unveiling and scaling disruptively ambitious and overwhelmingly beneficial opportunities that contribute to the rising tide of responsible engineering and consumer-centric design.

Engineering Privacy for Good Design

While the Internet of Things moves from hype to maturity, industrial innovators have already begun to make inroads into standardized techniques and operating guidelines for the introduction of simple, useful and attractive products for future decades

Now is the time to adopt the privacy principles that will effectively and elegantly spearhead consumer-centric design for the next few decades. Use the sample questions below to align your objectives with those of your audience. Create a privacy document that will practically map these principles to concrete approaches. Demonstrate to test audiences how responsible design leads to robust engineering and enhanced experiences. Finally, implement a knowledge sharing program with your product and software designers, project and program managers, marketers and promoters. It will create a cohesive web of consistently dependable information protection that renders and improves your core security controls.

The IOT Privacy Principles form a framework designed to scale to support your scope. You need to rally the right core group of people, awaken their talent and focus on what the audience deserves for themselves and those around them. Proactive design, default protection, inbuilt privacy, open, transparent, secure implementation. It's the best way to have a far reaching impact using a simple approach that is widely adopted. The rest is up to you.

Operational Application of PbD Principles to IOT

1. Anticipate and Eliminate Opportunities for Abuse
2. Configure Privacy by Default
3. Embed Integrity into Design
4. Push Optimized Experiences to Full Functionality
5. Clarify & Simplify for Protective Design
6. Control Monitoring and Awareness
7. Include Users as Stakeholders, not Victims

The Web of Things: A web-Connected World of Smart Devices

As more "things" on planet Earth are changed over to the stock of carefully associated Internet gadgets, the jobs and duties of web designers and innovation supervisors should develop in keeping pace with the consistently growing rundown of apparatuses and contraptions that require a web interface. This worldwide pattern is known as "The Internet of Things" or IOT, and as a dream has roused that equivalent introduce for "The Web of

Things", or WoT, and fuses comparable attributes and application models. This piece will analyze the specialized highlights that epitomize The Web of Things, and I will give instances of current applications being used today, and offer some cheerful prospects for the fate of the web and "things."

What is this Web of Things?

As I quickly referenced in my presentation over, the WoT is a piece of the IoT, and a few thoughts or dreams persevere about what each means regarding the thinking ahead and thought of how they are executed and their outcomes. The effect to human and computerized reasoning is another worry, not from only a philosophical point of view, but rather from scholarly, mechanical, and administration viewpoints also. As I've looked into the subject of both, plainly there is a quickened pace to change over "things" to getting to be "shrewd" web associated gadgets that make, store, and offer information; furthermore, these savvy gadgets can be customized to settle on choices dependent on the information it has made and information from different sources. Generally, we have an amalgam of innovations, hardware, apparatuses, frameworks, techniques, structures, and gadgets that when added to the web should be produced, executed, observed, looked after, overhauled, and represented. Straight to the point daCosta in his Net of Things Blog spot compares and differences the conventional ways to deal with advancement of the IOT/WoT with characteristic intuitive frameworks including the ways ants, honey bees, and super organisims coexist. Honesty's blog sub-heading aggregates up his way to deal with the current pattern: For some savants (and item chiefs), the Internet of Things is essentially somewhere else to apply a similar old conventional systems administration thoughts, for example, IPv6. Be that as it may, in reality, a totally extraordinary methodology is required if the IOT is genuinely to achieve its potential.

That approach will be educated by exercises gained from nature and other monstrous collaborating frameworks. Specialized administrators should figure out how to coordinate their present plans of action and web administration frameworks to acknowledge the fast pace as conventional gadgets keep on being received into the "shrewd" classification of web-empowered satisfaction. There is nobody estimate fits all arrangement, however there are endeavors to plot a uniform technique that underpins the procedure from an innovative out look.

A Uniform Technology

The binding together preface behind selection of the WoT is that all "things" will be associated with comparative innovation, with a uniform interface to access the global functionality among all smart devices and objects. Several projects are underway to achieve the goal of using HTTP as an application protocol rather than as a transport protocol similar to Web Services or Web API. The specialized perspectives additionally depend on the synchronous usefulness of savvy gadgets through what is known as a Representational State Transfer (REST), which is a style of programming engineering for dispersed frameworks including the World Wide Web (WWW), and is the dominating web administrations configuration show. The WoT display likewise depends on current Web syndication usefulness such as Atom, which is the standard for syndication groups, or Comet which is the standard for web server push innovation.

Architecture of Web of Things (WoT)

The Web of Things (WoT) is a term used to depict approaches, programming engineering styles and programming designs that permit certifiable items to be a piece of the World Wide Web. Also to what the Web (Application Layer) is to the Internet

(Network Layer), the Web of Things gives an Application Layer that disentangles the production of Internet of Things applications. The engineering proposes four layers or stages that are to be utilized:

1. Accessibility Layer

This layer manages the entrance of things to the Internet and guarantees they uncover their administrations by means of Web APIs. This is the center layer of the WoT as it guarantees things have a Web available API, changing them into programmable things. The entrance layer in the WoT is worked around two center examples: Firstly, all things ought to uncover their administrations through a Restful API (either specifically or through gateway). REST is an engineering style at the base of the programmable Web thanks to its implementation in HTTP 1.1. As an outcome, if things offer Restful APIs over HTTP, they get a URL and turn out to be consistently coordinated to the World Wide Web and its instruments, for example, programs, hyperlinked HTML pages and Java script applications. A few plans depicting how the administrations offered by things can be gotten to by means of REST have been proposed. Furthermore, the demand reaction nature of HTTP is frequently referred to as one of the constraints for IOT utilize cases as it doesn't coordinate the occasion driven nature of uses that are normal in the Wireless Sensor Networks.

To conquer this deficiency while maintaining an attention on cultivating combination with the Web, a few creators have recommended the utilization of HTML5 Web Sockets either locally or using interpretation merchants (e.g., deciphering from MQTT or COAP to Web Sockets).This supplements the REST API of things with a distribute buy in instrument that is to a great extent incorporated with the Web eco-framework. Some things can connect directly to the Internet (e.g., using Ethernet, Wi-Fi or

GSM/3G), however in different cases (for instance when gadgets are battery-controlled) gadgets can get to the Internet through Smart Gateways. Shrewd Gateway is convention interpretation portals at the edge of the system.

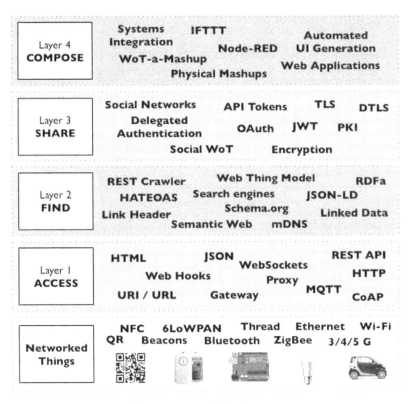

Source: Building the Web of Things: book.webofthings.io
Creative Commons Attribution 4.0

2. Findability layer

The focal point of this layer is to give an approach to discover and find things on the Web and henceforth is emphatically impacted by the semantic Web. The methodology here is to reuse Web semantic principles to depict things and their administrations. Specifically, individuals have been dealing withHTML5 Micro data integration, RDF RDFa, JSON-LD and EXI. This empowers scanning for things through web search tools and other Web lists and also empowering machine to machine association dependent on a little arrangement of all around characterized configurations and guidelines.

3. Sharing layer

The Web of Things is to a great extent dependent on the possibility of things pushing information to the Web where more knowledge and huge information examples can be connected for instance to enable us to deal with our health (Wearable's),optimize our energy consumption (Smart Grid), etc. This, however, can only happen in a large-scale way if some of the data can be efficiently shared across services. The sharing layer guarantees that information created by things can be partaken in a productive and secure way. A few methodologies towards a granular and social setting based sharing have been proposed, for example, the utilization of informal organization to construct a Social Web of Things.

4. Composition layer

The job of the last layer is to incorporate the administrations and information offered by things into more elevated amount Web apparatuses (examination programming, Mash up applications such as IFTTT), making it significantly more straightforward to make applications including things and virtual Web administrations. Instruments in the synthesis layer go from Web tool box (e.g., Java content SDKs offering larger amount abstractions) to dashboards with programmable widgets and Physical Mash up tools. Inspired by Web 2.0 participatory services and in particular Web Mash ups, the Physical Mash ups offer a unified view of the traditional Web and Web of Things and enable individuals to construct applications utilizing the

Web of Things administrations without requiring programming aptitudes.

Real-World Implementation Examples

Several executions are set up today that use the WoT sort of innovation, including remote DVR planning, remote home security frameworks checking and organization, and remote home power matrix utilization observing. These are just a few of the current implementations which bring us one step closer to the WoT, and it will be interesting to see how each evolves in the coming years as more devices are enhanced and functionality is improved. DIRECTV's web interface that enables clients to remotely set their DVR to record future projects utilizing the DVR Scheduler via any PC or cell phone is one precedent. The necessities to associate with the DVR remotely implies that you should possess a DIRECTV Plus DVR collector (R15, R16, R22), DIRECTV Plus HD DVR Receiver (HR20 or more), or TiVo Series 2 beneficiaries with 6.4a programming. To send a record ask for from directv.com requires a PC, Internet program, an Internet association, and a directv.com username and secret phrase. To send a record request from a cell phone requires a mobile phone, an Internet browser, a mobile phone data plan without restrictions on addresses you can visit, and a directv.com username and password.

UNIT - II

2. Software-Defined Networking

Programming characterized organizing (SDN) is a design that means to make systems light-footed and adaptable. The objective of SDN is to enhance organize control by empowering undertakings and specialist organizations to react rapidly to changing business necessities.

In a product characterized organize; a system architect or overseer can shape activity from a brought together control reassure without contacting singular switches in the system. The concentrated SDN controller guides the changes to convey arrange benefits wherever they're required, paying little respect to the explicit associations between a server and gadgets. This procedure is a move far from customary system engineering, in which singular system gadgets settle on activity choices dependent on their arranged directing tables.

2.1 History

The historical backdrop of SDN standards can be followed back to the division of the control and information plane originally utilized in people in general exchanged phone arrange as an approach to rearrange provisioning and the executives a long time before this design started to be utilized in information systems.

The Internet Engineering Task Force (IETF) started considering different approaches to decouple the control and sending capacities in a proposed interface standard distributed in 2004 fittingly named "Sending and Control Element Separation" (ForCES). The ForCES Working Group likewise proposed a buddy SoftRouter Architecture. Extra early guidelines from the IETF that sought after isolating control from information incorporate the Linux Netlink as an IP Services Protocol and A Path Computation Element (PCE)- Based Architecture.

These early endeavors neglected to pick up footing for two reasons. One is that numerous in the Internet people group saw isolating control from information to be unsafe, particularly attributable to the potential for a disappointment in the control plane. The second is that merchants were worried that making standard application programming interfaces (APIs) between the control and information planes would result in expanded rivalry.

The utilization of open source programming in split control/ information plane models follows its underlying foundations to the Ethane venture at Stanford's PC sciences division. Ethane's basic change configuration prompted the making of OpenFlow. An API for OpenFlow was first made in 2008. That equivalent year saw the production of NOX—a working framework for networks.

Work on OpenFlow proceeded at Stanford, incorporating with the formation of testbeds to assess utilization of the convention in a solitary grounds arrange, and in addition over the WAN as a spine for associating various grounds. In scholarly settings there were a couple of research and creation systems dependent on OpenFlow changes from NEC and Hewlett-Packard; and additionally dependent on Quanta Computer whiteboxes, beginning from around 2009.

Past scholarly world, the primary organizations were by Nicira in 2010 to control OVS from Onix, co-created with NTT and Google. A remarkable sending was Google's B4 arrangement in 2012. Later Google recognized their first OpenFlow with Onix organizations in their Datacenters in the meantime. Another realized extensive arrangement is at China Mobile.

The open Network Foundation was established into advance SDN and OpenFlow and the programming characterized organizing was shown by Avaya utilizing most limited way crossing over and OpenStack as a robotized grounds, expanding mechanization from the server farm to the eng gadget, expelling manual provisioning from administration conveyance.

SDN Architecture

A run of the mill portrayal of SDN design contains three layers: the application layer, the control layer and the foundation layer. The application layer, as anyone might expect, contains the normal system applications or capacities associations utilize, which can incorporate interruption discovery frameworks, stack adjusting or firewalls. Where a customary system would utilize a specific apparatus, for example, a firewall or load balancer, a product characterized arrange replaces the machine with an application that utilizes the controller to oversee information plane conduct.

The control layer speaks to the incorporated SDN controller programming that goes about as the cerebrum of the product characterized arrange. This controller dwells on a server and oversees arrangements and the stream of activity all through the system.

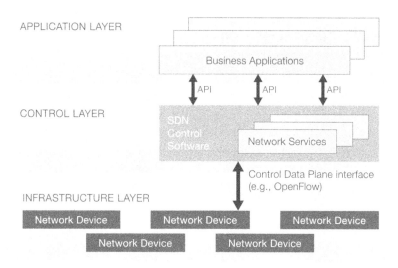

Figure: 2.1.1 SDN architecture

The foundation layer is comprised of the physical switches in the system.

These three layers convey utilizing particular northbound and southbound application How SDN functions. SDN incorporates a few kinds of advancements, including useful division, organize virtualization and computerization through programmability. Initially, SDN innovation concentrated exclusively on partition of the system control plane from the information plane. While the control plane settles on choices about how parcels should move through the system, the information plane really moves bundles from place to put.

In an exemplary SDN situation, a bundle touches base at a system switch, and guidelines incorporated with the switch's restrictive firmware advise the change where to forward the parcel. These bundle taking care of guidelines are sent to the change from the brought together controller. The switch - otherwise called an information plane gadget - questions the controller for direction as required, and it furnishes the controller with data about activity it handles. The switch sends each parcel setting off to a similar goal along a similar way and treats every one of the bundles precisely the same way.

Programming characterized organizing utilizes an activity mode that is once in a while called versatile or dynamic, in which a switch issues a course demand to a controller for a bundle that does not have an explicit course. This procedure is isolated from versatile steering, which issues course asks for through switches and calculations dependent on the system topology, not through a controller.

The virtualization part of SDN becomes an integral factor through a virtual overlay, which is a sensibly discrete system over the physical system. Clients can actualize end-to-end overlays to extract the fundamental system and section organize activity. This microsegmentation is particularly valuable for specialist co-ops and administrators with multi- inhabitant cloud situations and cloud administrations, as they can arrangement a different virtual system with explicit approaches for each occupant. programming interfaces (APIs). For instance, applications converse with the controller through its northbound interface, while the controller and switches convey utilizing southbound interfaces, for example, Open Flow - albeit different conventions exist.

There is as of now no formal standard for the controller's northbound API to coordinate OpenFlow as a general southbound interface. It is likely the OpenDaylight controller's northbound API may rise as a true standard after some time, given its expansive merchant bolster.

The accompanying rundown characterizes and clarifies the building segments:

SDN Application

SDN Applications are programs that explicitly, directly, and programmatically communicate their network requirements and desired network behavior to the SDN Controller via a Northbound Interface(NBI). In addition they may consume an abstracted view of the network for their internal decision-making purposes. An SDN Application consists of one SDN Application Logic and one or more NBI Drivers. SDN Applications may themselves expose another layer of abstracted network control, thus offering one or more higher-level NBIs through respective NBI agents.

SDN Controller

The SDN Controller is a logically centralized entity in charge of (i) translating the requirements from the SDN Application layer down to the SDN Datapaths and (ii) providing the SDN Applications with an abstract view of the network (which may include statistics and events). An SDN Controller consists of one or more NBI Agents, the SDN Control Logic, and the Control to Data-Plane Interface (CDPI) driver. Definition as a logically centralized entity neither prescribes nor precludes implementation details such as the federation of multiple controllers, the hierarchical connection of controllers, communication interfaces between controllers, nor virtualization or slicing of network resources.

SDN Datapath

The SDN Datapath is a logical network device that exposes visibility and uncontested control over its advertised forwarding and data processing capabilities. The logical representation may encompass all or a subset of the physical substrate resources. An SDN Datapath comprises a CDPI agent and a set of one or more traffic forwarding engines and zero or more traffic processing functions.

These engines and functions may include simple forwarding between the datapath's external interfaces or internal traffic processing or termination functions. One or more SDN Datapaths may be contained in a single (physical) network element—an integrated physical combination of communications resources, managed as a unit. An SDN Datapath may also be defined across multiple physical network elements. This logical definition neither prescribes nor precludes implementation details such as the logical to physical mapping, management of shared physical resources, virtualization or slicing of the SDN Datapath, interoperability with non-SDN networking, nor the data processing functionality, which can include OSI layer 4-7 functions.

SDN Control to Data-Plane Interface (CDPI)

The SDN CDPI is the interface defined between an SDN Controller and an SDN Datapath, which provides at least

- i. programmatic control of all forwarding operations,
- ii. capabilities advertisement,
- iii. statistics reporting, and
- iv. event notification. One value of SDN lies in the expectation that the CDPI is implemented in an open, vendor-neutral and interoperable way.

SDN Northbound Interfaces (NBI)

SDN NBIs are interfaces between SDN Applications and SDN Controllers and typically provide abstract network views and enable direct expression of network behavior and requirements. This may occur at any level of abstraction (latitude) and across different sets of functionality (longitude). One value of SDN lies in the expectation that these interfaces are implemented in an open, vendor-neutral and interoperable way.

How SDN Works

SDN envelops a few kinds of innovations, including practical division, organize virtualization and computerization through programmability.

Initially, SDN innovation concentrated exclusively on partition of the system control plane from the information plane. While the control plane settles on choices about how parcels should course through the system, the information plane really moves bundles from place to put. In an exemplary SDN situation, a bundle touches base at a system switch, and standards incorporated with the switch's exclusive firmware advise the change where to forward the parcel. These bundle taking care of guidelines are sent to the change from the incorporated controller.

The switch - otherwise called an information plane gadget - inquiries the controller for direction as required, and it furnishes the controller with data about activity it handles. The switch sends each bundle setting off to a similar goal along a similar way and treats every one of the parcels precisely the same way.

Programming characterized organizing utilizes an activity mode that is in some cases called versatile or dynamic, in which a switch issues a course demand to a controller for a parcel that does not have an explicit course. This procedure is independent from versatile steering, which issues course asks for through switches and calculations dependent on the system topology, not through a controller.

The virtualization part of SDN becomes possibly the most important factor through a virtual overlay, which is a coherently independent system over the physical system. Clients can actualize end-to-end overlays to digest the fundamental system and portion organize activity. This microsegmentation is particularly helpful for specialist co-ops and administrators with multi-occupant cloud conditions and cloud administrations, as they can arrangement a different virtual system with explicit strategies for each inhabitant.

Applications

SDMAN

Programming characterized portable systems administration (SDMN)is a way to deal with the plan of versatile systems where all convention explicit highlights are actualized in programming, amplifying the utilization of nonexclusive and ware equipment and programming in both the center system and radio access arrange It is proposed as an expansion of SDN worldview to fuse portable system explicit functionalities. Since 3GPP Rel.14, a Control User Plane Separation was presented in the Mobile Core Network models with the PFCP convention.

SD-WAN

A SD-WAN is a Wide Area Network (WAN) oversaw utilizing the standards of programming characterized organizing. The fundamental driver of SD-WAN is to bring down WAN costs utilizing more reasonable and industrially accessible rented lines, as an option or incomplete substitution of more costly MPLS lines. Control and the executives is managed independently from the equipment with focal controllers taking into consideration less demanding arrangement and organization.

SD-LAN

A SD-LAN is a Local zone organize (LAN) worked around the standards of programming characterized organizing, however there are enter contrasts in topology, arrange security, application perceivability and control, the executives and nature of administration. SD- LAN decouples control the executives, and information planes to empower an approach driven design for wired and remote LANs. SD-LANs are described by their utilization of a cloud the executives framework and remote network without the nearness of a physical controller.

Security using the SDN paradigm

SDN architecture may enable, facilitate or enhance network-related security applications due to the controller's central view of the network, and its capacity to reprogram the data plane at any time. While security of SDN architecture itself remains an open question that has already been studied a couple of times in the research community, the following paragraphs only focus on the security applications made possible or revisited using SDN.

Several research works on SDN have already investigated security applications built upon the SDN controller, with different aims in mind. Distributed Denial of Service (DDoS) detection and mitigation, as well as botnet and worm propagation, are some concrete use-cases of such applications: basically, the idea consists in periodically collecting network statistics from the forwarding plane of the network in a standardized manner (e.g. using Openflow), and then apply classification algorithms on those statistics in order to detect any network anomalies. If an anomaly is detected, the application instructs the controller how to reprogram the data plane in order to mitigate it.

Another kind of security application leverages the SDN controller by implementing some moving target defense (MTD) algorithms. MTD algorithms are typically used to make any attack on a given system or network more difficult than usual by periodically hiding or changing key properties of that system or network. In traditional networks, implementing MTD algorithms is not a trivial task since it is difficult to build a central authority able of determining - for each part of the system to be protected - which key properties are hid or changed. In an SDN network, such tasks become more straightforward thanks to the centrality of the controller. One application can for example periodically assign virtual IPs to hosts within the network, and the mapping virtual IP/real IP is then performed by the controller. Another application can simulate some fake opened/closed/filtered ports on random hosts in the network in order to add significant noise during reconnaissance phase (e.g. scanning) performed by an attacker.

Additional value regarding security in SDN enabled networks can also be gained using FlowVisor and FlowChecker respectively. The former tries to use a single hardware forwarding plane sharing multiple separated logical networks. Following this approach the same hardware resources can be used for production and development purposes as well as separating monitoring, configuration and internet traffic, where each scenario can have its own logical topology which is called slice. In conjunction with this approach FlowChecker realizes the validation of new OpenFlow rules that are deployed by users using their own slice.

SDN controller applications are mostly deployed in large-scale scenarios, which requires comprehensive checks of possible programming errors. A system to do this called NICE was described in Introducing an overarching security architecture requires a comprehensive and protracted approach to SDN. Since it was introduced, designers are looking at possible ways to secure SDN that do not compromise scalability. One architecture called SN-SECA (SDN+NFV) Security Architecture.

Group Data Delivery Using SDN

Appropriated applications that keep running crosswise over datacenters as a rule repeat information with the end goal of synchronization, blame strength, stack adjusting and getting information closer to clients (which diminishes idleness to clients and builds their apparent throughput). Additionally, numerous applications, for example, Hadoop, recreate information inside a datacenter over various racks to build adaptation to internal failure and make information recuperation simpler. These tasks require information conveyance from one machine or datacenter to numerous machines or datacenters. The procedure of dependably conveying information from one machine to various machines is alluded to as Reliable Group Data Delivery (RGDD).

SDN switches can be utilized for RGDD by means of establishment of standards that enable sending to different active ports. For instance, OpenFlow offers help for Group Tables since variant which makes this conceivable. Utilizing SDN, a focal controller can deliberately and keenly setup sending trees for RGDD. Such trees can be constructed while focusing on system blockage/stack status to enhance execution. For instance, MCTCP is a plan for conveyance to numerous hubs inside datacenters that depends on standard and organized topologies of datacenter systems while DCCast and QuickCast are approaches for quick and productive information and substance replication crosswise over datacenters over private WANs.

Benefits of Software Defined Networking

Software defined networking offers numerous benefits including on-demand provisioning, automated load balancing, streamlined physical infrastructure and the ability to scale network resources in lockstep with application and data needs. As noted on Enterprise Networking Planet, coupled with the ongoing virtualization of servers and storage, SDN ushers in no less than the completely virtualized data center, where end-to-end compute environments will be deployed and decommissioned on a whim.

SDN Challenges: Legacy Network Infrastructure

Inheritance arrange foundation is regularly a blend of seller arrangements, stages and convention arrangements making a definitive objective of a coordinated system biological system a troublesome procedure for some associations. As indicated by Enterprise Networking Planet, it is attainable, however maybe not ideal, to actualize programming characterized organizing on existing physical framework. Today, the venture and substantial clients hope to fabricate new SDN framework from the beginning.

SDN is short for programming characterized organizing. Programming characterized organizing (SDN) is a way to deal with utilizing open conventions, for example, OpenFlow, to apply all inclusive mindful programming control at the edges of the system to get to arrange switches and switches that normally would utilize shut and exclusive firmware.

A SDN application is a product program intended to play out an errand in a product characterized organizing (SDN) condition. SDN applications can supplant and develop capacities that are executed through firmware in the equipment gadgets of a customary system.

Programming characterized organizing (SDN) innovation is a way to deal with distributed computing that encourages arrange the board and empowers automatically productive system design with the end goal to enhance organize execution and monitoring.[1] SDN is intended to address the way that the static engineering of conventional systems is decentralized and complex while current systems require greater adaptability and simple investigating. SDN recommends to incorporate system knowledge in one system part by disassociating the sending procedure of system bundles (information plane) from the steering procedure (control plane). The control plane comprises of at least one controllers which are considered as the mind of SDN organize where the entire knowledge is fused. In any case, the knowledge centralization has its very own disadvantages with regards to security,[2] adaptability and elasticity[3]and this is the primary issue of SDN.

SDN was usually connected with the OpenFlow convention (for remote correspondence with system plane components to determine the way of system packetsacross organize switches) since the last's development in 2011. Be that as it may, since OpenFlow for some, organizations is not any more a selective arrangement, they included restrictive strategies. These incorporate Open Network Environment and Nicira's system virtualization stage.

SD-WAN applies comparable innovation to a wide zone arrange (WAN).

Network Function Virtualization

System capacities virtualization is a system design idea that utilizes the advances of IT virtualization to virtualize whole classes of system hub capacities into building hinders that may associate, or chain together, to make correspondence administrations. NFV depends upon, yet contrasts from, customary server-virtualization procedures, for example, those utilized in big business IT. A virtualized organize capacity, or VNF, may comprise of at least one virtual machines running diverse programming and procedures, over standard high-volume servers, switches and capacity gadgets, or even distributed computing foundation, rather than having custom equipment apparatuses for each system work.

For instance, a virtual session fringe controller could be conveyed to ensure a system without the regular expense and multifaceted nature of getting and introducing physical system insurance units. Different instances of NFV incorporate virtualized stack balancers, firewalls, interruption identification gadgets and WAN quickening agents.

System Function Virtualization expects to change the way, the system administrators designer systems, by developing standard IT virtualization innovation to merge many system hardware types onto industry standard high volume servers, switches and capacity, which could be situated in Data focuses, Network Nodes and at last client premises, as showed in Figure 1. These virtual machines can be instantiated on interest without the establishment of new gear. For instance, arrange administrators may run an open-source programming based firewall in a Virtual Machine (VM). without the requirement for establishment of new gear. At the end of the day, Network Function Virtualization advances the usage of system works in programming that can keep running on a scope of standard IT equipment in server farms and can be overseen (e.g. moved, or duplicated) without the need of changing the physical framework.

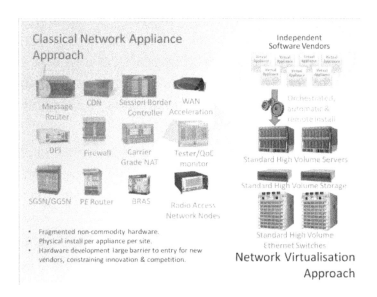

Figure 2.2: Vision for Network Functions Virtualization

Benefits of Network Function Virtualization

System capacities virtualization (NFV) is a rising subject inside the telecoms business, and in the course of recent years, it has turned into an impetus for major transformational changes in the system. Use of Network Functions Virtualization conveys numerous advantages to arrange administrators, adding to huge changes in the broadcast communications industry.

Advantages incorporate:-

- Reduced gear costs and lessened power utilization through combining hardware. Cost effectiveness is a principle driver of NFV.

- NFV permits to digest basic equipment, and empowers versatility, adaptability and mechanization. Enhances the adaptability of system benefit provisioning and decrease an opportunity to convey new administrations.

- Increased speed of arrangement by limiting the common system administrator cycle of advancement. Economies of scale required to cover interests in equipment based functionalities are not any more material for programming based advancement, making practical different methods of highlight development. System Functions Virtualisation will empower arrange administrators to altogether lessen the development cycle.

- The probability of running generation, test and reference offices on a similar foundation gives significantly more proficient test and combination, lessening advancement expenses and time to showcase.

- Services can be quickly scaled up/down as required. What's more, speed of administration sending is enhanced by provisioning remotely in programming with no site visits required to put in new equipment.

- Enabling a wide assortment of eco-frameworks and empowering receptiveness. It opens the virtual machine market to unadulterated programming contestants, little players and the scholarly world, urging more advancement to bring new administrations and new income streams rapidly at much lower chance.

- Reduced vitality utilization by misusing power the board includes in standard servers and capacity, and in addition remaining task at hand solidification and area enhancement. For instance, depending on virtualization methods, it is conceivable to focus the remaining burden on fewer servers amid off-top hours (e.g. medium-term) so the various servers can be turned off or put into a vitality sparing mode.

- Improved operational productivity by exploiting the higher consistency of the physical system stage and its homogeneity to other help stages.

Enablers for Network Function Virtualization

The Network Functions Virtualization (NFV) became achievable with several recent technology developments, such as given below.

Cloud Computing

System Functions Virtualization influences upon present day advancements, for example, those created for distributed computing. At the center of these cloud advances are virtualization instruments: equipment virtualization by methods for hypervisors, and additionally the use of virtual Ethernet switches (e.g. switch) for associating activity between virtual machines and physical interfaces. For correspondence arranged capacities, elite bundle preparing is accessible through rapid multi-center CPUs with high I/O transmission capacity, the utilization of brilliant Ethernet NICs for load sharing and TCP Offloading, and steering parcels straightforwardly to Virtual Machine memory, and survey mode Ethernet drivers (instead of hinder driven, for instance Linux NAPI and Intel's DPDK).

Cloud frameworks give strategies to improve asset accessibility and utilization by methods for coordination and the board components, appropriate to the programmed instantiation of virtual machines in the system, to the administration of assets by doling out virtual apparatuses to the right CPU center, memory and interfaces, to the re-introduction of fizzled VMs, to preview VM states and the relocation of VMs. At long last, the accessibility of open APIs for the executives and information plane control, as OpenFlow, OpenStack, Open Naas or OGF's NSI, give an extra level of incorporation of Network Functions Virtualization and distributed computing.

Industry Standard High Volume Servers

The utilization of industry standard high volume servers is a key component in the financial case for Network Functions Virtualization. An industry standard high volume server is a server manufactured utilizing institutionalized IT segments (for instance x86 engineering) and sold in the millions. A typical component of industry standard high volume servers is that there is focused supply of the subcomponents which are compatible inside the server.

System Appliances which rely upon the improvement of bespoke Application Specific Integrated Circuits (ASICs) will turn out to be progressively uncompetitive against broadly useful processors as the expense of creating ASICs increments exponentially with diminishing component measure. Shipper silicon will stay material for item works executed at scale while ASICs will even now be pertinent for a few kinds of high throughput applications.

Software Defined Networking (SDN)

Software defined networking (SDN) and NFV can be used independently, but SDN makes it much easier to implement and manage NFV. SDN manages network complexity via a network-wide software platform that enables centralized network coordination, control and programmability. SDN provides a programmable and customizable interface that controls and orchestrates the operation of a collection of devices at different levels of abstraction. With it, users can dynamically reconfigure the network to plumb in a function running on a server in the appropriate place in the network using just software mechanisms. Without it, NFV would require much more manual intervention to configure the network to appropriately plumb in software- instantiated functions.

Technical Requirement/Challenges for Network Function Virtualization

As an emerging technology in network industry, NFV brings several challenges to network operators, such as the guarantee of network performance for virtual appliances, their dynamic installation and migration, and their efficient placements etc. These challenges to implement the Network Functions Virtualization need to be addressed before implementing the same.

Interoperability and Compatibility

The key prerequisite/issue for NFV is to structure standard interfaces between a scope of virtual apparatuses as well as between the virtualized executions and the heritage gear. One of the objectives of NFV is to advance receptiveness, in this way arrange transporters may need to incorporate and work servers, hypervisors and virtual machines from various merchants in a multi-occupant NFV condition. Their consistent joining requires a brought together interface to encourage the interoperability among them. The created NFV arrangements should be good with existing Operation and Business Support Systems (OSS/BSS) and Element and Network Management Systems (EMS/NMS), and work in a half breed condition with both physical and virtual system capacities. Over the long haul, organize administrators must have the capacity to relocate easily from exclusive physical machines to open standard based virtual ones, since they will most likely be unable to keep refreshed all their current administrations and hardware in restrictive physical system apparatus based arrangements.

Performance Trade-Off

Since the Network Functions Virtualization approach depends on utilizing industry standard equipment (i.e. evading any exclusive equipment, for example, increasing speed motors) alongside a virtualized systems and apparatuses, a likely reduction in execution may emerge. The test is the manner by which to keep the execution corruption as little as conceivable by utilizing fitting hypervisors and present day programming innovations, with the goal that the antagonistic impacts on dormancy and throughput are limited. The accessible execution of the fundamental.

Migration from and co-existence of legacy while ensuring compatibility with existing platforms

Executions of Network Functions Virtualization (NFV) must exist together with system administrators' heritage arrange hardware and be perfect with their current Element Management Systems, Network Management Systems, OSS and BSS, and conceivably existing IT organization frameworks, if Network Functions Virtualization coordination and IT organization are to combine. The Network Functions Virtualization design must help a relocation way from the present exclusive physical system machine based answers for more open principles based virtual system apparatus arrangements. As such, Network Functions Virtualisation must work in a half and half system made out of traditional physical system machines and virtual system apparatuses. Virtual machines must, in this way, utilize/bolster existing North Bound Interfaces (for the executives and control) and interwork with physical apparatuses actualizing similar capacities.

Management and Orchestration

System Functions Virtualization displays a chance, through the adaptability managed by programming system apparatuses working in an open and institutionalized framework, to quickly adjust the board and coordination to North Bound Interfaces to all around characterized gauges and dynamic details. This will incredibly diminish the expense and time to incorporate new virtual machines into a system administrator's working condition. Programming Defined Networking (SDN) further stretches out this to streamlining the combination of bundle and optical switches into the framework e.g. A virtual machine or Network

Functions Virtualization arrangement framework may control the sending practices of physical switches utilizing SDN.

Security & Resilience

While sending virtualized organize capacities, administrators need to guarantee that the security highlights of their system won't be unfavorably influenced. NFV may acquire new security worries alongside its advantages. Beginning desires are that Network Functions Virtualizations enhances arrange strength and accessibility by permitting system capacities to be reproduced on interest after a disappointment. A virtual machine ought to be as secure as a physical apparatus if the foundation, particularly the hypervisor and its arrangement, is secure. System administrators will look for instruments to control and confirm hypervisor designs. They will likewise require security

Reliability and Stability

Dependability is a vital necessity for system administrators when offering explicit administrations (e.g., voice call and video on interest), regardless of through physical or virtual system machines. Bearers need to ensure that benefit unwavering quality and administration level understanding are not unfavorably influenced when advancing to NFV. To meet the unwavering quality prerequisite, NFV needs to incorporate the strength with programming when moving to mistake inclined equipment stages. Every one of these tasks make new purposes of disappointment that ought to be taken care of consequently.

Furthermore, guaranteeing administration security represents another test to NFV, particularly while reconfiguring or moving a substantial number of programming based virtual machines from various sellers and running on various hypervisors. System administrators ought to have the capacity to move VNF segments from one equipment stage onto an alternate stage while as yet fulfilling the administration progression req0uirement. They additionally need to determine the estimations of a few key execution pointers to accomplish benefit solidness and coherence, including most extreme non-deliberate parcel misfortune rate and call/session drop rate, greatest per-stream deferral and idleness variety, and most extreme time to recognize and recoup from disappointments.

Simplicity

It should be guaranteed that virtualized arrange stages will be less difficult to work than those that exist today. A huge and topical concentration for system administrators is along these lines, on disentanglement of the plenty of complex system stages and emotionally supportive networks which have advanced over many years of system innovation development, while keeping up congruity to help imperative income creating administrations. It is essential to abstain from exchanging one arrangement of operational migraines for an alternate however similarly obstinate arrangement of operational cerebral pains.

Framework

The NFV framework consists of three main components:

- Virtualized network functions (VNFs) are software implementations of network functions that can be deployed on a network functions virtualization infrastructure (NFVI).

- Network functions virtualization infrastructure (NFVI) is the totality of all hardware and software components that build the environment where VNFs are deployed. The NFV infrastructure can span several locations. The network providing connectivity between these locations is considered as part of the NFV infrastructure.

- Network functions virtualization management and orchestration architectural framework (NFV-MANO Architectural Framework) is the collection of all functional blocks, data repositories used by these blocks, and reference points and interfaces through which these functional blocks exchange information for the purpose of managing and orchestrating NFVI and VNFs.

- **The NFV Infrastructure (NFVI)** consists of physical networking, computing and storage resources that can be geographically distributed and exposed as a common networking/NFV infrastructure. It is the combination of both hardware and software resources which build up the environment in which VNFs are deployed, managed and executed. The NFVI can span across several locations i.e. places where NFVI-PoPs are operated. The network providing connectivity between these locations is regarded to be part of the NFVI.

- **Virtualized Network Functions (VNFs)** are software implementations or virtualization of network functions (NFs) that are deployed on virtual resources such as VM. Virtualized network functions, or VNFs, are responsible for handling specific network functions that run in one or more virtual machines on top of the hardware networking infrastructure, which can include routers, switches, servers, cloud computing systems and more. Individual virtualized network functions can be chained or combined together in a building block-style fashion to deliver full-scale networking communication services.

- **NFV Management and Orchestration (NFV MANO)** functions provide the necessary tools for operating the virtualized infrastructure, managing the life cycle of the VNFs and orchestrating virtual infrastructure and network functions to compose value-added end-to-end network services. NFV MANO focuses on all virtualization specific management task necessary in the NFV framework.

Virtualization provides the opportunity for a flexible software design. Existing networking services are supported by diverse network functions that are connected in a static way. NFV enables additional dynamic schemes to create and manage network functions. Its key concept is the VNF forwarding graph which simplifies the service chain provisioning by quickly and inexpensively creating, modifying and removing Virtualized Network Functions service chains. On one hand, we can compose several VNFs together to reduce management complexity, for instance, by merging the serving gateway (SGW) and Packet Data Network Gateway (PGW) of a 4G core network into a single box. On the other hand, we can decompose a VNF into smaller functional blocks for reusability and faster response time. However, we note that the actual carrier-grade deployment of VNF instances should be transparent to end-to-end services.

Distributed NFV

The underlying impression of NFV was that virtualized ability ought to be executed in server farms. This methodology works in many – however not all – cases. NFV presumes and accentuates the vastest conceivable adaptability with regards to the physical area of the virtualized capacities.

In a perfect world, in this manner, virtualized capacities ought to be found where they are the best and slightest costly. That implies a specialist co-op ought to be allowed to find NFV in every single conceivable area, from the server farm to the system hub to the client premises. This methodology, known as appropriated NFV, has been accentuated from the earliest starting point as NFV was being produced and institutionalized, and is noticeable in the as of late discharged NFV ISG records.

For a few cases there are clear points of interest for a specialist organization to find this virtualized usefulness at the client premises. These focal points go from financial aspects to execution to the plausibility of the capacities being virtualized.

NFV Modularity Benefits

When planning and building up the product that gives the VNFs, sellers may structure that product into programming parts (execution perspective of a product design) and bundle those segments into at least one pictures (sending perspective of a product engineering). These merchant characterized programming parts are called VNF Components (VNFCs). VNFs are actualized with at least one VNFCs and it is expected, without loss of sweeping statement, that VNFC occasions delineate to VM Images.

VNFCs ought to when all is said in done have the capacity to scale up as well as scale out. By having the capacity to allot adaptable (virtual) CPUs to every one of the VNFC occurrences, the system the board layer can scale up (i.e., scale vertically) the VNFC to give the throughput/execution and versatility desires over a solitary framework or a solitary stage. So also, the system the board layer can scale out (i.e., scale on a level plane) a VNFC by initiating various cases of such VNFC over numerous stages and subsequently connect with the execution and design details while not bargaining the other VNFC work dependable qualities.

Difference between SDN and NFV for IoT Basics of IoT
System Management with NETCONF

System capacities virtualization and programming characterized organizing are two firmly related innovations that regularly exist together, yet not generally. NFV and SDN are the two pushes toward system virtualization and robotization, yet the two innovations have distinctive objectives.

A SDN can be viewed as a progression of system objects -, for example, switches, switches and firewalls - that are conveyed in an exceptionally mechanized way. The computerization might be accomplished by utilizing business or open source apparatuses - like SDN controllers and OpenFlow - in view of the director's necessities. A full programming characterized system may cover just generally direct systems administration prerequisites, for example, VLAN and interface provisioning.

By and large, SDN will likewise be connected to server virtualization, giving the paste that sticks virtual systems together. This may include NFV, yet not really. NFV is the way toward moving administrations like load adjusting, firewalls and interruption anticipation frameworks from devoted equipment into a virtualized domain. This is, obviously, some portion of a more extensive development toward the virtualization of utilizations and administrations.

Capacities like storing and substance control can without much of a stretch be relocated to a virtualized situation, however won't really give any noteworthy decrease in working expenses until the point when some insight is presented. This is on the grounds that a straight physical to virtual, from an operational point of view, accomplishes little past the underlying decrease in power and rack-space utilization. Until the point that some unique knowledge is presented with a SDN innovation, NFV organize organizations acquire a large number of indistinguishable imperatives from customary equipment machine arrangements, for example, static, overseer characterized and oversaw strategies.

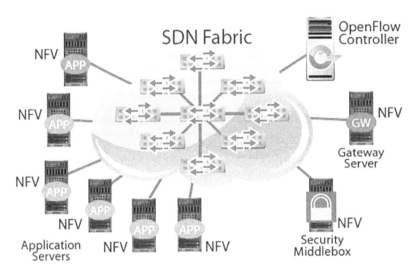

Figure: 2.3 How SDN and NFV work together

A decent model is virtualized application conveyance controllers (ADCs). With cautious design, it is conceivable to respond to the system state and turn up or down application servers as requests rise and fall. Customary equipment organizations have possessed the capacity to do this for some time, in any case, and the design is extremely static; it doesn't take into account the situation where the ADC itself ends up over-burden, or an extra application should be brought into generation rapidly.

How SDN and NFV Work Together

With SDN highlights driving a NFV arrange, a few valuable things begin to occur. The virtual overlay made by SDN helps arrangement and deal with the virtual system capacities with NFV. SDN additionally oversees activity stacks all the more productively, so the system can respond when things need to change at smaller scale and full scale levels. An extra example can be provisioned in a bunch of virtualized ADCs as the heap increments, and generation applications can without much of a stretch be cloned and redeployed in an advancement domain. The potential for SDN and NFV is interminable.

In this way, it's splendidly conceivable to have NFV without the consideration of an out and out programming characterized arrange. In any case, NFV and SDN are frequently conveyed together, and a product characterized organize that drives NFV is a ground-breaking mix.

Neither NFV nor SDN are turnkey benefits in mid 2014 - a lot of mix and approach configuration still need to occur. Gauges work for both SDN and NFV arrange structures is as yet continuous, and the two advances require more demonstrated organizations. Be that as it may, while the saddle isn't completely set up, NFV and SDN can turn into a reality for some ventures. So, the devices are quickly developing, and numerous merchants are putting up advancements for sale to the public that help SDN or NFV arrangements. At last, the usage of either or the two innovations will be driven by the business needs.

Differences Between SDN and Network Functions Virtualization

As server farm heads search for advancements that streamline organize capacities while offering lower costs, more noteworthy adaptability and enhancements in system nimbleness, two methodologies are being grasped in the systems administration world: Software Defined Networking (SDN) and Network Functions Virtualization (NFV). While both offer new and diverse approaches to configuration, execute and deal with the system and its administrations, both have the ability to fundamentally improve arrange execution.

To address bigger amounts of information being transmitted, put away and oversaw on high volume servers, switches, stockpiling innovation and in distributed computing conditions, SDN and NFV are progressively getting to be alluring alternatives to integrators and esteem included affiliates (VARs) who need to recognize techniques that compliment virtualization and system programmability.

There are a few explanations behind the development of SDN and NFV. Drivers of these innovations incorporate the development of huge information, cell phones, and the extension of disseminated databases and servers situated at various destinations and associated over long separations through open and private mists that require strong information the executives frameworks and access to transmission capacity on interest.

As indicated by an examination from Infonetics Research the worldwide bearer SDN and NFV equipment and programming business sector will develop from under $500 million out of 2013 to over $11 billion of every 2018.

As VARs set out on an arrangement to execute SDN and NFV, in any case, they ought to value the contrasts between these two systems administration approaches and perceive the manners by which both can help organize heads lift their administration abilities.

Both SDN and NFV depend on programming that works on product servers and switches, yet the two advancements work at various dimensions of the system.

SDN is intended to offer clients an approach to oversaw organize benefits through programming that makes arranges midway programmable, which takes into account quicker design. Basically, SDN makes the system programmable by isolating the framework that chooses where movement is sent (the control plane) from the fundamental framework that pushes parcels of information to explicit goals (the information plane). As system chairmen and VARs know, SDN is based on switches that can be customized through a SDN controller using an industry standard controller like OpenFlow.

On the other hand, NFV isolates arrange capacities from switches, firewalls, stack balancers and other devoted equipment gadgets and permits organize administrations to be facilitated on virtual machines. Virtual machines have a hypervisor, additionally called a virtual machine administrator, which enables different working frameworks to share a solitary equipment processor. At the point when the hypervisor controls arrange capacities those administrations that required devoted equipment can be performed on standard x86 servers.

As systems integrators and VARs work with network administrators to deploy these technologies, it's important to look at the differences between each. Here are five key differences to keep in mind:

1. The Basic Idea:

SDN separates control and data and centralizes control and programmability of the network. NFV transfers network functions from dedicated appliances to generic servers.

2. Areas of Operation

SDN operates in a campus, data center and/or cloud environment

NFV targets the service provider network

3. Initial Application Target.

SDN software targets cloud orchestration and networking NFV software targets routers, firewalls, gateways, WAN, CDN, accelerators and SLA assurance

4. Protocols

SDN – OpenFlow

NFV – None

5. Supporting organization

SDN: Open Networking Foundation (ONF)

NFV: ETSI NFV Working Group

For affiliates and frameworks integrators dealing with undertakings that execute NFV into the system, they ought to think about that on the grounds that NFV can include server limit through programming as opposed to acquiring more committed equipment gadgets to fabricate organize administrations, arrange managers can convey to the server farm cost decreases in capital and working costs.

Integrators ought to likewise think about that they are including esteem when they help organize directors design, oversee, secure and streamline arrange assets through SDN programs, which arrange chiefs can compose without anyone else in light of the fact that these projects don't rely upon exclusive programming.

As VARs and integrators pass on the advantages of SDN and NFV, they'll discover a wealth of approaches to assume a basic job in helping system overseers, and the organizations they work for, to set aside some cash while building a system that is less demanding to oversee, quicker to arrange and more brilliant at handling the developing information difficulties within recent memory.

Features	SDN	NFV
Focus or major role	SDN focuses on data center.	NFV focuses on service providers or operators.
Strategy	It splits the control and data forwarding planes.	It replaces hardware network devices with software.
protocol	Uses OpenFlow	Not finalized yet, does support OpenFlow
Where the applications will run?	Applications run on industry standard servers or switches	Applications run on industry standard servers
Prime intiative supporters	Vendors of enterprise networking software and hardware.	Telecom service providers or operators.
Business initiator	Corporate IT	Service provider
Customer benefit or end user benefit	Drives down complexity and cost and increases agility.	Drives down complexity and cost and increases agility.
Initial applications	Cloud orchestration and networking	routers, firewalls, gateways, CDN, WAN accelerators, SLA assurance
Formalization body	Open Networking Foundation (ONF)	ETSI NFV Working Group

Table: 2.3.2 Differences between SDN and NFV

Netconf Yang

This is a short introduction on the NETCONF information demonstrating dialect YANG. To take in more about YANG, investigate the instructional exercises and precedents at YANG Central. The clear asset is RFC 6020, which is a fantastic and very meaningful instructional booklet. On the off chance that you ask why NETCONF needs an information demonstrating dialect, look at the "Why YANG?" report at YANG Central.

The Basics

An information demonstrate depicts how information is spoken to and gotten to. In YANG, information models are spoken to by definition chains of importance called outline trees. Cases of mapping trees are called information trees and are encoded in XML.

YANG gives two develops to determine leaf hubs: leaf and leaf-list articulations. They vary in that a leaf hub has at most one example, while a leaf-list hub may have numerous occasions.

This YANG snippet specifies a flag called enabled that defaults to true:

```
leaf enabled {
    type boolean;
        default true;
}
Example XML instance:
    <enabled>false</enabled>
```

The following YANG example specifies a list of cipher names:

```
    leaf-list cipher {
type string; }
Example XML instance:
    <cipher>blowfish-cbc</cipher>
        <cipher>3des-cbc</cipher>
```

The number of valid entries in a leaf-list can be constrained by optional min-elements and max-elements

There are additionally two develops in YANG for determining non-leaf hubs: holder and rundown proclamations. They vary for the most part in that a compartment hub has at most one occurrence, while a rundown hub may have various cases (list sections are recognized by keys that separate them from one another).

The accompanying YANG precedent uses a holder proclamation to characterize a timeout component for a demand to a server. The timeout has two segments: get to timeout, which speaks to the most extreme time without server reaction, and retries, which speaks to the quantity of demand endeavors before surrendering.

```
container timeout {
    leaf access-timeout {
        type uint32;
}
            leaf retries {
                type uint8;
            }
        }
Example XML instance:
        <timeout>
            <access-timeout>60</access-timeout>
            <retries>2</retries>
</timeout>
```

The next example illustrates YANG lists. The entries in a list are identified by keys that distinguish them from each other. Here computer users are identified with their login name:

```
list user {
        key "login-name";
            leaf login-name {
        type string;
    }
    leaf full-name {
    type string;
    }
}
```

Example XML instances:

```
<user>
<login-name>hakanm</login-name>
<full-name>Hakan Millroth</fullname>
</user>
<user>
<login-name>mbj</login-name>
<full-name>Martin Bjorklund</fullname> </user>
```

The models so far have just utilized assembled-in YANG types. The arrangement of fabricated

- in types are like those of many programming dialects, however with a few contrasts because of uncommon prerequisites from the administration area. YANG likewise gives a component through which extra sorts might be characterized (these are called determined sorts). For instance, the accompanying characterizes a sort percent that is a confinement of the constructed

- in type uint8:

```
typedef percent {
    type uint8 {
range "0.. 100";
}
        }
```

The next example defines the type ip-address as the union of two other derived types (union is a built-in type):

```
typedef ip-address {
type union {
    type ipv4-address;
        type ipv6-address;
}
    }
```

More Data Structuring Features

A decision hub in the construction tree characterizes an arrangement of choices, just a single may exist at any one time. A decision comprises of various branches, characterized with case substatements. The hubs from at most one of the decision's branches exist in the information tree (the decision hub itself does not exist in the information tree). Model

```
choice route-distinguisher
    { case ip-address-based {
        leaf ip-address {
type ipv4-address;
}
leaf ip-address-number {
type uint16;
}
}
case asn32-based {
leaf asn32 {
type uint32;
}
leaf two-byte-number { type uint16;
}}}
Example XML instantiation:
    <asn32>12356789</asn32>
<two-byte-number>2468</two-byte-number>
```

A grouping defines a reusable collection of nodes. Here we define a grouping endpoint comprising two leaf nodes:

```
grouping endpoint {
    leaf address {
type ip-address;
}
```

```
leaf port {
type port-number;
}
}
```

The utilizations explanation is utilized to reference a gathering definition, duplicating the hubs characterized by the gathering into the present pattern tree. Proceeding with the model, we can reuse the endpoint gathering in characterizing the source and goal of an association:

```
container connection {
container source {
uses endpoint {
refine port {
default 161;
}
}
}
container destination {
uses endpoint {
refine port {
default 161;
}
}
}
}
```

Here we have used the (optional) refine statement. Example XML instance:

```
<connection>
<source>
<address>192.168.0.3</address>
<port>8080</port>
```

```
</source>
<destination>
<address>192.168.0.4</address>
<port>8080</port>
</destination>
</connection>
```

The nearness explanation offers semantics to the presence of a compartment in the information tree (regularly a holder is only an information organizing component). It takes as a contention a documentation string that depicts what the model architect expect the hub's quality to imply:

```
container logging {
presence "Enables logging"; leaf directory {
type string;
default "/var/log/myapplication";
}
}
```

An alternative to using presence is to define a leaf (called, for example, enabled or disabled or on or off) conveying the presence of the container.

References

The leafref fabricated •-in type is utilized to reference a specific leaf occasion in the information tree, as determined by a way. This way is indicated utilizing the XML Path Language (XPath), in a documentation that is like the punctuation for registry ways in Unix/Linux. Think about this model:

```
leaf interface-name {
type leafref {
path "/interface/name";
}
}
```

Here interface-name is referencing another leaf using an absolute path. The nextexample instead lets reference a leaf using a relative path:

```
leaf interface-name {
type leafref {
path "../interface/name";
}
}
```

There is an analogous referencing construct for list keys called key ref.

Data Constraints

YANG underpins a few kinds of limitations that express semantic properties of the information being demonstrated.

Information hubs can speak to either arrangement information or state information. The config explanation indicates whether the definition it happens in speak to arrangement information (config=true) or status information (config=false). On the off chance that config isn't determined, the default is equivalent to the parent pattern hub's config esteem. In the event that the best hub does not indicate a config articulation, the default is config=true.

YANG gives an obligatory explanation to express that a hub must exist in the information tree (it is additionally conceivable to have discretionary hubs). The accompanying precedent demonstrates the utilization of config and compulsory:

```
leaf host-name {
type string; mandatory true; config true;
}
```

The unique statement ensures unique values within list siblings. Here is an example of its use (note that the constraint specifies that the combination of two leaf values, ip and port, must be unique):

```
list server {
key "name";
unique "ip port";
leaf name {
type string;
}
leaf ip {
type ip-address;
}
leaf port {
type port-number;
}
}
```

The must statement expresses constraints that must be satisfied by each data node in the structure where it is defined. The must constraints are expressed using XPath expressions. The following examples models an IP address that does not belong to the 192.* or 127.* networks:

```
leaf mirrorIp {
    type ip-address;
    default 0.0.0.0;
    must "false() = starts-with(current(), '192')" { error-message
    "The mirrorIp is in the forbidden "+"192.* network";
}
    must "false() = starts-with(current(), '127')" { error-
    message "The mirrorIp is in the occupied "+"127.* network";

}
}
```

Modules

YANG sorts out information models into modules and submodules. A module can import information from different modules, and incorporate information from submodules. Other than pattern definitions, a module contains header proclamations (yang-•-version, namespace, prefix), linkage articulations (import and incorporate), meta data (association, contact), and an update history.

All hubs characterized in a module have a place with a predefined XML namespace, which is indicated by the URI of the namespace. It is great practice to have a one-•-to-•-one correspondence among modules and namespaces.

In the event that an import or incorporate explanation incorporates an amendment date substatement, definitions are taken from the predefined update of the foreign made or included module. By bringing in determined module modifications one can enable distributed modules to develop freely after some time. YANG gives unmistakable principles to how distributed modules can develop after some time and still be in reverse good (to distort, it is conceivable to include new definitions, yet not to erase old definitions or change effectively distributed definitions).

Here is a case of a module definition:

```
module acme-module {
namespace    "http://acme.example.com/module";    prefix
acme;
import "yang-types" {
prefix yang;
}
include "acme-system";
```

organization "ACME Inc."; contact joe@acme.example.com; description "The module for entities implementing the ACME products";
revision 2007-06-09 {
description "Initial revision.";
}......
}

The module chain of importance can be increased, enabling one module to add information hubs to the progressive system characterized in another module (without changing the expanded module). Increase can be restrictive, utilizing when explanations, with new hubs seeming just if certain conditions are met.

In the accompanying precedent we (unequivocally) increase a nonexclusive switch module to an information display for a RIP directing stack:

```
module rip_router {
    import router {
        prefix r;
    }
    augment "/r:system/r:router" {
        container rip {
            leaf version {... }
            list network-ip {... }
            list network-ifname {... }
            list neighbor {... }
}...
    }
```

Note that the import statement assigns the prefix r to the imported module router. When we then reference identifiers from that module we must use the prefix, as in

/r:system/r:router.

This example also illustrates a common YANG design pattern with a top-level container (rip in this case).

RPCs and Notifications

YANG allows the definition of NETCONF RPCs, extending the base set of operations provided by the NETCONF standard. Input and output parameters are modeled using YANG data definition statements. In the following example we model a new RPC for activating software images:

```
rpc activate-software-image {
    input {
leaf image-name {
type string;
        }
        }
output {
leaf status {
type string;
}
}
        }
```

YANG data definition statements can also be used to model the names and content of NETCONF notifications. Here is an example where we reuse the definition of a connection from above:

```
notification link-failure {
        description "A link failure has been detected";
        container link {
            uses connection
        }
}
```

This example also illustates the use of description statement. All YANG data definition statements (leaf, list, leaf-list, etc) can include description statements.

YANG

YANG is a particular dialect speaking to information structures in a XML tree organize. The information demonstrating dialect accompanies various inherent information types. Extra application explicit information types can be gotten from the worked in information types. More intricate reusable information structures can be spoken to as groupings. YANG information models can utilize XPATH articulations to characterize imperatives on the components of a YANG information display.

Many system the board conventions have related information displaying dialects. The primary generally sent Internet standard for system the executives was the Simple Network Management Protocol (SNMP). The information displaying dialect related with SNMP was known as the Structure of Management Information (SMI).

Not long after the advancement of the NETCONF convention in the IETF, it turned out to be certain that an information demonstrating dialect was expected to characterize information models controlled by the NETCONF convention. A plan group made a suggestion that turned into the premise of the YANG language.The syntactic structure and the base kind framework was basically obtained from SMIng. Notwithstanding, in view of the exercises gained from the SMIng venture, no endeavors were made to make YANG convention impartial. Rather, YANG integrates with ideas of the NETCONF convention, for example, the suspicion that information show occasions can be serialized into XML.

YANG is an information demonstrating dialect for the NETCONF design the board convention. Together, NETCONF and YANG give the instruments that organize directors need to robotize setup assignments crosswise over heterogeneous gadgets in a product characterized arrange (SDN).

The YANG information demonstrating dialect gives portrayals of a system's hubs and their collaborations. Every YANG module characterizes a chain of command of information that can be utilized for NETCONF-based activities - including arrangement, state information, Remote Procedure Calls (RPCs) and notices. Modules can import information from other outside modules and incorporate information from sub-modules.

YANG was created by the IETF NETCONF Data Modeling Language Working Group (NETMOD) to be effectively perused by people and as of this composition, Cisco, Juniper and Ericsson all help NETCONF and YANG. The YANG detail is distributed as RFC 6020 and YANG types as RFC 6021.

YANG (Yet Another Next Generation) is an information demonstrating dialect for the meaning of information sent over the NETCONF arrange design convention. The YANG information displaying dialect was created by the NETMOD working gathering in the Internet Engineering Task Force (IETF) and was distributed as RFC 6020 in October 2010. The information demonstrating dialect can be utilized to show both setup information and also state information of system components. Besides, YANG can be utilized to characterize the configuration of occasion warnings discharged by system components and it enables information modelers to characterize the mark of remote method calls that can be conjured on system components by means of the NETCONF convention. The dialect, being convention autonomous, would then be able to be changed over into any encoding configuration, e.g. XML or JSON, that the system setup convention bolsters.

YANG is a particular dialect speaking to information structures in a XML tree design. The information displaying dialect accompanies various inherent information types. Extra application explicit information types can be gotten from the worked in information types. More intricate reusable information structures can be spoken to as groupings. YANG information models can utilize XPATHexpressions to characterize limitations on the components of a YANG information display.

History

Many system the board conventions have related information displaying dialects. The principal broadly conveyed Internet standard for system the executives was the Simple Network Management Protocol (SNMP). The information displaying dialect related with SNMP was known as the Structure of Management Information (SMI). The SMI dialect itself depended on the 1988 rendition of the Abstract Syntax Notation One (ASN.1). The present rendition of the SMI dialect, SMIv2 characterized in RFC 2578, RFC 2579, RFC 2580, has formed into an all- encompassing subset of ASN.1.

In the late 1990s, a venture was begun to make a trade for SMIv2, which was called SMIng. One inspiration was to decouple SMIng from the administration convention SNMP and to give SMIng a syntactic structure that is both simple to parse for PC projects and simple to learn for individuals acquainted with programming dialects that utilization a C-like documentation. While the SMIng venture did not prevail in the IETF, the SMIng determinations were distributed as exploratory archives in May 2004 (RFC 3780, RFC 3781).

Not long after the advancement of the NETCONF convention in the IETF, it turned out to be certain that an information displaying dialect was expected to characterize information models controlled by the NETCONF convention. A plan group made a recommendation that turned into the premise of the YANG language.[4] The syntactic structure and the base sort framework was basically acquired from

SMIng. Be that as it may, in view of the exercises gained from the SMIng venture, no endeavors were made to make YANG convention nonpartisan. Rather, YANG integrates with ideas of the NETCONF convention, for example, the supposition that information display occurrences can be serialized into XML. Institutionalization of YANG began with the development of the NETMOD working gathering in April 2008. The YANG 1.0 particular was distributed as RFC 6020 in October 2010. As of late, the NETMOD working gathering has been chipping away at YANG 1.1, which has been distributed in August 2016 in RFC 7950.

Example

The accompanying YANG module precedent games demonstrates an information show for group activities. The module proclaims a namespace and a prefix and imports the sort library module ietf-yang-types before characterizing the sort season. It at that point characterizes a compartment sports that incorporates a rundown of people and a rundown of groups. A group has a rundown of players that reference people through the leafref type and its way limitation.

```
module example-sports {
    namespace "http://example.com/example-
    sports"; prefix sports;
    import ietf-yang-types { prefix yang; }
    typedef season {
type string;
    description
    "The name of a sports season, including the type and
    the year,
    e.g, 'Champions League 2014/2015'.";
}
```

```
container sports {
    config true;
list person {
    key name;
    leaf name { type string; }
    leaf birthday { type yang:date-and-time; mandatory true; }
    }
    list team {
        key name;
        leaf name { type string; }
        list player {
            key "name season";
            unique number;
            leaf name { type leafref { path "/sports/person/
            name"; } } leaf season { type season; }
            leaf number { type uint16; mandatory true; }
            leaf scores { type uint16; default 0; }
            }
        }
    }
}
```

YANG Modules Overview

YANG information models involve modules and submodules and can characterize arrangement and state information, warnings, and RPCs for use by NETCONF-based activities. A YANG module characterizes an information show through its information, and the various leveled association of and imperatives on that information. Every module is extraordinarily recognized by a namespace URI.

A module characterizes a solitary information display. Be that as it may, a module can reference definitions in different modules and submodules by utilizing the import articulation to import outer modules or the incorporate proclamation to incorporate at least one submodules. Also, a module can expand another information show by utilizing the increase explanation to characterize the situation of the new hubs in the information display pecking order and the when proclamation to characterize the conditions under which the new hubs are legitimate. A module utilizes the element articulation to determine parts of a module that are restrictive and the deviation proclamation to indicate where the gadget's execution may go astray from the first definition.When you import an outer module, you characterize a prefix that is utilized while referencing definitions in the foreign made module. We prescribe that you utilize indistinguishable prefix from that characterized in the foreign made module to maintain a strategic distance from clashes.

YANG models information utilizing a various leveled, tree-based structure with hubs. YANG characterizes four hubs types. Every hub has a name, and relying upon the hub type, the hub may either characterize an esteem or contain an arrangement of youngster hubs. The hubs types are:

- leaf hub—Contains a solitary estimation of an explicit kind
- leaf-list hub—Contains a succession of leaf hubs
- container hub—Contains a gathering of related hubs containing single tyke hubs, which can be any of the four hub types
- list hub—Contains an arrangement of rundown passages, every one of which is particularly distinguished by at least one key leafs

In YANG, each leaf and leaf-list hub incorporates the sort articulation to distinguish the information type for substantial information for that hub. YANG characterizes an arrangement of inherent kinds and furthermore gives the typedef proclamation to characterizing a got sort from a base sort, which can be either a worked in sort or another inferred sort.

As a matter of course, a hub characterizes design information. A hub characterizes state information on the off chance that it is labeled as config false. Setup information is returned utilizing the NETCONF <get-config> task, and state information is returned utilizing the NETCONF <get> activity.

Netopeer

Netopeer is an arrangement of NETCONF devices based on the libnetconf library. It enables administrators to interface with their NETCONF-empowered gadgets and in addition designers to permit control their gadgets by means of NETCONF. More data about NETCONF convention can be found at NETCONF WG.

With the encounters from Netopeer, we have moved our exercises to deal with up and coming age of this NETCONF toolset dependent on libyang library. Netopeer2 is develop enough to be utilized as a substitution of the first Netopeer apparatuses. In this manner, the Netopeer is not any more created neither kept up.

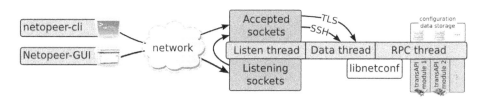

Figure: Tools Overview

Netopeer-CLI

CLI interface enabling client to associate with a NETCONF-empowered gadget and to acquire and control its design information.

- Man Pages
- netopeer-cli(1)

Netopeer-server

The fundamental Netopeer server following the incorporated engineering. netopeer-server should keep running as a framework benefit controlling a gadget. Of course, we give precedent modules to control a few zones of a GNU/Linux work area (organize interfaces, parcel channel and generally speaking framework data). The netopeer-server enables you to just change the modules to utilize your very own control modules.

As a major aspect of the Netopeer server, there is an arrangement of the accompanying apparatuses:

- netopeer-server as the principle benefit daemon incorporating the SSH/TLS server.
- netopeer-supervisor as an instrument to deal with the netopeer-server's modules.
- netopeer-configurator as an apparatus for the server previously run setup.
- Man Pages
- netopeer-server(8)
- netopeer-manager(1)
- netopeer-configurator(1)

Running the server in docker

This storehouse has a Dockerfile that can be utilized to make a holder that manufactures netopeer-server and begins the administration. You require a linux with working docker establishment to utilize it.

To fabricate the holder:

git clone
https://github.com/CESNET/netopeer.git album netopeer
docker fabricate - t
netopeer. To begin it:
docker run - it - rm - p 8300:830 - name netopeer

The line above maps netopeer's netconf port to 8300 on the host. You can associate with that port with ncclient with no client or secret phrase (as long as you have a substantial private key on the host).

TransAPI modules

Netopeer ventures gives a few fundamental transAPI modules that, other than their usefulness, fill in as models for composing the libnetconf transAPI modules. These modules are situated inside the transAPI/registry.

cfgsystem

TransAPI module executing ietf-framework information demonstrate following RFC 7317.

Netopeer GUI

The Apache module with an online GUI enabling client to associate with a NETCONF-empowered gadget and to acquire and control its design information from a graphical interface.

This part is accessible as an independent venture at GitHub.

Interoperability

In November 2012, preceding the IETF 85 meeting, a portion of these devices were partaking in NETCONF Interoperability Testing.

All apparatuses are based over the libnetconf library and enables you to utilize the accompanying NETCONF highlights:

- NETCONF v1.0 and v1.1 compliant (RFC 6241)
- NETCONF over SSH (RFC 6242) including Chunked Framing Mechanism
- DNSSEC SSH Key Fingerprints (RFC 4255)
- NETCONF over TLS (RFC 5539bis)
- NETCONF Writable-running capability (RFC 6241)
- NETCONF Candidate configuration capability (RFC 6241)
- NETCONF Validate capability (RFC 6241)
- NETCONF Distinct startup capability (RFC 6241)
- NETCONF URL capability (RFC 6241
- NETCONF Event Notifications (RFC 5277 and RFC 6470)
- NETCONF With-defaults capability (RFC 6243)
- NETCONF Access Control (RFC 6536)
- NETCONF Call Home (Reverse SSH draft, RFC 5539bis)
- NETCONF Server Configuration (IETF Draft)

Simple Network Management Protocol (SNMP) is an Internet Standard convention for gathering and arranging data about oversaw gadgets on IP systems and for adjusting that data to change gadget conduct. Gadgets that regularly bolster SNMP incorporate link modems, switches, switches, servers, workstations, printers, and the sky is the limit from there.

SNMP is broadly utilized in system the executives for system checking. SNMP uncovered administration information as factors on the oversaw frameworks composed in an administration data base (MIB) which depict the framework status and setup. These factors would then be able to be remotely questioned (and, in a few conditions, controlled) by overseeing applications. Three critical adaptations of SNMP have been produced and sent. SNMPv1 is the first form of the convention. Later forms, SNMPv2c and SNMPv3, include enhancements in execution, adaptability and security. SNMP is a segment of the Internet Protocol Suite as characterized by the Internet Engineering Task Force (IETF). It comprises of an arrangement of benchmarks for system the executives, including an application layer convention, a database pattern, and an arrangement of information objects.

Overview and basic concepts

In average employments of SNMP, at least one regulatory PCs called directors have the assignment of observing or dealing with a gathering of hosts or gadgets on a PC arrange. Each overseen framework executes a product part called a specialist which reports data by means of SNMP to the director.

An SNMP-managed network consists of three key components:

- Managed devices
- Agent – software which runs on managed devices
- Network management station (NMS) – software which runs on the manager

An oversaw gadget is a system hub that actualizes a SNMP interface that permits unidirectional (read-just) or bidirectional (read and compose) access to hub explicit data. Overseen gadgets trade hub explicit data with the NMSs. At times called organize components, the oversaw gadgets can be any sort of gadget, including, however not restricted to, switches, get to servers, switches, link modems, spans, centers, IP phones, IP camcorders, PC hosts, and printers. A specialist is a system the executives programming module that lives on an oversaw gadget. A specialist has nearby learning of the executives data and makes an interpretation of that data to or from a SNMP-explicit shape. A system the executives station executes applications that screen and control oversaw gadgets. NMSs give the majority of the preparing and memory assets required for system the executives. At least one NMSs may exist on any overseen arrange.

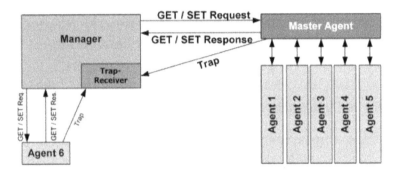

Management Information Base

SNMP operators uncover the executives information on the oversaw frameworks as factors. The convention additionally allows dynamic administration undertakings, for example, arrangement changes, through remote alteration of these factors. The factors open by means of SNMP are composed in pecking orders. SNMP itself does not characterize which factors an oversaw framework should offer. Or maybe, SNMP utilizes an extensible plan which enables applications to characterize their own progressions. These chains of importance are depicted as an administration data base (MIB). MIBs depict the structure of the administration information of a gadget subsystem; they utilize a various leveled namespace containing object identifiers.

Protocol Details

SNMP works in the application layer of the Internet convention suite. All SNMP messages are transported by means of User Datagram Protocol (UDP). The SNMP specialist gets asks for on UDP port 161. The director may send demands from any accessible source port to port 161 in the operator. The operator reaction is sent back to the source port on the administrator. The administrator gets notices (Traps and InformRequests) on port 162. The specialist may produce notices from any accessible port. At the point when utilized with Transport Layer Security or Datagram Transport Layer Security, asks for are gotten on port 10161 and warnings are sent to port 10162.SNMPv1 indicates five center convention information units (PDUs). Two different PDUs, GetBulkRequest and InformRequest were included SNMPv2 and the Report PDU was included SNMPv3. All SNMP PDUs are built as pursues:

The seven SNMP PDU types as distinguished by the PDU-type field are as per the following:

GetRequest

A supervisor to-specialist demand to recover the estimation of a variable or rundown of factors. Wanted factors are determined in factor ties (the esteem field isn't utilized). Recovery of the predetermined variable qualities is to be done as a nuclear task by the specialist. A Response with current qualities is returned.

SetRequest

An administrator to-specialist demand to change the estimation of a variable or rundown of factors. Variable ties are indicated in the body of the demand. Changes to every predetermined variable are to be made as a nuclear task by the specialist. A Response with (current) new qualities for the factors is returned.

GetNextRequest

A director to-specialist demand to find accessible factors and their qualities. Returns a Response with variable official for the lexicographically next factor in the MIB. The whole MIB of an operator can be strolled by iterative use of GetNextRequest beginning at OID 0. Lines of a table can be perused by indicating section OIDs in the variable ties of the demand.

GetBulkRequest

A director to-specialist ask for various emphasess of GetNextRequest. An enhanced adaptation of GetNextRequest. Returns a Response with various variable ties strolled from the variable official or ties in the demand. PDU explicit non-repeaters and max-reiterations fields are utilized to control reaction conduct. GetBulkRequest was presented in SNMPv2.

Reaction

Returns variable ties and affirmation from operator to supervisor for GetRequest, SetRequest, GetNextRequest, GetBulkRequest and InformRequest.Error revealing is given by blunder status and mistake list fields. In spite of the fact that it was utilized as a reaction to the two gets and sets, this PDU was called GetResponse in SNMPv1.

Trap

Nonconcurrent notice from operator to supervisor. While in other SNMP correspondence, the supervisor effectively asks for data from the specialist, these are PDUs that are sent from the operator to the director without being expressly asked. SNMP traps empower an operator to advise the administration station of noteworthy occasions by method for a spontaneous SNMP message. Trap PDUs incorporate current sysUpTime esteem, an OID distinguishing the kind of device and discretionary variable ties. Goal tending to for devices is resolved in an application-explicit way regularly through snare design factors in the MIB. The arrangement of the device message was changed in SNMPv2 and the PDU was renamed SNMPv2-Trap.

InformRequest

Recognized nonconcurrent warning. This PDU was presented in SNMPv2 and was initially characterized as administrator to supervisor correspondence. Later usage have relaxed the first definition to enable specialist to director interchanges. Director to-chief notices were at that point conceivable in SNMPv1 utilizing a Trap, however as SNMP regularly keeps running over UDP where conveyance isn't guaranteed and dropped parcels are not announced, conveyance of a Trap was not ensured. Illuminate Request settles this as an affirmation is returned on receipt. https://en.wikipedia.org/wiki/Simple_Network_Management_ Protocol cite_note-cisco_a-6 RFC 1157 indicates that a SNMP execution must acknowledge a message of somewhere around 484 bytes long. By and by SNMP usages acknowledge longer messages. Whenever actualized effectively, a SNMP message is disposed of if the translating of the message comes up short and hence distorted SNMP asks for are overlooked. An effectively decoded SNMP ask for is then verified utilizing the network string. In the event that the confirmation comes up short, a snare is produced demonstrating a validation disappointment and the message is dropped.

UNIT - III

The 'Thing' in IoT can be any gadget with any sort of inherent sensors with the capacity to gather and exchange information over a system without manual mediation. The installed innovation in the protest causes them to associate with interior states and the outside condition, which thus helps in choices makingprocess.

More or less, IoT is an idea that associates every one of the gadgets to the web and let them speak with one another over the web. IoT is a mammoth system of associated gadgets – all of which assemble and share information about how they are utilized and the situations in which they are worked.

Thusly, every one of your gadgets will gain from the experience of different gadgets, as people do. IoT is attempting to extend the reliance in human-i.e. interact, contribute and work together to things. I realize this sounds somewhat convoluted, how about we comprehend this with a model.

An engineer presents the application with a record containing the models, rationale, blunders and special cases dealt with by him to the analyzer. Once more, if there are any issues Tester conveys it back to the Developer. It takes numerous cycles and thusly a brilliant application is made.

Likewise, a room temperature sensor assembles the information and sends it over the system, which is then utilized by different gadget sensors to alter their temperatures as needs be. For instance, fridge's sensor can accumulate the information in regards to the outside temperature and as needs be alter the cooler's temperature. So also, your forced air systems can likewise modify its temperature in like manner. This is the means by which gadgets can associate, contribute and work together.

3.1 Developing of Internet of Things

From an improvement point of view, making IoT gadgets relies on inserted programming. There are both programming and equipment points to think about while making an IoT model— the little PC implanted in the protest or gadget, and the product that makes it run. As referenced over, this incorporates things like wearables, associated home gadgets, circuit structure, GPS programming, 3D plan, and the sky is the limit fromthere.

Luckily, a significant number of these product frameworks and programming improvement packs (SDKs) now utilize programming dialects and working frameworks that engineers as of now use for versatile and web advancement, which opens the field up to a lot more designers.

In case you're making a completely fledged dispersed IoT benefit, there are numerous points to consider: improvement of the installed gadget itself, the IT and systems administration benefits that control it, information and examination, and plan and advancement of a coordinated UI (e.g., a versatile application to control your home's indoor regulator).

You'll need to:

- Choose your hardware platform (i.e., your processing board)

- Develop the application software, including any back-end and networking support

- Create the integratedUI

- Develop the APIs, beacons, web sockets, and procedure calls that enable the high-level communications that occur between devices

- Establish security, data storage, and analytics measures

What is IoT Design?

Planning for the Internet of Things (IoT) is the structuring of associated items. IoT frameworks join physical and computerized segments that gather information from physical gadgets and convey significant, operational bits of knowledge. These segments include: physical gadgets, sensors, information extraction and anchored correspondence, entryways, cloud servers, investigation, and dashboards. Not exclusively should every one of these segments should be structured, however their interdependencies should likewise be completely represented.

For item and building groups planning IoT frameworks, the center test lies in taking IoT utilize cases and transforming them into an associated framework – with full incorporation, the privilege IoT correspondence conventions, security, and an easy to use look and feel. For mechanical assembling, IoT item configuration is otherwise called Industry 4.0 structure.

3.2 Industry 4.0 Design Principles

There are four universal design principles shaping IoT design today:

a) Interoperability

At the most essential dimension, an associated framework requires sensors, machines, hardware, and destinations, to impart and trade information. Interoperability is the hidden guideline all through all Industry 4.0 structure forms.

b) Information transparency

The quick development of associated gadgets implies constant connecting between the physical and computerized universes. In this specific situation, data straightforwardness implies that physical procedures ought to be recorded and put away basically, making a Digital Twin.

C) Technicalassistance

A driving advantage of IoT, specialized help alludes to the capacity of associated frameworks to give and show information that encourages individuals to settle on better operational choices and unravel issues quicker. Moreover, IoT-empowered things should help individuals in difficult errands to enhance efficiency and security.

d) Decentralized decisions

The last guideline of Industry 4.0 structure is for the associated framework to go past helping and trading information, to have the capacity to settle on choices and execute necessities as indicated by its characterized rationale.

3.3 Transitioning to IoT Product Design

New innovation layers engaged with IoT configuration require new ranges of abilities also.Very nearly 33% of organizations today come up short on the full assets expected to plan and convey IoT items, for example, information incorporation know-how, web and portable application advancement, information investigation, and security.Looked with the abilities hole, numerous organizations source extra accomplices. These new, multidisciplinary groups should proficiently work together all through the plan procedure.

3.4 IoT Design Complexity

IoT items are significantly more unpredictable, and with the additional multifaceted nature come the danger of making mistakes in plan. All through the plan procedure, the expenses of slip-ups raise.

To approve the plan and guarantee there are no holes in the information streams or utilize cases, groups can use an IoT test system. With IoT recreation, a computerized model of the planned framework enables organizations to imagine framework conduct and error confirmation the rationale in front of improvement.

3.5 IoT Design Tools

Best-in-class Industrial IoT stages give the required devices to help fast and precise IoT structure:

a) Visual Modeling

A key device for quickening the plan procedure, visual IoT displaying gives a canvas to characterize the mechanics, gadgets, information network, investigation, and dashboards of the whole framework.

Visual IoT displaying empowers groups to flawlessly expand their CAD models – which cover mechanics and hardware – to the full IoT demonstrate, with all its additional innovation layers and utilize cases.

3.6 IoT Simulation

To rapidly and effectively approve the IoT framework configuration, groups should search for a stage with IoT reenactment abilities. Here, a computerized model is utilized to envision how associated gadgets, edge and cloud servers, web and versatile applications collaborate with one another when an occasion is activated, and iteratively refine the model dependent on the reproduction runs.

Another sort of reproduction – IoT investigation recreation – gives groups a way to envision the in-advertise bits of knowledge their IoT framework will convey, including the dashboards and cautions, taken from their model. This guarantees every single required datum sources have been represented in the structure preceding advancement.

3.6.1 The Physical Design of IoT

As we enter another age in which uncommon information is traded between frameworks, the expanding interest for availability arrangements carries with it new prerequisites for item capacities and abilities.

When organizations start the physical plan of their IoT framework, regardless of whether by retrofitting existing items or growing new ones, there are a large group of elements they have to represent at the beginning. Here, physical structure implies more than making associated items, however shaping a by and large keen framework.

Mechanical machines, for example, must have sensors equipped for producing fundamentally more information than any time in recent memory, and to send the data safely for examination and activity.

Correct situation of sensors on the gadget, and the capacity of the sensors to work in outrageous conditions must be considered.

Choosing which IoT correspondence convention to use for information coordination is another choice organizations look toward the start of IoT structure.

To improve the complexities that emerge in the physical structure process, organizations swing to advancement stages which center around both IoT plan and IoT conveyance. These stages guarantee that the physical structure ascribes essential for frameworks to appropriately work and impart, are for all intents and purposes spoke to in the frameworkshow.

3.6.2 What is the Best IoT Designmethodology?

There are a few ways to deal with IoT configuration went for defeating the difficulties that IoT presents. Here we propose a blend of strategies which together quicken and help to guarantee accomplishment for the structureprocedure.

a) Taking a Lean, Agile Design Approach

A few item advancement systems have been adjusted for effective IoT plan and conveyance. The main methodology today is Stage-Gate, in which groups do errands dependent on an itemized arrangement, audit their results, achieve an entryway concentrated on investigation, and at exactly that point move onto the following stage.

To apply this procedure of advancement to IoT configuration, groups can use visual demonstrating and virtual prototyping to recreate the framework configuration, present it inside, and repeat dependent on criticism.

b) Incorporating "Design Thinking"

The center rule of configuration believing is to factor individuals, innovation, and business into all item structure choices. This methodology is client driven and sees the client's needs as a urgent thought all through the item improvement process. For IoT structure, this is particularly essential as it strengthens the idea that an IoT framework isn't an objective in it of itself, but instead a business answer for explicit client needs.Regardless of which procedure groups decide for doing their IoT structure, in the event that it considers nonstop survey and emphasis dependent on business prerequisites and client needs, it's destined for success.

For more data about IoT configuration, visit our library of free IoT assets. In case you're investigating approaches to configuration better for Industry 4.0, don't hesitate to get in touch with us to discover how the Seebo stage can make your IoT configuration process quicker and less demanding.

3.7 Case Study on IoT System for Weathermonitoring

The framework proposed in this paper is a propelled answer for checking the climate conditions at a specific place and make the data unmistakable anyplace on the planet. The innovation behind this is Internet of Things (IoT), which is a progressed and effective answer for interfacing the things to the web and to associate the whole universe of things in a system. Here things may be whatever like electronic contraptions, sensors and car electronic hardware. The framework manages observing and controlling the natural conditions like temperature, relative stickiness and CO level with sensors and sends the data to the page and afterward plot the sensor information as graphical insights. The information refreshed from the actualized framework can be available in the web from anyplace on the planet.

3.7.1 Introduction

The web of Things (IoT) is viewedas a development and money related wave in the overall information industry after the Internet. The IoT is an insightful framework which relates everything to the Internet with the true objective of exchanging information and passing on through the information recognizing devices according to agreed traditions. It achieves the target of sharp perceiving, discovering, following, watching, and managing things. It is a growth and augmentation of Internet-based framework, which develops the correspondence from human and human to human and things or things and things. In the IoT perspective, numerous articles incorporating us will be related into frameworks in some shape. It is a present correspondence worldview that imagines a not so distant future, in which the objects of standard everyday presence will be furnished with microcontrollers, handsets for electronic correspondence, and sensible tradition stacks that will make them prepared to talk with one another and with the customers, transforming into a fundamental bit of the Internet. The IoT idea,consequently, goes for making the Internet considerably more vivid and unavoidable. Moreover, by enabling straightforward get to and relationship with a wide combination of devices, for instance, for instance, home mechanical assemblies, observation cameras, checking sensors, actuators, grandstands, vehicles, and so on, the IoT will empower the progression of different applications that make usage of the conceivably colossal whole and arrangement of data made by such inquiries give new organizations to subjects, associations, and open associations. Present developments in innovation primarily center on controlling and checking of various exercises. These are progressively rising to achieve the human needs. The greater part of this innovation is centered on productive checking and controlling diverse exercises. A productive ecological checking framework is required to screen and evaluate the conditions if there should be an occurrence of surpassing the recommended dimension of parameters (e.g., commotion, CO and radiation levels). At the point when the items like condition furnished with sensor gadgets, microcontroller and different programming applications turns into a self-ensuring and self-checking condition and it is likewise called as shrewd condition. In such condition when some occasion happens the caution or LED alarms naturally. The impacts because of the ecological changes on creatures, plants and people can be checked and controlled by keen natural observing framework. By utilizing inserted insight into nature makes the earth intuitive with different goals, this is one of the application that brilliant condition targets. Human needs requests distinctive sorts of observing frameworks these are relies upon the kind of information accumulated by the sensor devices.Event Detection based and Spatial Process Estimation are the two classifications to which applications are ordered. At first the sensor gadgets are conveyed in condition to distinguish the parameters (e.g., Temperature, Humidity and CO etc.)Whilethe information procurement, calculation and controlling activity (e.g., the varieties in the temperature and CO levels regarding the predetermineddimensions).

Sensor gadgets are set at various areas to gather the information to anticipate the conduct of a specific zone of intrigue. The fundamental point of the this paper is to plan and actualize an effective observing framework through which the required parameters are checked remotely utilizing web and the information accumulated from the sensors are put away in the cloud and to extend the evaluated pattern on the internet browser. An answer for checking the temperature, mugginess and CO levels i.e., any parameter esteem crossing its limit esteem ranges, for instance CO levels in air in a specific territory surpassing the ordinary dimensions and so on.In the earth utilizing remote implanted figuring framework is proposed in this paper. The arrangement additionally gives a shrewd remote observing to a specific territory of intrigue. In this paper we additionally present a slanting aftereffects of gathered or detected information as for the typical or determined scopes of specific parameters. The inserted framework is a reconciliation of sensor gadgets, remote correspondence which empowers the client to remotely get to the different parameters and store the information incloud.

3.7.2 SystemArchitecture

The executed framework comprises of a microcontroller (ESP8266) as a primary preparing unit for the whole framework and all the sensor and gadgets can be associated with the microcontroller. The sensors can be worked by the microcontroller to recover the information from them and it forms the investigation with the sensor information and updates it to the web through Wi-Fi module associated with it.

a) Wi-Fi Module

Here we utilized ESP8266 Wi-Fi module which is having TCP/IP convention stack incorporated on chip. So it can furnish any microcontroller to get associated with Wi-Fi arrange. ESP8266 is a prearranged SOC and any microcontroller needs to speak with it through UART interface.. It works with a supply voltage of 3.3v. The module is arranged with AT directions and the microcontroller ought to be customized to send the AT directions in an expected succession to design the module in customer mode. The module can be utilized in both customer and server modes.

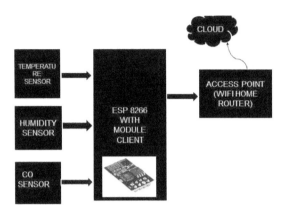

b) Sensors

The framework comprises of temperature and stickiness sensor (DHT 11 and CO sensor (MQ 6). These 2 sensors will quantify the essential ecological components temperature, mugginess and the CO levels. This sensors will gives the simple voltage speaking to one specific climate factor. The microcontroller will changes over this simple voltage into computerized information.

c) Temperature Sensor and Humidity Sensor

The DHT11 is a basic, ultra insignificant exertion electronic temperature and dampness sensor. It uses a capacitive dampness sensor and a thermistor to measure the encompassing air, and discharges a computerized information on the information stick (no simple data pins required). The principle authentic downside of this sensor is you can simply get new data from it once like clockwork, so while using our library, sensor readings can be up to 2 seconds old. It takes a shot at 3 to 5V control supply. Useful for 20-80% stickiness readings with 5% precision and for 0- 50°C temperature readings ±2°Cexactness.

d) Carbon Monoxide (CO) Sensor

Carbon Monoxide (CO) sensor, suitable for sensing CO concentrations in the air.Carbon monoxide sensor, reasonable for detecting CO fixation in air. The MQ-6 can detect CO- gas fixation some place in the scope of 20 to 2000ppm. This sensor has a high affectability and brisk response time. The sensor's yield is an analog opposition. The drive circuit is especially clear; you ought to just control the radiator twist with 5V, incorporate a heap obstruction, and partner the yield to an ADC. The standard reference procedure for the estimation of carbon monoxide focus in air relies upon the ingestion of infrared radiation by the gas in a no dispersive photometer.This system is sensible for stable foundation satsettled sitechecking stations. Evenmore starting late, advantageous carbon monoxide analyzers with information logging have ended up being open for individual introduction watching. These estimations rely upon the electrochemical reactions between carbon monoxide and de-ionized water, which are recognized by incredibly arranged sensors. Nowadays the assurance, quality and affectability of the electrochemical analyzers are inside the points of interest of the reference method and, together with the information logging frameworks, they fit into a little backpack or even a parcel.

Conversion factors

1 ppm = $1.145mg/m^3$

1 mg/mg = 0.873 ppm

e) Thing Speak

As indicated by its engineers, "Thing Speak" is an open source Internet of Things (IOT) application and API application and API to store and recover information from things utilizing the HTTP convention over the Internet or by means of Local Area Network. Thing Speak empowers the making of sensor logging applications, area following applications, and an informal organization of things with notices". Thing Speak has incorporated help from the numerical registering programming MATLAB from MathWorks permitting Thing Speak clients to break down and envision transferred information utilizing Matlab without requiring the buy of a Matlab permit from Mathworks.

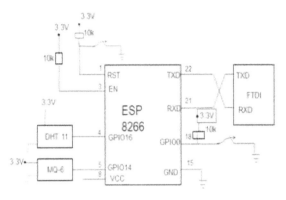

Fig: Circuit Diagram of the system

3.7.3 Simulation Results

In the wake of detecting the information from various sensor gadgets, which are set specifically region of intrigue. The detected information will be naturally sent to the web server, when a legitimate association is built up with separate device.The web server page which will enable us to screen and control the framework. The site page gives the data about the temperature, stickiness and the CO level varieties in that specific area, where the inserted observing framework is set. The detected information will be put away in cloud (Google Spread Sheets). The information put away in cloud can be utilized for the examination of the parameter and nonstop observing reason. The temperature and stickiness levels and CO levels in air at customary time interims.

All the above data will be put away in the cloud, with the goal that we can give inclining of temperature and moistness levels and CO levels in a specific territory anytime of time.

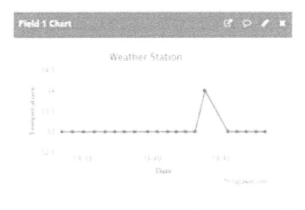

Fig. 6(a) Simulation of temprature v/s time

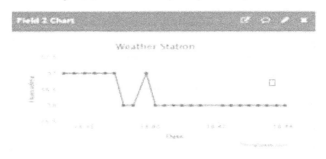

Fig. 6(b) Simulation of humidity v/s time

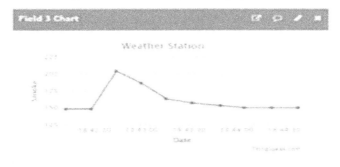

Fig. 6(c) Simulation of smoke content v/s time

3.7.4 Conclusion

By keeping the installed gadgets in nature for checking empowers self security (i.e., brilliant condition) to the earth. To execute this need to convey the sensor gadgets in nature for gathering the information and investigation. By sending sensor gadgets in the earth, we can bring nature into genuine i.e. it can collaborate with different protests through the system. At that point the gathered information and examination results will be accessible to the end client through the Wi- Fi. The savvy approach to screen condition and a productive, minimal effort installed framework is given distinctive models in this paper. In the proposed design elements of various modules were talked about. The temperature, mugginess and CO esteem can be checked with Internet of Things (IoT) idea tentatively tried for observing three parameters. It likewise sent the sensor parameters to the cloud (Google Spread Sheets). This information will be useful for future examination and it very well may be effortlessly shared to opposite end clients. This model can be additionally extended to screen the creating urban areas and mechanical zones for climate observing. To protect thepublic health from pollution, this model gives a proficient and ease answer for persistent checking ofcondition.

3.8 Home Automation Using IoT

This far reaching manual for IoT and home robotization covers regularly utilized structures, stages, sensors, and prototyping systems.

What truly would urge somebody to really build up an entire IoT-based home robotization framework? Would it be able to be the need to enhance the wellbeing of your home, or might it be able to be the longing to carry on with a Jetson-like life that twenty to thirty year olds dependably longed for?

It is hard to state. Frequently, it is much harder to envision the innovation that is required to manufacture a home robotization stage.

Because of the multifaceted nature presented by programming, equipment, and systems administration environments, it turns out to be critical to learn, comprehend, and use the comfortable innovation for your savvy home item.

We plan to address a portion of the worries with this article. What will you realize here?

- Home Automation: How to begin fromzero
- Home mechanization sensors andconventions
- Home mechanization structures, entryways, and stages

3.8.1 IoT Home Automation: Getting Started

Home automation has three major parts:

- Hardware
- Software/Apps
- Communicationprotocols

Every one of these parts is similarly vital in building a really keen home involvement for your clients. Having the correct equipment empowers the capacity to build up your IoT model iteratively and react to innovation turns effortlessly. A convention chose with the correct testing and watchful thought encourages you stay away from execution bottlenecks that generally would limit the innovation and gadget mix abilities with sensors and IoT portals. Another imperative thought is the firmware that lives in your equipment dealing with your information, overseeing information exchange, firmware OTA updates, and performing other basic tasks to make things talk

3.8.2 Applications of Home Automation

Reconstructing buyer desires, home computerization has been anticipated to target wide cluster applications for the new advanced shopper. A portion of the zones where buyers can hope to see home computerization drove IoT-empowered network are:

- Lightingcontrol
- HVAC
- Lawn/Gardening management
- Smart HomeAppliances
- Improved Home safety andsecurity
- Home air quality and water quality monitoring
- Natural Language-based voiceassistants
- Better Infotainment delivery
- AI-driven digitalexperiences
- SmartSwitches
- SmartLocks
- Smart EnergyMeters

The rundown is as yet not comprehensive and will develop over an opportunity to oblige new IoT utilize cases. Since you know about home robotization applications, we should have a point by point take a gander at what segments are engaged with building a regular home computerization model.

3.8.3 Home Automation Components

We have discussed them previously, yet we should unmistakably isolate our parts that will at long last help you manufacture a sensible model of what significant segments are associated with building a brilliant home. The real parts can be broken into:

- IoT sensors
- IoT gateways
- IoT protocols
- IoT firmware
- IoT cloud and databases
- IoT middleware (ifrequired)

IoT sensors engaged with home computerization are in thousands, and there are several home mechanization passages also. The majority of the firmware is either written in C, Python, Node. js, or some other programming dialect. The greatest players in IoT cloud can be isolated into a stage as-a-benefit (PaaS) and foundation as-a-benefit(IaaS).

3.8.4 Major IoT PaaS Providers

- AWSIoT
- Azure IoT
- Thingworx
- Ubidots
- Thingspeak
- Carriots
- Konekt
- TempoIQ
- Xively
- IBMBluemix

3.8.5 Characteristics of IoT Platforms

Once more, these stages are to a great degree separated over the IoT application and security- related highlights that they give. A couple of these stages are open source.

Let's have a look at what you should expect from a typical IoT platform:

- Device security and authentication
- Message brokers and messagequeuing
- Deviceadministration
- Support towards protocols like CoAP, MQTT, and HTTP
- Data collection, visualization, and simple analysis capabilities
- Integrability with other web services
- Horizontal and verticalscalability
- Web Socket APIs for real-time for real-time information flow

Aside from what we referenced above, more stage manufacturers are publicly releasing their libraries to engineers. Take for instance the Dallas temperature library for DS18B20 for Arduino was immediately ported as a result of open source improvement to another rendition that helped engineers to coordinate DS18B20 with Linkit One. Understanding these things ends up pivotal as IoT will in general develop consistently and having a similarly responsive stage makes it business safe to continue. Allows now profoundly assess every one of these segments, beginning with IoTsensors.

3.8.6 Home Automation Sensors

There are likely a huge number of such sensors out there that can be a piece of this rundown, yet since this is a presentation towards keen home innovation, we will keep it brief. We will separate IoT sensors for home robotization by their detectingcapacities:

- Temperaturesensors
- Luxsensors
- Water levelsensors
- Air composition sensors

- Video cameras for surveillance
- Voice/Sound sensors
- Pressure sensors
- Humidity sensors
- Accelerometers
- Infrared sensors
- Vibrations sensors
- Ultrasonic sensors

Contingent on what you require, you may utilize one or a significant number of these to manufacture a genuinely brilliant home IoT item. We should examine probably the most normally utilized home robotization sensors.

3.8.6.1 Temperature Sensors

The market is brimming with them, yet the celebrated temperature sensors are DHT11/22, DS18B20, LM35, and MSP430 arrangement from TI. The MSP430 arrangement is more precise than the rest, and yet, it is a standout amongst the most costly to prototyping or beginning item testing purposes. MSP430 beat all temperature sensors, as the exactness and battery utilization is negligible with them.

The DHT11 has an exceptionally confined temperature range and experiences exactness issues. DHT22, then again, is somewhat more precise yet at the same time, doesn't make it as the inclination. The DS18B20, then again, is more exact, rather than advanced temperature sensors like the DHT22 and 11. Dallas temperature sensors are simple and can be to a great degree precise down to Observe that regularly, the temperatures that you straightforwardly sense from these sensors may not be extremely exact, and you would once in a while observe 1000 F or more prominent qualities regardless of what you are doing.

There's a whole rationale that circumvents building temperature sensors that we will address in another blog entry.

3.8.6.2 Lux Sensors

Lux sensors measure the radiance and can be utilized to trigger different capacities extend from cross-approving developments to turn the lights on in the event that it turns out to be excessively dull. Probably the most prevalent light sensors are TSL2591 and BH1750. Ongoing tests to incorporate TSL2591 and BH1750 into low-fueled IoT gadgets have observed them to work genuinely well for most utilize cases. Here's an examination done by Robert and Tomas that indicates how these two look at against a spectrometer and a photodiode. To get a smart thought of whether these two sensors would address your issues, we would recommend luminance tests pursued by normalizations of the information to watch deviations under different circumstances.

3.8.6.3 Water Level Sensors

While building your model, you may consider a strong state eTape fluid dimension sensor or, similar to other people, simply utilize a HC-SR04 ultrasonic sensor to quantify the water level. Then again, in different situations where those two don't do the trick, one needs to use something that can convey an a lot higher execution. Buoy level sensors and different ICs like LM1830 offer a more exact estimation ability to IoT engineers — in spite of the fact that, they are significantly substantially more costly thanothers.

3.8.6.4 Air Composition Sensors

There are two or three explicit sensors that are utilized by designers to gauge explicit segments noticeable all around:

- CO monitoring byMiCS-5525

- MQ-8 to measure Hydrogen gaslevels

- MiCS-2714 to measure nitrogenoxide

- MQ135 to sense hazardous gas levels (NH_3, NOx, Alcohol, Benzene, smoke, CO_2

The majority of these are sensors have a warming time, which additionally implies that they require a specific time before they really begin conveying precise qualities.

These sensors principally depend on their surface to distinguish gas segments. When they at first begin detecting, there's continually something that is there on their surface, a type of testimony that requires some warming to leave. Consequently, after the surface gets sufficiently warmed, genuine qualities begin to appear.

3.8.6.5 Video Cameras for Surveillance and Analytics

A scope of webcams and cameras explicit to equipment advancement packs are generally utilized in such situations. Equipment with USB ports offer to incorporate camera modules to manufacture usefulness. Be that as it may, using USB ports isn't exceptionally productive, particularly on account of constant video exchange or any sort of video handling. Take the Raspberry Pi for instance. It accompanies a camera module (Pi cam) that interfaces utilizing a flex connector specifically to the board without utilizing the USB port. This makes the Pi cam to a great degree productive.

3.8.6.6 Sound Detection

Sound recognition assumes a fundamental job in everything from observing infants to consequently turning lights on and off to naturally identifying your puppy's sound at the entryway and opening it up for your pet. Some generally utilized sensors for sound location incorporate the SEN-12462 and EasyVR Shield for fast prototyping. These sensors aren't on a par with mechanical review sensors like those from 3D Signals, which can identify even ultra-low dimensions of commotion and adjust between different clamor levels to develop even machine breakdesigns.

3.8.6.7 Humidity Sensors

These sensors bring the capacity of detecting mugginess/RH levels noticeable all around to brilliant homes. The exactness and detecting accuracy depends a considerable measure on numerous components, including the general sensor structure and position. In any case, certain sensors like the DHT22 and 11, worked for fast prototyping, will dependably perform inadequately when contrasted with superb sensors like HIH6100 and Dig RH. While building an item to detect mugginess levels, guarantee that there's no confined layer of dampness that is clouding the genuine outcomes. Likewise, remember that in certain little spaces, the stickiness may be too high toward one side when contrasted with the others.

When you take a gander at free and open spaces where the air parts can move much uninhibitedly, the circulation around the sensor can be relied upon to be uniform and, therefore, will require less restorative activities for the correct alignment.

3.8.7 Home Automation Protocols

A standout amongst the most critical parts of building a home computerization item is to consider conventions — conventions that your gadget will use to convey to passages, servers, and sensors. A couple of years prior, the best way to do as such was by either utilizing Bluetooth, Wi-Fi, or GSM. In any case, due to included costs cell SIM cards and low execution of Wi-Fi, most such arrangements didn't work. Bluetooth endure and later developed as Bluetooth Smart or Bluetooth Low Energy. This acquired a great deal of network the "portable server controlled economy." Essentially, your telephone would go about as a middleware getting information from BLE-fueled sensors and sending it over to theweb.

When looking at the major home automation protocols, the following top the list:

- Bluetooth Low Energy or Bluetooth Smart: Wireless protocol with mesh capabilities, security, data encryption algorithms, and much more. Ideal for IoT-based products for smarthomes.

- Zigbee: Low cost, mesh networked, and low power radio frequency-based protocol for IoT. Different Zigbee versions don't talk to eachother.

- X10: A legacy protocol that utilizes powerline wiring for signaling andcontrol.

- Insteon: Communicates with devices both wirelessly and withwires.

- Z-wave: Specializes in home automation with an emphasis onsecurity.

- Wi-Fi: Needs noexplanation.

- UPB: Uses existing power lines installed in a home. Reducescosts.

- Thread: A royalty-free protocol for smart home automation, uses a 6 low pan.

- ANT: An ultra low-power protocol helping developers build low-powered sensors with a mesh distribution capabilities.

- 6 low pan

3.8.8 Home Automation: Which Protocol is the Best?

While there are some protocols that clearly offer much more, it is always important to start from your smart home development needs and then move towards narrowing down the solutions.

The commonly preferred protocols are Bluetooth Low Energy, Z-wave, Zigbee, and Thread. The protocol selection can now be narrowed down by the following factors:

- Ability to perform identity verification
- Quality of sensor networks
- Data transferrate
- Security level
- Network topology required
- Density of objects around
- Effective Distance to be covered

3.8.9 Home Automation Architecture

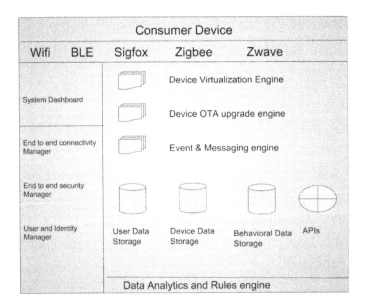

This architecture supports the following considerations for home automation solutions:

- End to end security mechanisms involving multilevel authentication
- End to end data encryption, including the linklayer
- Flexible and configurable access and authorization control
- Powerful cloudinfrastructure
- Network agnostic with built-in feedback loops
- Configurable cloud-based rules engine
- API end points
- Data scalability
- No SQL databases

3.8.10 Home Automation Gateways

For developing a home automation product, often a standalone product sending data to a server is not enough. Due to battery and protocol limitations, the data from a sensor or sensors present in a home has been routed through an IoT gateway.

To select the perfect gateway for your IoT home automation, consider some of these factors:

- Communication protocols supported
- Real-time capabilities
- MQTT, CoAP, and HTTPS support
- Security and configuration
- Modularity

When it comes to building IoT gateways, modularity and hybrid IoT protocol support top the list when a product is in the early stages of market introduction.Either create a gateway from the ground up using existing hardware stacks for prototyping (using Raspberry Pi, Intel Edison, etc). Then, when a PoC is validated, you can create your own custom hardware.Or, you can use existing gateway modules like Ingincs BLE gateway. These gateways are extremely easy to customize and connect with your cloud services and devices. However, they may or may not offer the same level of support that you need to build certain features.

For example, a gateway with a bad networking queue may result in traffic congestion, or it may not support the required protocols that you wish to use. Further, pivoting with these gateways to some other technology stack may become very difficult. It should be emphasized that they are extremely good for robust prototypingneeds.

3.8.11 Home Automation Programming Languages

The accompanying programming dialects command the home robotization space: Python, Embedded C, C, Shell, Go, and JavaScript (Node.js). This has fundamentally occurred because of the sheer advancement of the dialects for comparative utilizecases.

3.8.12 Home Automation Frameworks

In the event that you want to construct everything for home mechanization (conventions, equipment, programming, and so on.) all alone, that is somewhat farfetched. Everybody, from high-development new companies to billion-dollar buyer centered endeavors, is currently utilizing the assistance of home robotization structures to assemble associated items to amuse shoppers.There are in excess of 15 diverse keen home systems accessible for IoT engineers to utilize and assemble their up and coming age of associated home items. A portion of these systems are open source and some are shut source. How about we view some of them in the areas thatpursue.

3.8.13 Open Source IoT Platforms andFrameworks

Anticipating doing a no-nonsense model? There's no compelling reason to record everything without any preparation. On account of a cluster of wonderful commitments, we have open source stages that can get your home mechanization items ready for action in a matter of moments. Our top picks are:

- Home Assistant
- Calaos
- Domoticz
- Open HAB: Supports Raspberry Pi, written in Java and has design tools to build your own mobile apps by tweaking UI.
- Open Motics [Asked their developer, waiting for them to respond (devconfirmed)]
- Linux MCE
- PiDome
- MisterHouse
- Smart homatic

We should investigate the significant home robotizationIoT stages.

3.8.13.1 Home Assistant

Backings Raspberry Pi, utilizes Python, and the OS is Hassbian. It has disentangled computerization decides that designers can use to assemble their home robotization item, sparing them a large number of lines of code. How Home Assistant functions:

- Home control: Responsible for collecting information and storingdevices.

- Home automation triggers commands based on userconfigurations.

- Smart home triggers based on past userbehavior.

As designers, it is critical for us to comprehend the engineering of Home Assistant for us to assemble high-performing items over it. How about we examine the engineering that makes control and data stream conceivable. Home control comprises of five segments:

- Components
- Statemachine
- Eventbus
- Serviceregistry
- Timer

The center engineering of Home Assistant:

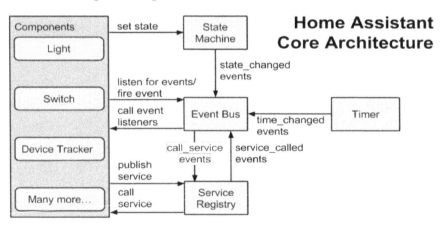

Fig. Core Architecture of Home Assistant

These segments cooperating make a consistent offbeat framework for shrewd home IoT. In the prior rendition of Home Assistant center, the center regularly needed to stopwhile searching for new gadget data. In any case, with the new forms of Home Assistant, a regressive perfect API, and an async center have been presented, making things significantly quicker for IoT applications.

The best part about home right hand's center engineering is the manner by which painstakingly it has been structured and created to help IoT at home.

3.8.13.2 Open HAB

An understanding architecture of OpenHAB:

- Modularity: It is realized with the bundle concept
- Runtime dynamics: So that software components can be managed atruntime
- Service orientation: There are services for various components to speak with each other and exchange information

Further relying on the OGSi framework, it leverages the following layers stacked together:

- Modular layer: Manages dependencies between bundles
- Life cycle layer: Controls the life cycle of thebundles
- Service layers: Defines a dynamic model of communication between various modules
- Actual services: This is the application layer, using all other layers
- Security layer: Optional, leverages Java 2 security architecture and manages permissions from different modules.

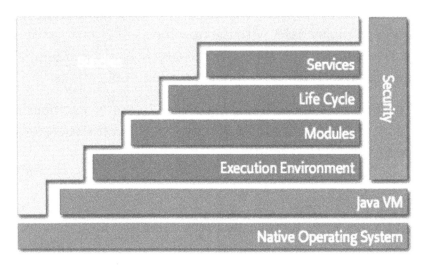

Fig: OGSi framework

OpenHAB features:

- Plug in frame work
- Rules engine
- Logging mechanism
- UI abstraction: A tree structure for UI Widgets, Item UI providers, and dynamic UI configuration
- UI implementations are available for the web, Android, and iOS
- Designer tools availability

OpenHAB has been fundamentally just been seen as a venture for the specialist developer, and even numerous parts of openhab. org pass on the equivalent. Be that as it may, we have watched an alternate exertion as of late from OpenHAB in building the engineer economy for building IoT savvyhomes.

Take this gradually developing GitHub repo discussing OpenHAB cloud, for instance.

As indicated by the archive, OpenHAB cloud design will look something like this:

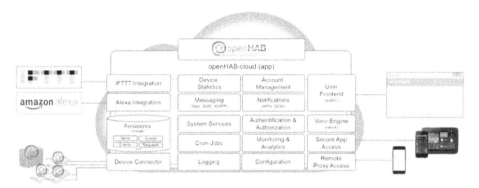

Fig: OpenHAB

Great enough that some open stage out there is considering framework administrations, Cron employments, logging, and so forth. Further, how about we take a gander at the structures and innovations that openHAB will bolster: Node.js, Express.js, Nginx, MongoDB, Redis, Socket.IO.

Not at all like Home Assistant's immense integrability, openHAB is as of now restricted to:

- IFTTT
- Amazon Alexa
- AWS EC2 [AWS Multi-AZ isn't compatible for multiple time zoneavailability]
- AWS IoT withopenHAB
- MQTT support

OpenHAB is amazingly incredible, and yet exceptionally constrained as far as reconciliation. The group behind openHAB is amazingly encouraging and have just passed on their plans to open up openHAB to other joining capacities rightaway.

3.8.13.3 Calaos

Calaos was created at first by an organization that shut in 2013, yet home computerization from that point forward has developed, and it is being kept up and updated by engineers. While now being open source, it encourages premade source code to:

- Create sweet homeenvironments
- Control music
- Automation rules that focus on time, mood, orambiance
- Easyconfiguration

Calaos underpins the accompanying equipment:

- Premoboard
- Cubieboard
- RaspberryPi
- Intel-basedmachines

Their absence of help towards creating private IoT applications limits their utilization by designers to manufacture astounding answers for buyers.

3.8.13.4 Domoticz

Domoticz enables you to screen and arrange your gadgets and sensors with the least difficult conceivable structure. Sufficiently noteworthy that the whole task is to a great degree lightweight, it further is upheld by high inerrability with outsiders and highlights like auto- learning switches.

This stage has been intended to work with working frameworks like Linux and Windows. Convention capacities of Domoticz include: Z-wave, Bluetooth, Apple Homekit, X10, and MQTT Equipment reconciliation abilities of Domoticz:

- RFXCOMtransceiver
- ESP2866 Wi-Fi module
- P1 smartmeter
- Youlessmeter
- Pulsecounters
- 1-Wire
- Philips Hue
- Essent Ethermostat

Domiticz can be utilized to make any kind of administrations that you can consider, extending from a brilliant climate gadget to a Telegram bot. As of now, not very many individuals think about the engineering of Domoticz, making it to a great degree hard to construct applications on it without going out on a limb in building the item itself. For instance, the whole structure of general engineering feels a little abnormal when you take a gander at the idea of a sensor to control to an actuator. It is by all accounts missing.Building propelled applications with Domoticz should be possible utilizing C++, lula, PHP, shell, and soon.

3.8.14 Block chainin IoT

Purchasers, particularly the individuals who experienced childhood in the advanced time, comprehend the significance of security. With the advancement of IoT, security has become the dominant focal point for practical organization situations. Arrangement of blockchain into home systems should effortlessly be possible with a $35 Raspberry Pi. A blockchain anchored layer among gadgets and portals can be actualized without a gigantic redo of the current code base.

Basically, blockchain is an innovation that would be a usage that most clients won't think about, however it will assume an immense job later on to console them with progressive and new plans of action like powerful leasing for Airbnb. Up until now, interoperability issues and broken conventions appeared to have hampered the development of IoT-based shrewd homes. However, as innovation is advancing and more processing force can be created with low-fueled gadgets, home computerization will bit by bit turn into an innovation that will simple for us to construct and produce for regularly.

3.9 Case Studies Illustrating IOT Design: Cities

The Internet-of-Things (IoT) is the novel bleeding edge innovation which proffers to associate plenty of advanced gadgets enriched with a few detecting, activation and processing capacities with the Internet, along these lines offers complex new administrations with regards to a savvy city. The engaging IoT administrations and enormous information examination are empowering keen city activities everywhere throughout the world. These administrations are changing urban areas by enhancing foundation, transportation frameworks, decreased movement clog, squander the board and the nature of human life. In this paper, we devise a scientific categorization to best deliver a conventional diagram of IoT worldview for shrewd urban areas, incorporated data and correspondence advances (ICT), organize types, conceivable chances and significant prerequisites. Additionally, a diagram of the a la mode endeavors from standard bodies is exhibited. Afterward, we give a diagram of existing open source IoT stages for acknowledging brilliant city applications pursued by a few model contextual investigations. Also, we abridge the most recent collaborations and activities overall taken to advance IoT with regards to keen urban communities. At long last, we feature a few difficulties with the end goal to give future researchheadings.

This contextual analysis has displayed ongoing patterns and headways in IoT empowered shrewd urban areas worldview. We formulated a scientific classification for IoT put together keen urban areas based with respect to correspondence conventions, real specialist organizations, arrange types, standard bodies and real administration necessities for the comprehension of the peruser. In light of the led think about, we presumed that brilliant city applications depend on a few remote advancements, for example, IEEE 802.11p, WAVE, SIGFOX, 6LoWPAN, LTE/LTE-A. Besides, we examined significant open IoT stages for the simplicity of scientists. Also, various detailed contextual investigations of a few most up to date IoT organizations and research ventures are displayed to uncover an expanding pattern of IoT arrangements. At last, we uncover a few open research issues, for example, multi-seller interoperability, minimal effort, low power utilization and security which request significant considerations from our exploration network.

3.10 Case Study Illustrating IoT Design: Environment

Savvy learning conditions (SLEs) are physical spaces improved with computerized and setting explicit parts (sensors and actuators, for example) that encourage better and quicker learning. This takes into consideration half breed learning approaches that switch among formal and casual settings, free and class getting the hang of, shifting learning times and places, and simple and computerized learning groups. These learning situations make ready for mixture cooperative energies between the physical and computerized world. Shrewd learning situations additionally adjust to students' needs by taking data from the earth, handling it, and utilizing it to start suitable advances, for example, suggestions.

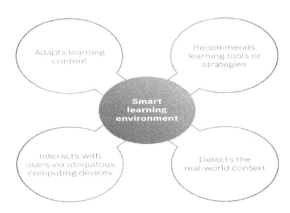

Fig. 3.6.1.1

3.10.1 Human Centered Design

Savvy learning situations ought to dependably start with the requirements of their clients. With the end goal to have the capacity to provide food explicitly to singular partner needs and exercises, the initial step ought to be to do a complete investigation of the necessities, setting, and condition. This structures the reason for building up a customized learning condition that underpins autonomous learning and can be connected with formal learningsituations.

3.10.1.1 Learning and workmethods

Computerized change calls for new aptitude in zones, for example, specialized, strategies, media, and data. Progressively, learning is integral, on interest, and deep rooted, happening both in the working environment and moving, and no longer solely in formal instructional courses in conventional classrooms. Building up this ability requires new learning methods (e.g. free learning or configuration considering) that offer instructive assortment while additionally being supplemented by expert learning backing, training, and tutoring. This implies formal learning time inside a physical learning space converges with casual exercises outside of the classroom, making half and half learning situations. Learning material ends up concentrated and more customized, obscuring the limits between getting the hang of, working, and a person's private life.

3.10.1.2 Learning and corporateculture

Each association has its own way of life – shifting work strategies, methods, and procedures that must be considered. Imaginative learning situations depend on a culture of trust and input, and additionally a high level of individual duty.

3.8.2 Smart IT infrastructure

Brilliant IT foundation is the center of the shrewd learning condition and is right now alluded to as a "computerized operator" or "advanced colleague." It involves explicit equipment and programming parts and also the going with interfaces, which shape the premise of keen information trade. The savvy IT framework assembles accessible and required information in a cloud; this is the place all learning/work materials and learning results are put away (in a somewhat robotized process) and available wherever you go. The coordination of semantic ideas enhancements and connections learning content with further wellsprings of data. For example, a student may enter the expression "IoT." They are then given significant indexed lists as indicated by classification (thinks about, networks, introductions, congresses, and so forth.) and information of distribution.

Access to fantastic substance is empowered through availability both with inside learning stages, for example, Moodle and outer assets, for example, online libraries, master databases, and pro gatherings, for example, ResearchGate. The keen IT framework works as the interface among inner and outer datasets, and sorts out the majority of the important data as per the client's needs.

A case of an accessible model for "shrewd suggestion frameworks" is the OER EEXCESS venture, which expects to associate significant online assets and get substance to clients without them trawling through an assortment of stages to get it. The code is open source and accessible by means of GitHub. This video clarifies how everythingfunctions:

An essential component of the Internet of Things is incorporating innovation into ordinary things to make them "keen protests." The point is to improve regular articles, for example by furnishing a window with sensors and actuators so it very well may be mechanized to give an additional advantage, (for example, windows that open consequently when air quality isn't helpful for learning).

In this situation, innovation works subtly out of sight, which is additionally a worry from a structure point of view. The more brilliant the innovation, the less detectable it is. It turns into a piece of the design and decorations, incorporated into dividers, tables, seats, and comparable things. Different models incorporate amplifiers coordinated into dividers and couches, or multifunctional segments that give a screen when required, and at different occasions fill in as racks or an intuitive divider.

3.10.3 Digital & physical equipment

A key piece of planning a space is its hardware – furniture, innovation, and even plants, to give some examples. First there are the conventional simple things, for example, tables, seats, stools, couches, flip diagrams, parcels, pens, paper, post it notes, and so forth. At that point there is the innovation, for example, PCs, projectors, sound and meeting frameworks – and keen gadgets. These savvy gadgets incorporate brilliant pens, tablets, 3D printers, cell phones, keen TVs, control dividers, shrewd sheets, and savvy windows, which open naturally to let in outside air. These components can be inventively joined, as in cooperating spaces, for example, the Fab Lab Berlin or Impact HUB. Over this, savvy learning conditions highlight computerized devices (programming applications), which constantly bolster the learning and workprocess.

One model are applications that share learning results with an (inside) "network of training," and also pre-introduced instruments that enable clients to make and alter photographs, illustrations, and recordings amid the learning procedure. Essentially, it incorporates any application that guides data preparing and adds to network with others (just whenever wanted, obviously). Consistently, there is a decent review of apparatuses significant to learning and work practice gathered by Jane Heart – while a diagram by Robin Good records in excess of 550 work devices.

3.10.4 Workplace architecture

Work environment engineering affects learning society. Anybody can see the contrast between working in a plain old office and, for example, a Google office. Obviously, these are two boundaries – the key is to locate the correct parity. The key components are a charming, present day configuration joined with multifunctional decorations that can be rapidly and effectively adjusted to a scope of learning and work situations. It is likewise worth considering creative ideas, for example, up cycling, in which for example beds are made into tables orretires.

To conclude our consideration of these 6 key areas, I recommend the following actions in developing a smart learning environment:

3.11 Case Study Illustrating IoT Design: Agriculture

With the developing appropriation of the Internet of Things (IoT), associated gadgets have entered each part of our life, from wellbeing and wellness, home computerization, car and coordinations, to brilliant urban areas and modern IoT.

Subsequently, it is just coherent that IoT, associated gadgets, and computerization would discover its application in horticulture and, all things considered, colossally enhance numerous aspects of the cultivating practice. How might despite everything one depend on steeds and furrows when self-driving vehicles and augmented reality are never again a science fiction dream yet an ordinary event? Cultivating has seen various innovative changes in the most recent decades, winding up more industrialized and innovation driven. By utilizing different keen agribusiness devices, agriculturists have increased better command over the way toward raising animals and developing yields, making it more unsurprising and proficient.

In this article, we will investigate the IoT utilize cases in farming and look at their advantages. On the off chance that you are thinking about putting resources into shrewd cultivating or intending to fabricate an IoT answer for agribusiness, make a plunge.

3.11.1 What is Smart Agriculture? The Definition and Market Size

There are numerous approaches to allude to current farming. For instance, AgriTech alludes to the general use of innovation to agribusiness.

Savvy horticulture, then again, is generally used to signify the utilization of IoT arrangements in farming.

Albeit savvy horticulture IoT, and additionally modern IoT, aren't as prominent as shopper associated gadgets, the market is still exceptionally powerful. The selection of IoT answers for agribusiness is continually developing. In particular, BI Intelligence predicts that the quantity of horticulture IoT gadget establishments will hit 75 million by 2020, becoming 20% every year. In the meantime, the worldwide shrewd farming business sector measure is relied upon to triple by 2025, achieving $15.3 billion (contrasted with being somewhat over $5 billion of every 2016). Since the market is as yet creating, there are as yet abundant open doors for organizations willing to participate. Building IoT items for farming inside the coming years can separate you as an early adopter and, all things considered, enable you to make ready to progress. In any case, for what reason would it be advisable for you to consider building an IoT application for horticulture in any case?

3.11.2 The Benefits of Smart Farming: How IoT is Shaping Agriculture

Innovations and IoT can possibly change horticulture in numerous perspectives. Specifically, there are five different ways IoT can enhance farming:

- **Data, tons of data, collected by smart agriculture sensors,** e.g. climate conditions, soil quality, product's development advancement or cow's wellbeing. This information canbe utilized to follow the condition of your business when all is said in done, and also staff execution, gear proficiency, and so on.

- **Better control over the internal processes and, as a result, lower production risks**. The capacity to predict the yield of your generation enables you to anticipate better item circulation. On the off chance that you know precisely how much yields you will collect, you can ensure your item won't lie aroundunsold.

- **Cost management and waste reduction thanks to the increased control over production**. Being ready to perceive any inconsistencies in the harvest development or domesticated animal's wellbeing, you will have the capacity to alleviate the dangers of losing youryield.

- **Increased business efficiency through process automation**. By utilizing shrewd gadgets, you can mechanize different procedures over your generation cycle, e.g. water system, preparing, or bugcontrol.

- **Enhanced product quality and volumes**. Accomplish better authority over the creation procedure and keep up higher principles of product quality and development limit through robotization.

Accordingly, these variables can in the end lead to higher income.

Since we have illustrated how IoT can be favorably connected in the circle of farming, we should investigate how the recorded advantages can discover their application, in actuality.

3.11.3 IoT Use Cases in Agriculture

There are many types of IoT sensors and IoT applications that can be used in agriculture:

3.11.3.1 Monitoring of Climate Conditions

Likely the most well known brilliant agribusiness contraptions are climate stations, joining different keen cultivating sensors. Situated over the field, they gather different information from the earth and send it to the cloud. The gave estimations can be utilized to outline atmosphere conditions, pick the fitting products, and take the expected measures to enhance their ability (i.e. exactness cultivating). A few instances of such agribusiness IoT gadgets are all METEO, Smart Elements, and Pycno.

3.11.3.2 Green House Automation

Notwithstanding sourcing ecological information, climate stations can consequently change the conditions to coordinate the given parameters. In particular, nursery computerization frameworks utilize a comparable guideline.

For example, Farmapp and Growlink are likewise IoT agribusiness items offering such capacities among others.

GreenIQ is likewise an intriguing item that utilizes keen agribusiness sensors. It is a shrewd sprinklers controller that enables you to deal with your water system and lighting frameworks remotely.

3.11.3.3 Crop Management

One more kind of IoT item in agribusiness and another component of exactness cultivating is edit the executives gadgets. Much the same as climate stations, they ought to be put in the field to gather information explicit to trim cultivating; from temperature and precipitation to leaf water potential and generally edit wellbeing, these would all be able to be utilized to promptly gather information and data for enhanced cultivating rehearses. Accordingly, you can screen your product development and any irregularities to adequately avoid sicknesses or invasions that could hurt your yield. Arable and Semios can fill in as great portrayals of how this utilization case can be connected, all things considered.

3.11.3.4 Cattle Monitoring and Management

Much the same as harvest observing, there are IoT agribusiness sensors that can be joined to the creatures on a ranch to screen their wellbeing and log execution. This works comparatively to IoT gadgets for pet consideration.

For instance, SCR by Allflex and Cowlar utilize savvy farming sensors (neckline labels) to convey temperature, wellbeing, action, and nourishment bits of knowledge on every individual cow, and also aggregate data about the crowd.

3.11.3.5 End-to-End Farm ManagementSystems

A more intricate way to deal with IoT items in agribusiness can be spoken to by the alleged homestead efficiency the board frameworks. They more often than exclude various agribusiness IoT gadgets and sensors, introduced on the premises and in addition an amazing dashboard with diagnostic capacities and in-fabricated bookkeeping/detailing highlights.

This offers remote ranch observing capacities and enables you to streamline a large portion of the business activities. Comparative arrangements are spoken to by FarmLogs and Cropio.

Notwithstanding the recorded IoT farming use cases, some conspicuous open doors incorporate vehicle following (or even mechanization), stockpiling the board, coordinations, and so forth.

3.11.4 Four Things to Consider Before Developing Your Smart Farming Solution

As we can see, the use cases for IoT in agriculture are endless. There are many ways smart devices can help you increase your farm's performance and revenue. However, agriculture IoT apps development is no easy task. There are certain challenges you need to be aware of if you are considering investing in smartfarming.

3.11.4.1 Hardware

To build an IoT solution for agriculture, you need to choose the sensors for your device (or create a custom one). Your choice will depend on the types of information you want to collect and the purpose of your solution. In any case, the quality of your sensors is crucial to the success of your product— it will depend on the accuracy of the collected data and itsreliability.

3.11.4.2 The Brain

Data analytics should be at the core of every smart agriculture solution. The collected data itself will be of little help if you cannot make sense of it. Thus, you need to have powerful data analytics capabilities and apply predictive algorithms and machine learning in order to obtain actionable insights based on the collecteddata.

3.11.4.3 Maintenance

Maintenance of your hardware is a challenge that is of primary importance for IoT products in agriculture, as the sensors are typically used in the field and can be easily damaged. Thus, you need to make sure your hardware is durable and easy to maintain. Otherwise, you will need to replace your sensors more often than you would like.

3.11.4.4 Mobility

Smart farming applications should be tailored for use in the field. A business owner or farm manager should be able to access the information on site or remotely via a smartphone or desktop computer. Plus, each connected device should be autonomous and have enough wireless range to communicate with the other devices and send data to the central server.

3.11.4.5 Infrastructure

To ensure that your smart farming application performs well (and to make sure it can handle the data load), you need a solid internal infrastructure. Furthermore, your internal systems have to be secure. Failing to properly secure your system only increases the likeliness of someone breaking into it, stealing your data, or even taking control of your autonomoustractors.

3.12 Case Study Illustrating IOT design: Productivity Applications

The best way for organizations to look at the potential of IoT deployments to succeed in their digital transformation efforts, optimize their efficiency and better serve their customers is by understanding the business rationale behind Internet of Things examples and real cases in practice.

Add to that the several IoT use cases (areas where IoT is and can be deployed such as manufacturing operations, precision farming, smart lighting, smart buildings and so forth, not real deployments), an understanding of the essence of the Internet of Things and its applications, a good mix of common business sense, sound advice, and lessons from success stories, and the Internet of Things becomes tangible instead of just a term and set oftechnologies.

3.12.1 Internet of Things benefits and business drivers across industries

Great and compelling Internet of Things models begin with difficulties or potentially ultimate objectives as a main priority. While taking a gander at the approaches to accomplish these true objectives, new open doors regularly emerge. By and large these rotate around taking advantage of new incomes, essentially client confronting and frequently shared, in an 'as an administrationeconomy'.

There are plentiful of IoT models crosswise over different enterprises. Some are pilot ventures, others are completely operational, versatile and driving business and client esteem. From assembling IoT cases in Industry 4.0 and precedents in transportation and coordinations. (Logistics 4.0) and utilities to buyer IoT, human services IoT, retail, keen city applications and cross-industry IoT utilize cases: there are constantly functional genuine Internet of Things models out there, in spite of the fact that they aren't generally that simple to discover. As the Internet of Things, from a genuine utilization point of view, is a piece of a greater picture and gets its incentive from the difficulties and true objectives obviously not all ventures are moving at a similar speed. This implies in a few businesses you'll discover moreprecedents.

Be that as it may, the pith of versatile IoT organizations, from the business and result point of view, realizes no industry fringes. The difficulties and chances are regularly quite all inclusive. At last, we talk about offering better client benefit, taking advantage of new wellsprings of information, experiences and significant knowledge, advancement, profitability upgrade and horde different objectives that are normal crosswise over areas.

At the end of the day: when you search for instances of Internet of Things arrangements that work or are in a pilot organize, surely don't constrain your journey to models from your industry. The client is one and has comparative desires, paying little heed to industry. Business difficulties and openings are more differing yet at the same time: there is continually something to be educated.

UNIT - IV

Introduction

Python is a clear and amazing object situated programming dialect comparable to perl,ruby scheme or java.

A portion of python's prominent highlights:

- Utilizes a rich linguistic structure influencing the projects you to compose less demanding to peruse.

- Is a simple to utilize dialect that makes it easy to get your program working. This makes python perfect for model advancement and other adhoc programming errands without compromising practicality.

- Comes with a vast standard library that bolsters numerous common programming errands such as connecting to web servers, searching content with regular expressions, reading and modifying files.

- Python's interactive mode makes it simple to test short pieces of code. There's additionally a packaged advancement condition called IDLE.

- Effectively reached out by including new modules executed in a compiled dialect such as c or c++

- Can also be inserted into an application to give a programmable interface.

- Runs anyplace, including Mac OS X, Windows, Linux, and Unix with unofficial builds additionally accessible for Android and IOS.

- Is free programming in two detects. It doesn't cost anything to download or utilize Python, or to incorporate it in your application. Python can likewise be uninhibitedly changed and re-dispersed, on the grounds that while the language is copyrighted it's accessible under an open source permit.

Some programming-language highlights of Python are:

- A assortment of essential data types are accessible: numbers (skimming point, complex, and boundless length long whole numbers), strings (both ASCII and Unicode), lists, and dictionaries.

- Python bolsters object-oriented programming with classes and multiple inheritance.

- Code can be gathered into modules and packages.

- The language underpins raising and catching exceptions, bringing about cleaner error handling.

- Data types are emphatically and powerfully typed. Blending contrary types (e.g. endeavoring to include a string and a number) makes an exception be raised, so errors are gotten sooner.

- Python contains advanced programming features, for example, generators and list comprehensions.

Python gives heaps of highlights that are recorded underneath.

- **Easy to Learn and Use:** Python is anything but difficult to learn and utilize. It is developer friendly and high level programming language.

- **Expressive Language:** Python language is more expressive implies that it is more understandable and intelligible.

- **Interpreted Language:** Python is a translated language i.e. translator executes the code line by line at once. This makes investigating simple and along these lines appropriate for learners.

- **Cross-platform Language:** Python can run similarly on various platforms such as Windows, Linux, Unix and Macintosh etc. Along these lines, we can state that Python is a versatile language.

- **Free and Open Source:** Python language is freely accessible at offical web address.The source-code is additionally accessible. Hence it is open source.

- **Object-Oriented Language:** Python supports object oriented language and concepts of classes and objects come into existence.

- **Extensible:** It infers that different languages such as C/C++ can be utilized to compile the code and hence it tends to be utilized further in our python code.

- **Large Standard Library:** Python has a huge and expansive library and prvides rich arrangement of module and functions for quick application improvement.

- **GUI Programming Support:** Graphical user interfaces can be created utilizing Python.

- **Integrated:** It tends to be effectively integrated with languages like C, C++, JAVA etc.

4.1 Data Types in Python

Each value in Python has a data type. Since everything is an object in Python programming, data types are really classes and variables are example (object) of these classes. There are different data types in Python. A portion of the essential types are recorded underneath.

4.1.1 Python Numbers:

An integer, floating point numbers and complex numbers falls under Python numbers class. They are defined as int, float and complex class in Python.

We can utilize the type() function to realize which class a variable or a value has a place with and the isinstance() function to check if an object has a place with a specific class.

```
a = 5
print(a, "is of type", type(a))
a = 2.0
print(a, "is of type", type(a))
a = 1+2j
print(a, "is complex number?", isinstance(1 + 2j,complex))
```

Integers can be of any length, it is just constrained by the memory accessible.

A floating point number is exact up to 15 decimal places. Integer and floating points are isolated by decimal points. 1 is integer, 1.0 is floating point number.

Complex numbers are written in the shape, x + yj, where x is the real part and y is the imaginary part. Here are a few models:

```
>>> a = 1234567890123456789
>>> a
1234567890123456789
>>> b = 0.1234567890123456789
>>> b
0.12345678901234568
>>> c = 1+2j
>>> c
(1+2j)
```

Notice that the float variable b got truncated.

4.1.2 Python List

List is an ordered sequence of items. It is a standout amongst the most utilized data type in Python and is entirely adaptable. Every one of the items in a list doesn't should be of a similar type. Declaring a list is truly straight forward. Items isolated by commas are enclosed within brackets [ ].

>>> a = [1, 2.2, 'python']

We can utilize the slicing operator [ ] to separate a item or a range of items from a list. Index begins from 0 in Python.

```
a = [5, 10, 15, 20, 25, 30, 35, 40]
# a[2] = 15
print("a[2] =", a[2])
# a[0:3] = [5, 10, 15]
print("a[0:3] =", a[0:3])
# a[5:] = [30, 35, 40]
print("a[5:] =", a[5:])
```

Lists are mutable, meaning; value of components of a list can be adjusted.

```
>>> a = [1,2,3]
>>> a[2]=4
>>> a
[1, 2, 4]
```

4.1.3 Python Tuple

Tuple is an ordered sequence of items same as list. The just distinction is that tuples are unchanging. Tuples once made can't be altered.

Tuples are utilized to write-protect data and are normally quicker than list as it can't change progressively.

It is defined within parentheses ( ) where items are isolated by commas.

>>> t = (5,'program', 1+3j)

We can utilize the slicing operator [] to extricate items however we can't change its value.

```
t = (5,'program', 1+3j)
# t[1] = 'program'
print("t[1] =", t[1])
# t[0:3] = (5, 'program', (1+3j))
print("t[0:3] =", t[0:3])
# Generates error
# Tuples are immutable
t[0] = 10
```

4.1.3 Python Strings

String is sequence of Unicode characters. We can utilize single quotes or double quotes to speak to strings. Multi-line strings can be indicated using triple quotes, "or".

>>> s = "This is a string"
>>> s = "'a multiline

Like list and tuple, slicing operator [ ] can be utilized with string. Strings are unchanging.

```
s = 'Hello world!'
# s[4] = 'o'
print("s[4] =", s[4])
# s[6:11] = 'world'
print("s[6:11] =", s[6:11])
# Generates error
# Strings are unchanging in Python
s[5] ='d'
```

4.1.5 Python Set

Set is an unordered gathering of interesting items. Set is defined by values isolated by comma inside braces { }. Items in a set are not ordered.

a = {5,2,3,1,4}
# printing set variable print("a =", a)
# data type of variable a print(type(a))

We can perform set operations like union, intersection on two sets. Set have unique values. They dispense with duplicates.

```
>>> a = {1,2,2,3,3,3}
>>> a
{1, 2, 3}
```

printing set variable print("a =", a)
data type of variable a print(type(a))

We can perform set operations like union, intersection on two sets. Set have unique values. They dispense with duplicates.

Since, set are unordered gathering, indexing has no significance. Henceforth the slicing operator [ ] does not work.

```
>>> a = {1,2,3}
>>> a[1]
Traceback (most recent call last): File
"<string>", line 301, in runcode
File "<interactive input>", line 1, in <module>
```

4.1.6 Python Dictionary

Dictionary is an unordered gathering of key-value pairs. It is commonly utilized when we have a colossal measure of information. Dictionaries are enhanced for retrieving information. We should realize the key to retrieve the value.

In Python, dictionaries are characterized inside braces { } with every item being a couple in the frame key and value. Key and value can be of any kind.

```
>>> d = {1:'value','key':2}
>>> type(d)
<class 'dict'>
```

We utilize key to recover the separate value. Be that as it may, not a different way.

```
d = {1:'value', 'key':2}
print(type(d))
print("d[1] = ", d[1]);
print("d['key'] = ", d['key']);
# Generates error
print("d[2] = ", d[2]);
```

4.1.7 Conversion between data types

We can change over between various data types by utilizing diverse type conversion functions like int(), float(), str() and so on.

```
>>> float(5)
5.0
```

Conversion from float to int will truncate the value (make it more like zero).

```
>>> int(10.6) 10
>>> int(-10.6)
```

Conversion to and from string must contain perfect values.

```
>>> float('2.5') 2.5
>>> str(25) '25'
>>> int('1p')
Traceback (most recent call last): File
"<string>", line 301, in runcode
```

We can even change over one arrangement to another.

```
>>> set([1,2,3])
{1, 2, 3}
>>> tuple({5,6,7})
(5, 6, 7)
>>> list('hello')
```

To change over to dictionary, every component must be a pair

```
>>> dict([[12][34]])
{1: 23: 4}
>>> dict([(326)(444)])
```

4.2 Data Structures

There are many data structures accessible. The builtins data structures are: lists, tuples, dictionaries, strings, sets and frozensets.

Lists, strings and tuples are requested successions of objects. Not at all like strings that contain just characters, list and tuples can contain any type of objects. Lists and tuples resemble arrays. Tuples like strings are immutables. Lists are mutables so they can be expanded or lessened voluntarily. Sets are impermanent unordered arrangement of interesting components though frozensets are changeless sets.

4.2.1 Lists

In python, lists are a piece of the standard dialect. You will discover them all over. Like nearly everything in Python, lists are objects. Lists are encased in brackets:

l = [1,2,"a"]

There are numerous strategies related to them. Some of which are introduced here beneath.

Quick example:

```
>>> l = [1, 2, 3]
>>> l[0] 1
>>> l.append(1)
>>> l
[1, 2, 3, 1]
```

Difference between append () and extend ():

Lists have a few methods among which the append () and extend () methods. The previous appends an object as far as possible of the list (e.g., another list) while the later appends every component of the iterable object (e.g., another list) as far as possible of the list.

For instance, we can append an object (here the character 'c') as far as possible of a basic list as pursues:

```
>>> stack = ['a','b']
>>> stack.append('c')
>>> stack ['a', 'b', 'c']
```

Nonetheless, in the event that we need to append a few objects contained in a list, the outcome of course (or not...) is:

```
>>> stack.append(['d', 'e', 'f'])
>>> stack
['a', 'b', 'c', ['d', 'e', 'f']]
```

The object ['d', 'e', 'f'] has been appended to the current list. In any case, it happens that occasionally what we need is to append the components one by one of a given list rather the list itself. You can do that manually obviously, yet a superior arrangement is to utilize the extend() method as below:

```
>>> stack = ['a', 'b', 'c']
>>> stack.extend(['d', 'e','f'])
>>> stack
['a', 'b', 'c', 'd', 'e', 'f']
```

Other list methods index

The index() methods looks for a component in a list. For example:

```
>>> my_list = ['a','b','c','b', 'a']
>>> my_list.index('b') 1
```

It returns the index of the solitary occurence of 'b'. On the off chance that you need to determine a range of legitimate index, you can demonstrate the start and stop lists:

```
>>> my_list = ['a','b','c','b', 'a']
>>> my_list.index('b', 2)
3
```

In the event that the component isn't discovered, an error is raised. **insert**

You can evacuate component yet additionally insert component wherever you need in a list:

```
>>> my_list.insert(2, 'a')
>>> my_list
['b','c','a','b']
```

The insert() methods insert an object before the index gave. **remove**

Thus, you can evacuate the first occurence of a component as below:

```
>>> my_list.remove('a')
>>> my_list ['b', 'c', 'b', 'a']
```

Pop

Or then again evacuate the last component of a list by utilizing:

```
>>> my_list.pop() 'a'
>>> my_list ['b', 'c', 'b']
```

Which additionally returns the value that has been evacuated?

Count

You can count the number of element of a kind:

```
>>> my_list.count('b')
2
```

Sort

There is a **sort()** method that performs an in-place sorting:

```
>>> my_list.sort()
>>> my_list ['a', 'b', 'b', 'c']
```

Here, it is very basic since the elements are generally characters. For standard types, the sorting functions admirably. Envision now that you have some non-standard types. You can overwrite the function used to play out the examination as the first argument of the sort() method.

There is likewise the possiblity to sort in the reverse order:

```
>>> my_list.sort(reverse=True)
>>> my_list ['c', 'b', 'b', 'a']
```

Reverse

Finally, you can reverse the element in-place:

```
>>> my_list = ['a', 'c','b']
>>> my_list.reverse()
>>> my_list ['b', 'c', 'a']
```

Operators

The + operator can be utilized to **extend** a list:

```
>>> my_list = [1]
>>> my_list += [2]
>>> my_list [1, 2]
>>> my_list += [3, 4]
>>> my_list [1, 2, 3, 4]
```

The * operator ease the generation of list with same values

```
>>> my_list = [1, 2]
>>> my_list = my_list * 2
>>> my_list [1, 2, 1, 2]
```

Slicing

Slicing uses the symbol: to access to part of a list:

```
>>> list[first index:last index:step]
>>> list[:]
>>> a = [0, 1, 2, 3, 4, 5]
[0, 1, 2, 3, 4, 5]
>>> a[2:] [2, 3, 4, 5]
>>> a[:2]
[0, 1]
>>> a[2:-1]
[2, 3, 4]
```

As a matter of course the first index is 0, the last index is the last one…, and the step is 1. The step is optional. So the following slicing is equivalent:

```
>>> a = [1, 2, 3, 4, 5, 6, 7, 8]
>>> a[:]
[1, 2, 3, 4, 5, 6, 7, 8]
>>> a[::1]
[1, 2, 3, 4, 5, 6, 7, 8]
>>> a[0::1]
[1,2,3,4,5,6,7,8]
```

List comprehension

Customarily, a bit of code that loops over an arrangement could be composed as below:

```
>>> evens = []
>>> for i in range(10):
... if i % 2 == 0:
... evens.append(i)
>>> evens [0, 2, 4, 6, 8]
```

This may work, yet it really makes things slower for Python in light of the fact that the interpreter takes a shot at each loop to determine what part of the grouping must be changed. A list comprehension is the correct solution:

```
>>> [i for i in range(10) if i % 2 == 0]
[0, 2, 4, 6, 8]
```

Other than the way that it is more effective, it is likewise shorter and involves less components. **Filtering Lists**

```
>>> li = [1, 2]
>>> [elem*2 for elem in li if elem>1] [4]
```

Lists as Stacks

The Python documentation gives a case of how to utilize lists as stacks, that is a last-in, first-out data structures (LIFO).

An item can be added to a list by using the append() method. The last item can be expelled from the list by using the pop() method without passing any index to it.

```
>>> stack = ['a','b','c','d']
>>> stack.append('e')
>>> stack.append('f')
>>> stack
['a', 'b', 'c', 'd', 'e', 'f']
>>> stack.pop() 'f'
>>> stack
['a, 'b', 'c', 'd', 'e']
```

Lists as Queues

Another use of list, again displayed in Python documentation is to utilize lists as queues, that is a first in - first out (FIFO).

```
>>> queue = ['a', 'b', 'c', 'd']
>>> queue.append('e')
>>> queue.append('f')
>>> queue
['a', 'b', 'c', 'd', 'e', 'f']
>>> queue.pop(0) 'a'
```

How to copy a list

There are three ways to copy a list:

```
>>> l2 = list(l)
>>> l2 = l[:]
>>> import copy
>>> l2 = copy.copy(l)
```

Don't do l2 = l, which is a reference, not a copy.

The preceding techniques for copying a list make shallow copies. It implies that nested objects won't be copied. Think about this precedent:

```
>>> a = [1, 2, [3, 4]]
>>> b = a[:]
>>> a[2][0] = 10
>>> a
[1, 2, [10, 4]]
>>> b
[1, 2, [10, 4]]
```

To get around this issue, you should play out a profound copy:

```
>>> import copy
>>> a = [1, 2, [3, 4]]
>>> b = copy.deepcopy(a)
>>> a[2][0] = 10
>>> a
[1, 2, [10, 4]]
>>> b
[1, 2, [3, 4]]
```

Inserting items into a sorted list:

The **bisect** module provides tools to manipulate sorted lists.

```
>>> x = [4, 1]
>>> x.sort()
>>> import bisect
>>> bisect.insort(x, 2)
>>> x [1, 2, 4]
```

To know where the index where the value would have been inserted, you could have utilize:

```
>>> x = [4, 1]
>>> x.sort()
>>> import bisect
>>> bisect.bisect(x, 2)
2
```

4.2.2 Tuples

In Python, tuples are part of the standard dialect. This is a data structure fundamentally the same as the list data structure. The main contrast being that tuple manipulation are quicker than list in light of the fact that tuples are permanent.

Constructing tuples

To create a tuple, place values within brackets:

```
>>> l = (1, 2, 3)
>>> l[0] 1
```

It is likewise conceivable to make a tuple without parentheses, by using commas:

```
>>> l = 1, 2
>>> l (1, 2)
```

On the off chance that you need to make a tuple with a single component, you should utilize the comma:

>>>singleton = (1,)

You can repeat tuples by multiplying a tuple by a number:

Note that you can concatenate tuples and utilize augmented assignment (*=, +=):>>> s1 = (1,0)

```
>>> s1 += (1,)
>>> s1
(1, 0, 1) >>> s1 = (1,0)
>>> s1 += (1,)
>>> s1 (1, 0, 1)
>>> s1 = (1,0)
>>> s1 += (1,)
>>> s1 (1, 0, 1)
```

Tuple methods:

Tuples are advanced, which makes them extremely basic objects. There are two methods accessible as it were:

* index, to find occurence of a value
* count, to count the number of occurence of a value

```
>>> l = (1,2,3,1)
>>> l.count(1) 2
>>> l.index(2) 1
```

Interests of tuples

Thus, Tuples are helpful because that there are

* faster than lists
* protect the data, which is immutable
* tuples can be used as keys on dictionaries

In addition, it can be utilized in various valuable ways:

Tuples as key/value pairs to build dictionaries

```
>>> d = dict([('jan', 1), ('feb', 2), ('march', 3)])
>>> d['feb'] 2
```

Signing multiple values:

```
>>> (x,y,z) = ('a','b','c')
>>> x
'a'
>>> (x,y,z) = range(3)
>>> x 0
```

Tuple Unpacking:

Tuple unpacking permits to extracts tuple components consequently is the list of variables on the left has same number of components from the length of the tuple

```
>>> data = (1,2,3)
>>> x, y, z = data
>>> x 1
```

Tuple can be utilize as swap function:

This code reverses the contents of 2 variables x and y:

```
>>> (x,y) = (y,x)
```

Consider the following function:

```
def swap(a, b)
(b,a) = (a,b)
then:
a = 2
b = 3
swap(a, b)
```

a is still 2 and b still 3 !! a and b are indeed passed by value not reference.

Length:

To find the length of a tuple, you can utilize the len() function:

```
>>> t= (1,2)
>>> len(t) 2
```

Slicing (extracting a segment):

```
>>> t = (1,2,3,4,5)
>>> t[2:]
(3, 4, 5)
```

Copy a tuple: To copy a tuple, just utilize the assignement:

```
>>> t = (1, 2, 3, 4, 5)
>>> newt = t
>>> t[0] = 5
>>> newt (1, 2, 3, 4, 5)
```

You can't copy a list with the = sign since lists are mutables. The = sign makes a reference not a copy. Tuples are unchanging in this manner a = sign does not make a reference but rather a copy of course.

Tuples aren't totally unchangeable !!

In the event that a value within a tuple is impermanent, you can transform it:

```
>>> t = (1, 2, [3, 10])
>>> t[2][0] = 9
>>> t
(1, 2, [9, 10])
```

Convert a tuple to a string:

You can change over a tuple to a string with either:

>>>str(t) or >>>'t'

Math and Comparison

Comparison operators and mathematical functions can be used on tuples. Here are some examples:

```
>>> t = (1, 2, 3)
>>> max(t) 3
```

4.2.4 Dictionary

A dictionary is an arrangement of items. Every item is a pair made of a key and a value. Dictionaries are not arranged. You can access to the list of keys or values independently.

```
>>> d = {'first':'string value', 'second':[1,2]}
>>> d.keys() ['first', 'second']
>>> d.values() ['string value', [1, 2]]
```

You can access to the value of a given key as below:

```
>>> d['first'] 'string value'
```

Warning: You cannot have duplicate keys in a dictionary

Warning: Dictionaries have no concept of order among components.

Methods to query information:

In addition to keys and values methods, there is likewise the items method that returns a list of items of the frame (key, value). The items are not returned in a particular order:

```
>>> d = {'first':'string value', 'second':[1,2]}
>>> d.items()
[('a', 'string value'), ('b', [1, 2])]
```

The iter items method works similarly, however restores an iterator instead of a list. See iterators section for an example.

You can check for the presence of a specific key with has key:

```
>>> d.has_key('first')
True
```

The expression d.has_key(k) is equivalent to k in d. The decision of which to utilize is to a great extent a matter of taste.

In order to get the value corresponding to an explicit key, utilize get or pop:

```
>>> d.get('first') # this method can set an optional value, if the
                       key is not found
'string value'
```

It is useful for things like adding up numbers:

sum[value] = sum.get(value, 0) + 1

The difference between **get** and **pop** is that **pop** also removes the corresponding item from the dictionary:

```
>>> d.pop('first') 'string value'
>>> d
{'second': [1, 2]}
```

Finally, **popitem** removes and returns a pair (key, value); you do not choose which one because a dictionary is not sorted

```
>>> d.popitem() ('a', 'string value')
>>> d
{'second': [1, 2]}
```

Methods to create new dictionary:

Since dictionaries (like different sequences) are objects, you ought to be careful when using the artificiality sign:

```
>>> d1 = {'a': [1,2]}
>>> d2 = d1
>>> d2['a'] = [1,2,3,4]
>>> d1['a]
[1,2,3,4]
```

To create a new object, use the **copy** method (shallow copy):

    >>>d2 = d1.copy()

copy.deepcopy()

You can clear a dictionary (i.e., remove all its items) using the **clear()** method:

```
>>> d2.clear()
{}
```

The **clear()** method deletes all items whereas **del()** deletes just one:

```
>>> d = {'a':1, 'b':2, 'c':3}
>>> del d['a']
>>> d.clear()
```

Create a new item with default value (if not provided, None is the default):

```
>>> d2.setdefault('third', '')
>>> d2['third'] "
```

Create a dictionary given a set of keys:

>>> d2.fromkeys(['first', 'second']) another syntax is to start from an empty dictionary:

```
>>> {}.fromkeys(['first', 'second'])
{'first': None, 'second': None}
```

Simply keep in,ind thqt the fromkeys() method makes another dictionary with the given keys, each with a default corresponding value of None.

Combining dictionaries:

Given 2 dictionaries d1 and d2, you can include all sets of key/ value from d2 into d1 by utilizing the update method (instead of looping and assigning each pair yourself:

```
>>> d1 = {'a':1}
>>> d2 = {'a':2; 'b':2}
>>> d1.update(d2)
>>> d1['a'] 2
>>> d2['b'] 2
```

The items in the provided dictionary are added to the former one, overwriting any items there with the equivalent keys.

Iterators:

Dictionary gives iterators over values, keys or items:

```
>>> [x for x in t.itervalues()] ['string value', [1, 2]]
>>>
>>> [x for x in t.iterkeys()] ['first', 'csecond']
>>> [x for x in t.iteritems()] [('a', 'string value'), ('b', [1, 2])]
```

Views:

viewkeys, viewvalues, viewitems are set-like objects giving a view on D's keys, values or items.

Comparison:

You can think about dictionaries! Python first looks at the sorted key-value pairs. It first sorts dictionaries by key and compare their initial items. On the off chance that the items have different values, Python makes sense of the comparison between them. Something else, the second items are compared and so on.

Strings

To put it plainly, strings are permanent arrangement of characters. There are a great deal of methods to ease control and production of strings as appeared here as below.

Creating a string (and special characters)

Single and double quotes are uncommon characters. There are utilized to defined strings. There are really 3 different ways to define a string using either single, double or triple quotes:

```
Text = 'The surface of the circle is 2 pi R ='
Text = "The surface of the circle is 2 pi R ='
Text = '''The surface of the circle is 2 pi R ='''
```

In fact the most recent is commonly written using triple double quotes:

Text = """The surface of the circle is 2 pi R ="""

Strings in double quotes work precisely equivalent to in single quotes yet permit to insert single quote character inside them.

The interest of the triple quotes ("'or"') is that you can determine multi-line strings. Also, single quotes and double quotes can be utilized uninhibitedly within the triple quotes:

text = """"a string with special character "and" inside"""

The "and" characters are part of the Python language; they are unique characters. To insert them in a string, you need to escape them (i.e., with a \ character before them to indicate the extraordinary idea of the character). For instance:

text = "a string with escaped special character\", \ "inside"

There are a few of other unique characters that must be escaped away to be included in a string. See The print statement for more information. To include unicode, you should go before the string with the u character:

```
>>>u"\u0041"
A
```

Note: Unicode is a single character set utilized to refer 65536 different characters.

So also, you may see strings gone before by the r character to indicate that the string must be interpreted for what it's worth without interpreting the special character \. This is helpful for docstrings that contain latex code for instance:

> r "\textbf{this is bold text in LaTeX}"

The print statement for more information about string format and printing. Strings are immutable

You can allows to any character utilizing slicing:

> text[0] text[-1]
> text[0:]

However, you can't change any character:

text[0] = 'a' *#this is incorrect.*

Formatter:

In Python, the % sign gives you a chance to deliver formatted outcome. A fast model will outline how to print an formatted string:

>>> **print**("%s" % "some text") "some text"
The syntax is simply: string % values

In the event that you have in excess of one value, they ought to be put within brackets:

>>> **print**("%s %s" % ("a", "b"))

The string contains characters and conversion specifiers (here %s) To get away from the sign %, simply double it:

> >>> **print** "This is a percent sign: %%"
> This is a percent sign: %

There are distinctive methods for formatting a string with arguments. The one dependent on a string method called format() is increasingly normal:

```
>>> "{a}!={b}".format(a=2, b=1)
2!=1
```

Operators:

The mathematical operators + and * can be utilized to make new strings:

```
t = 'This is a test' t2 = t+t
t3 = t*3
```

and comparison operators >, >=, ==, <=, < and != can be utilized to compare strings. Methods

The string methods are various, be that as it may, a significant number of them are similar (as you will find in this page).

Methods to query information

There are a few of methods to check the type of alpha numeric characters present in a string:

isdigit(), isalpha(), islower(), isupper(), istitle(), isspace(), str. isalnum():

```
>>> "44".isdigit() # is the string made of digits only ?
True
>>> "44".isalpha() # is the string made of alphabetic characters
                   only ?
False
>>> "44".isalnum() # is the string made of alphabetic characters
                   or digits only ?
True
>>> "Aa".isupper() # is it made of upper cases only ?
False
```

```
>>> "aa".islower() # or lower cases only ?
True
>>> "Aa".istitle() # does the string start with a capital letter ?
True
>>> text = "There are spaces but not only"
>>> text.isspace() # is the string made of spaces only ?
False
```

You can check the occurrence of a character with count() or get the length of a string with len():

```
>>> mystr = "This is a string"
>>> mystr.count('i') 3
>>> len(mystr) 16
```

Methods that arrival an altered variant of the string

The following methods return changed copy of the original string, which is permanent. To begin with, you can change the cases using **title()**, **capitalize()**, **lower()**, **upper()** and **swapcase()**

```
>>> mystr = "this is a dummy string"
>>> mystr.title() # return a titlecase version of the string
'This is a Dummy String'
>>> mystr.capitalize() # return  a  string  with  first  letter
                                  capitalised only.
'This is a dummy string'
>>> mystr.upper() # return a capitalised version of the string
'THIS IS A DUMMY STRING'
>>> mystr.lower() # return a copy of the string converted to
                              lower case
'This is a dummy string'
```

```
>>> mystr.swapcase() # replace lower case by upper case and
                      vice versa
'THIS IS A DUMMY STRING'
```

Second, you can add trailing characters with **center()** and **just()** methods:

```
>>> mystr = "this is a dummy string"
>>> mystr.center(40) # center the string in a string of length 40
' this is a dummy string '
>>> mystr.ljust(30) # justify the string to the left (width of 20)
'this is a dummy string '
>>> mystr.rjust(30, '-') # justify the string to the right (width of 20)
'--------this is a dummy string'
```

There is also a **zfill()** methods that adds zero to the left, which is equivalent to.rjust(width, '0'): or remove trailing spaces with the **strip()** methods:

```
>>> mystr.zfill(30)
'00000000this is a dummy string'
```

```
>>> mystr = "string with left and right spaces"
>>> mystr.strip()
'string with left and right spaces'
>>> mystr.rstrip()
'string with left and right spaces'
>>> mystr.lstrip()
'string with left and right spaces'
```

or expand tabs with **expandtabs()**:

```
>>> 'this is a \t tab'.expandtabs()
'this is a tab'
```

You can remove some specific characters with **translate()** or replace words with **replace()**:

```
>>> mystr = "this is a dummy string"
>>> mystr.replace('dummy', 'great', 1) # the 1 means replace
                                        only once
'this is a great strin
>>> mystr.translate(None, 'aeiou') ths s dmmy strng
```

Finally, you can separate a string with respect to a single separator with **partition()**:

```
>>> mystr = "this is a dummy string"
>>> t.partition('is')
('th', 'is', ' is a line')
>>> t.rpartition('is') ('this ', 'is', ' a line')
```

Methods to find position of substrings:

The are methods, for example, endswith(), startswith(), find() and index() that permit to look for substrings in a string.

```
>>> mystr = "This is a dummy string"
>>> mystr.endswith('ing') # may provide optional start and
                           end indices
True
>>> mystr.startswith('This') # may provide start and end indices
True
>>> mystr.find('is') # returns start index of 'is' first occurence
2
>>> mystr.find('is', 4) # starting at index 4, returns start index
                        of 'is' first occurence
5
```

```
>>> mystr.rfind('is') # returns start index of 'is' last occurence
5
>>> mystr.index('is') # like find but raises error when substring
                                is not found
2
>>> mystr.rindex('is') # like  rfind  but  raises  error  when
                            substring is not found
5
```

Methods to construct or break down a string:

A helpful function is the split() methods that splits a string according to a character. The inverse function exist and is called join().

```
>>> message = ' '.join(['this','is', 'a', 'useful', 'method'])
>>> message
'this is a useful method'
>>> message.split(' ')
['this', 'is', 'a', 'useful', 'method']
```

The split() function can be applied to a limited number of times if necessary. In any case, it begins from the left. On the off chance that you need to begin from the right, utilize rsplit() instead:

```
>>> message = ' '.join(['this','is', 'a', 'useful', 'method'])
>>> message.rsplit(' ', 2) ['this is a', 'useful', 'method']
```

On the off chance that a string is multi-lines, you can split it with splitlines():

```
>>> 'this is an example\n of\ndummy sentences'.splitlines()
['this is an example', ' of', 'dummy sentences']
```

you can keep the endline character by giving True as a optional argument., note that **split()** removes the splitter:

```
>>> "this is an exemple".split(" is ")
['this', 'an exemple']
```

On the off chance that you need to keep the splitter also, utilize partition()

```
>>> "this is an exemple".partition(" is ")
('this', ' is ', 'an exemple')
```

Encoding/Decoding/Unicode:

We've perceived how to make a unicode by adding the letter u before a string:

s = u"\u0041"

The function unicode() changes over a standard string to unicode string using the encoding indicated as a argument (default is the default string encoding):

s = unicode("text", "ascii")

In order to make sense of the default encoding, type:

```
>>> import sys
>>> sys.getdefaultencoding() 'ascii'
```

Here are a few encodings:

ascii, utf-8, iso-8859-1, latin-1, utf-16, unicode-escape.

The unicode function takes likewise a third argument set to: 'strict', 'ignore' or 'replace'. Give us a chance to take another example with accents:

```
>>> # Let us start wil a special character.
>>> text = u"π"
>>> # to obtain its code (in utf-8), let us use the encode function
>>> encoded = text.encode("utf-8")
>>> decoded = text.decode("utf-8")
```

Sets

Sets are built from a sequence (or some other iterable object). Since sets can't have copied, there are normally used to manufacture sequence of unique items (e.g., set of identifiers).

```
>>> a = set([1, 2, 3, 4])
>>> b = set([3, 4, 5, 6])
>>> a | b # Union
{1, 2, 3, 4, 5, 6}
>>> a & b # Intersection
{3, 4}
>>> a < b # Subset
False
>>> a - b # Difference
{1, 2}
>>> a ^ b # Symmetric Difference
{1, 2, 5, 6}
```

the intersection, subset, difference and symmetric difference can be called with method rather that symbols. See underneath for examples.

Ordering

Similarly likewise with dictionaries, the ordering of set components is quite arbitrary, and shouldn't be depended on.

Operators

As mentioned in the quick example session, every operator is related to an symbol (e.g., and) and a method name (e.g. union).

```
>>> a = set([1, 2, 3])
>>> b = set([2, 3, 4])
>>> c = a.intersection(b) # equivalent to c = a & b
>>> a.intersection(b) set([2, 3])
>>> c.issubset(a)
True
>>> c <= a
True
>>> c.issuperset(a) False
>>> c >= a
False
>>> a.difference(b) set([1])
>>> a - b set([1])
>>> a.symmetric_difference(b) set([1, 4])
>>> a ^ b set([1, 4])
```

You can likewise copy a set using the copy method:

```
>>> a.copy()
set([1, 2, 3])
```

Frozensets

Sets are changeable, and may along these lines not be utilized, for instance, as keys in dictionaries.

Another issue is that sets themselves may just contain unchanging (hashable) values, and along these lines may not contain different sets.

```
>>> a = frozenset([1, 2, 3])
>>> b = frozenset([2, 3, 4])
>>> a.union(b) frozenset([1, 2, 3, 4])
```

Set of Sets:

Sets may just contain unchanging (hashable) values, and in this way may not contain different sets, in which case frozensets can be helpful. Think about the following example:

```
>>> a = set([1, 2, 3])
>>> b = set([2, 3, 4])
>>> a.add(b)
>>> a.add(frozenset(b))
```

Using set as key in a dictionary:

On the off chance that you need to utilize a set as a key dictionary, you will require frozenset:

```
>>> fa = {frozenset([1,2]): 1}
>>> fa[ frozenset([1,2]) ] 1
```

Methods:

Frozensets have less methods than sets. There are a few operators like sets (intersection(), association(), symmetric_difference(), difference(), issubset(),isdisjoint(), issuperset()) and a copy() method.

Control Flow Statements:

A program's control flow is the order in which the program's code executes. The control flow of a Python program is managed by conditional statements, loops, and function calls. This session covers the if statement and for and while loops;

The if Statement:

Frequently, you have to execute a few statements just if some condition holds, or pick statements to execute depending on a several mutually exclusive conditions. The Python compound statement if, which utilizes if, elif, and else clauses, lets you restrictively execute blocks of statements. Here's the syntax for the if statement:

```
if expression: statement(s)
elif expression: statement(s)
elif expression: statement(s)
...
else:
statement(s)
```

The elif and else statements are discretionary. Note that not at all like a few languages, Python does not have a switch statement, so you should utilize if, elif, and else for all conditional processing. Here's a typical if statement:

```
if x < 0: print "x is negative"
elif x % 2: print "x is positive and odd" else: print "x is even
and non-negative"
```

At the point when there are multiple statements in a clause (i.e., the clause controls a block of statements), the statements are put on discrete logical lines after the line containing the clause's keyword (known as the header line of the clause) and indented rightward from the header line. The block terminates when the indentation returns to that of the clause header (or further left from that point). At the point when there is only a single basic statement, as here, it can follow the: on indistinguishable logical line from the header, however it can likewise be put on a different logical line, instantly after the header line and indented rightward from it. Numerous Python professionals consider the separate-line style more readable:

```
if x < 0:
print "x is negative" elif x % 2:
print "x is positive and odd"
else:
print "x is even and non-negative"
```

You can utilize any Python expression as the condition in an if or elif statement. When you utilize an expression thusly, you are utilizing it in a Boolean context. In a Boolean context, any value is taken as either true or false. As we talked about before, any non-zero number or non- void string, tuple, rundown, or word reference assesses as evident. Zero (of any numeric type), None, and empty strings, tuples, lists, and dictionaries assess as false. When you need to test a value x in a Boolean context, utilize the following coding style:

```
if x:
```

This is the clearest and most Pythonic frame. Try not to utilize:

```
if x is True:
if x = = True: if bool(x):
```

There is a vital distinction between saying that an expression "returns True" (meaning the expression returns the value 1 intended as a Boolean outcome) and saying that an expression "evaluates as true" (meaning the expression returns any outcome that is valid in a Boolean setting). When testing an expression, you care about the last condition, not the former.

In the event that the expression for the if clause evaluates as true, the statements following the if condition execute, and the whole if statement ends. Something else, the expressions for any elif conditions are evaluated in order. The statements following the first elif condition whose condition is valid, assuming any, are executed, and the whole if statement ends. Something else, if an else clause exists, the statements following it are executed.

The while Statement

The while statement in Python supports repeated execution of a statement or block of statements that is controlled by a conditional expression. Here's the syntax for the while statement:

```
while expression: statement(s)
```

A while statement can likewise include an else condition and break and continue statements, as we'll examine in a matter of seconds. Here's an ordinary while statement:

```
count = 0 while x > 0:
x = x // 2 # truncating division count += 1
print "The approximate log2 is", count
```

In the first place, expression, which is known as the loop condition, is evaluated. On the off chance that the condition is false, the while statement ends. In the event that the loop condition is fulfilled, the statement or statements that involve the loop body are executed. At the point when the loop body finishes executing, the loop condition is assessed again, to check whether another cycle ought to be performed. This procedure continues until the point when the loop condition is false, at which point the while statement ends.

The loop body ought to contain code that in the long run makes the loop condition false, or the loop will never end except if a special case is raised or the loop body executes a break statement.

A loop that is in a function's body additionally ends if a returns statement executes in the loop body, as the entire function ends for this situation.

The for Statement

The for statement in Python supports repeated execution of a statement or block of statements that is controlled by an iterable expression. Here's the language structure for the for statement: Note that the in keyword is part of the syntax of the for statement and is functionally inconsequential to the in operator utilized for membership testing. A for statement can likewise include an else condition and break and continue statements, as we'll examine in no time.

```
for letter in "ciao":
print "give me a", letter, "..."
```

iterable might be any Python expression reasonable as a contention to built-in function iter, which returns an iterator object (explained in detail in the following section). target is ordinarily an identifier that names the control variable of the loop; the for statement progressively rebinds this variable to every thing of the iterator, in order. The statement or statements that include the loop body execute once for every item in iterable (except if the loop ends because an exception is raised or a break or return statement is executed).

An objective with multiple identifiers is additionally permitted, similarly as with an unpacking task. For this situation, the iterator's items must then be sequences,each with a similar length, equivalent to the number of identifiers in the target. For instance, when d is a dictionary, this is a typical way to loop on the items in d:

```
for key, value in d.items( ):
if not key or not value: del d[key] # keep only true keys and
values
```

The items method returns a list of key/value sets, so we can utilize a for loop with two identifiers in the target to unpack every item into key and value.

In the event that the iterator has a mutable underlying object, that object must not be changed while a for loop is in progress on it. For instance, the past example can't utilize iteritems instead of items. iteritems returns an iterator whose underlying object is d, so therefore the loop body can't transform d (by deld[key]). items returns a list, however, so d isn't the underlying object of the iterator and the loop body can changed.

The control variable might be bounce back in the loop body, however is bounce back again to the following item in the iterator at the following emphasis of the loop. The loop body does not execute at all if the iterator yields no items. For this situation, the control variable isn't bound or bounce back in any way by the for statement. On the off chance that the iterator yields at least one item, in any case, when the loop statement terminates, the control variable remains bound to the last value to which the loop statement has bound it. The following code is thus correct, as long as someseqis not empty:

```
for x in someseq: process(x)
print "Last item processed was", x
```

Iterators:

An iterator is any object i to such an extent that you can call i.next( ) with no arguments. i.next( ) returns the following item of iterator I, or, when iterator i has no more items, raises a

StopIteration exception. When you write a class, you can enable instances of the class to be iterators by defining such a method next. Most iterators are built by implicit or explicit calls to built-in function iter. Calling a generator additionally returns an iterator, as we'll talk about later in this section.

The for statement implicitly calls iter to get an iterator. The following statement:

```
for x in c:
  statement(s)
```

is equivalent to:

```
_temporary_iterator = iter(c) while True:
try: x = _temporary_iterator.next( )
except StopIteration: break
statement(s)
```

Along these lines, if iter(c) returns an iterator i such that i. next( ) never raisesStopIteration (an infinite iterator), the loop for x in c: never terminates (unless) the statements in the loop body contain appropriate break or return statements or spread special cases). iter(c), in turn, calls special method c. iter ( ) to obtain and return an iterator on c. We'll speak more about the special method iter.

Iterators were first introduced in Python 2.2. In prior versions, for x in S: required S to be a sequence that was indexable with logically bigger indices 0, 1,..., and raised an IndexError when indexed with an as too large index. On account of iterators, the for statement would now be able to be utilized on a container that isn't an sequence, such as a dictionary, as long as the container is iterable (i.e., it defines a iter special method with the goal that function iter can acknowledge the container as the argument and return an iterator for the container). Built-in functions that used to require a sequence argument currently likewise accept any iterable.

range and xrange:

Looping over a sequence of integers is a typical assignment, so Python gives built-in functions range and xrange to create and return integer sequences. The simplest, most colloquial approach to loop n times in Python is:

```
for i in xrange(n):
    statement(s)
```

range(x) returns a list whose items are consecutive integers from 0(included) up to x (rejected). range(x, y) returns a list whose items are consecutive integers from x (included) up to y (barred). The outcome is the empty list if x is more noteworthy than or equivalent to y. range(x, y, step) returns a list of integers from x (included) up to y (prohibited), such that the distinction between every two nearby items in the list is step. In the event that step is under 0, range tallies down from x to y. range returns the empty list when x is more noteworthy than or equivalent to y and step is more prominent than 0, or when x is not exactly or equivalent to y and step is under 0. On the off chance that progression levels with 0, range raises an exception.

While range returns an ordinary list object, usable for all reasons, xrange returns a special- purpose object, explicitly intended to be utilized in iterations like the for statement indicated previously. xrange devours less memory than range for this explicit utilize. Leaving aside memory utilization, you can utilize range wherever you could utilize xrange.

The break Statement

The break statement is permitted just inside a loop body. At the point when break executes, the loop terminates. In the event that a loop is nested inside other loops, break terminates just the innermost nested loop. In practical utilize, a break statement is normally inside some clause of an if statement in the loop body with the goal that it executes restrictively.

One regular utilization of break is in the execution of a loop that chooses on the off chance that it should continue looping just amidst each loop iteration:

```
while True: # this loop can never terminate naturally x =
            get_next( )
y = preprocess(x)
if not keep_looping(x, y): break process(x, y)
```

The continue Statement

The continue statement is permitted just inside a loop body. Whenever continue executes, the present emphasis of the loop body terminates, and execution continues with the next iteration of the loop. In practical utilize, a continue statement is generally inside some clause of an if statement in the loop body so that it executes conditionally.

The continue statement can be utilized instead of profoundly nested if statements within a loop. For instance:

```
for x in some_container:
if not seems_ok(x): continue
lowbound, highbound = bounds_to_test( )
if x<lowbound or x>=highbound: countinue
if final_check(x):
do_processing(x)
```

This equivalent code does conditional processing without continue:

```
for x in some_container:
if seems_ok(x):
    lowbound, highbound = bounds_to_test( )
    if lowbound<=x<highbound:
        if final_check(x):
```

Both versions function identically, so which one you use is a matter of personal preference.

The else Clause on Loop Statements

Both the while and for statements may alternatively have a trailing else clause. The statement or statements after the else execute when the loop terminates normally (toward the finish of the for iterator or when the while loop condition turns out to be false), however not when the loop terminates rashly (by means of break, return, or a special case). At the point when a loop contains at least one break statements, you regularly need to check whether the loop terminates normally or rashly. You can utilize an else clause on the loop for this purpose:

```
for x in some_container:
if is_ok(x): break # item x is satisfactory, terminate loop
else:
    print "Warning: no satisfactory item was found in
        container" x = None
```

The pass Statement

The body of a Python compound statement can't be empty—it must contain no less than one statement. The pass statement, which performs no action, can be utilized as a placeholder when a statement is syntactically required yet you don't have anything explicit to do. Here's a example of using go in a conditional statement as a part of somewhat convoluted logic, with totally unrelated conditions being tried:

```
if condition1(x): process1(x)
elif x>23 or condition2(x) and x<5:
    pass # nothing to be done in this case elif condition3(x):
    process3(x) else:
    process_default(x)
```

The try Statement

Python supports exception handling with the try statement, which includestry, except, finally, and else clauses. A program can explicitly raise an exception with the raise statement. When a exception is raised, ordinary control flow of the program stops and Python searches for a suitable exception handler.

Functions:

Functions are a fundamental part of the Python programming language: you may have just experienced and utilized a portion of the numerous phenomenal functions that are built-in in the Python language or that accompany its library ecosystem. In any case, as a Data Scientist, you'll always need to compose your very own functions to solve those issues that your data poses to you.

Functions in Python

You utilize functions in programming to package an set of instructions that you need to utilize more than once or that, due to their complexity, are better independent in a sub - program and called when required. That implies that a function is a bit of code written to carry out a specified task. To do that explicit specific task, the function may or probably won't require multiple inputs. At the point when the task is done, the function can or cannot return one or more values.

There are three types of functions in Python:

- Built-in functions, for example, help() to request for help, min() with getting the minimum value, print() to print an object to the terminal,... You can find an overview with more of these functions here.

- User-Defined Functions (UDFs), which are functions that users make to enable them to out; And

- Anonymous functions, which are likewise called lambda functions due to they are not announced with the standard def keyword.

Functions Vs Methods

A technique refers to a function which is part of a class. You get to it with an instance or object of the class. A function doesn't have this confinement: it just alludes to a standalone function. This implies all methods are functions yet not all functions are methods. Think about this model, where you initially define a function plus() and then a Summation class with an sum() method:

```
# Define a function 'plus()'
def plus(a,b):
return a + b
# Create a 'Summation' class
class Summation(object):
def sum(self, a, b):
self.contents = a + b
return self.contents
```

On the off chance that you presently need to call the sum() method that is part of the Summation class, you initially need to define an instance or object of that class. In this way, how about we define such an object:

```
# Instantiate `Summation`
class to call `sum()`
sumInstance = Summation()
sumInstance.sum(1,2)
```

Keep in mind that this instantiation a bit much for when you need to call the function add()! You would have the capacity to execute plus(1,2) in the DataCamp Light code chunk without any problems!

Parameters Vs Arguments

Parameters are the names utilized when defining a function or a method, and into which arguments will be mapped. As it were, arguments are the things which are provided to any function or method call, while the function or method code alludes to the arguments by their parameter names.

Consider the following example and think back to the above DataCamp Light chunk: you pass two arguments to the sum() method of the Summation class, despite the fact that you recently defined three parameters, in particular, self, a and b.

What happened to self?

The first argument of each class method is dependably a reference to the present instance of the class, which for this situation is Summation. By convention, this argument is called self.

This all implies you don't pass the reference to self for this situation since self is the parameter name for a certainly passed argument that alludes to the instance through which a method is being invoked. It gets inserted implicitly into the argument list.

How To Define A Function: User-Defined Functions (UDFs)

The four stages to defining a function in Python are the following:

1. Use the keyword def to proclaim the function and line this up with the function name.

2. Add parameters to the function: they ought to be within the enclosures of the function. End your line with a colon.

3. Add statements that the functions ought to execute.

4. End your function with an return statement, if the function should yield something. Without the return statement, your function will return an object None.

```
def hello():
print("Hello World") return
```

Obviously, your functions will get more complex as you go along: you can include for loops, flow control... and more to it to make it more fine-grained:

```
def hello( ):
name = str(input("enter your name:"))
if name:
pint ("hello" +str(name))
else:
print("hello world")
return
hello()
```

In the above function, you request that the user give a name. On the off chance that no name is given, the function will print out "Hello World". Something else, the user will get a customized

—Hello‖ response.

Keep in mind likewise that you can define at least one function parameters for your UDF. You'll take in more about this when you handle the Function Arguments section. Also, you can or can not return one or multiple values as the outcome of your function.

The return Statement

Note that as you're printing something in your UDF hello(), you don't really need to return it. There won't be any distinction between the function above and this one:

```
def hello_noreturn():
print("Hello World")
```

In any case, on the off chance that you need to continue to work with the outcome of your function and try out some operations on it, you should utilize the return statement to return a value, for example, a String, an integer, ... Think about the following situation, where hello() restores a String "hello", while the function hello_noreturn() returns None:

```
def hello():
print("Hello World")
return("hello")
def hello_noreturn():
print("Hello World")
hello() * 2 # Multiply the output of 'hello()' with 2
hello_noreturn() * 2 # (Try to) multiply the output of
                            'hello_noreturn()' with 2
```

The second function gives you a mistake since you can't perform any operations with a None. You'll get a TypeError that says that you can't do the multiplication operation for NoneType (the None that is the outcome of hello_noreturn()) and int (2).

Tip functions quickly leave when they go over an return statement, regardless of whether it implies that they won't return any value:

```
def run():
for x in range(10): if x == 2:
return print("Run!")
```

Something else that merits mentioning when you're working with the return statement is the way that you can utilize it to return multiple values. To do this, you make utilization of tuples.

Keep in mind that this data structure is fundamentally the same as that of a list: it can contain multiple values. Nonetheless, tuples are unchanging, which implies that you can't alter any values that are put away in it! You develop it with the assistance of double parentheses(). You can unpack tuples into multiple variables with the assistance of the comma and the assignment operator.

Look at the following example to understand how your function can return multiple values:

```
# define plus()
def plus(a,b):
sum = a+b
return (sum, a)
# Call `plus()` and unpack variables sum, a = plus(3,4)
# print sum()
Print(sum)
```

Note that the return statement return sum, a would have same outcome as return (sum, a): the previous really packs sum and an into a tuple in the hood!

How to Call a Function

In the past sections, you have seen a lot of examples already of how you can call a function. Calling a function implies that you execute the function that you have defined - either directly from the Python prompt or through another function (as you will find in the section "Nested Functions").

Call your newly defined function hello() by basically executing hello(), simply like in the Data Camp Light chunk as follows:

hello()

Function Arguments in Python

Prior, you learned about the distinction among parameters and arguments. To put it plainly, arguments are the things which are given to any function or method call, while the function or method code refers to the arguments by their parameter names. There are four types of arguments that Python UDFs can take:

Default arguments
Required arguments
Keyword arguments
Variable number of arguments

Default Arguments

Default arguments are those that take a default value if no argument value is passed during the function call. You can assign this default value by with the assignment operator =, much the same as in the following example:

```
# Define `plus()` function def plus(a,b = 2):
return a + b
# Call `plus()` with only `a` parameter plus(a=1)
# Call `plus()` with `a` and `b` parameters
plus(a=1, b=3)
```

Required Arguments

As the name kind of gives away, the required arguments of a UDF are those that must be in there. These arguments should be passed during the function call and in precisely the right order, much the same as in the below example:

```
# Define `plus()` with required arguments
def plus(a,b):
return a + b
```

You need arguments that map to a as well as the b parameters to call the function without occurring any errors. In the event that you switch around an and b, the outcome won't be different, however it may be on the off chance that you change plus() to the following:

```
# Define `plus()` with required arguments
def plus(a,b):
return a/b
```

In the event that you need to ensure that you call every one of the parameters organized appropriately, you can utilize the keyword arguments in your function call. You utilize these to distinguish the arguments by their parameter name. How about we take the example from above to make this clearer:

```
# Define `plus()` function
def plus(a,b):
return a + b
# Call `plus()` function with parameters plus(2,3)
# Call `plus()` function with keyword arguments
                plus(a=1, b=2)
```

Note that by using the keyword arguments, you can likewise switch around the order of the parameters and still get a similar outcome when you execute your function:

```
# Define `plus()` function
def plus(a,b):
return a + b
# Call `plus()` function with keyword arguments
                plus(b=2, a=1)
```

Variable Number of Arguments:

In cases where you don't have a clue about the exact number of arguments that you need to pass to a function, you can utilize the following syntax with *args:

```
# Define `plus()` function to accept a variable number of
                arguments
def plus(*args):
return sum(args)
# Calculate the sum plus(1,4,5)
```

The asterisk (*) is put before the variable name that holds the values of all nonkeyword variable arguments. Note here that you should have passed *varint, *var_int_args or some other name to the plus() function.

Tip: Try replacing *args with another name that includes the asterisk. You'll see that the above code continues working!

212 | A Beginners Guide to Internet of Things

You see that the above function makes utilization of the built-in Python sum() function to sum every one of the arguments that passed to plus(). In the event that you might want to avoid this and build the function totally yourself, you can utilize this option:

```
# Define `plus()` function to accept a variable number of
                        arguments
def plus(*args):
total = 0
for i in args: total += i
return total
# Calculate the sum plus(20,30,40,50)
```

Global Vs Local Variable

All in all, variables that are defined inside a function body have a local scope, and those defined outside have a global scope. That implies that local variables are defined within a function block and must be accessed to inside that function, while global variables can be accessed by all functions that may be in your script:

```
# Global variable `init` init = 1
# Define `plus()` function to accept a variable number of
                        arguments
def plus(*args):
# Local variable `sum()` total = 0
for i in args: total += i
return total
# Access the global variable
print("this is the initialized value" + str(init))
# (Try to) access the local variable
print("this is the sum" + str(total))
```

You'll see that you'll get a Name Error that says that the name 'total' isn't defined when you try to print out the local variable total that was defined inside the function body. The init variable, then again, can be printed out with no issues.

Anonymous Functions in Python:

Anonymous functions are additionally called lambda functions in Python due to that instead of declaring them with the standard def keyword, you utilize the lambda keyword.

double = lambda x: x*2 double(5)

In the DataCamp Light chunk above, lambda x: x*2 is the anonymous or lambda function. x is the argument, and x*2 is the expression or instruction that gets evaluated and returned. What's uncommon about this functions is that it has no name, similar to the examples that you have found in the first part of this functions tutorial. In the event that you would need to write the above function in a UDF, the outcome would be the following:

def double(x):
return x*2

How about we consider another case of a lambda function where you work with two arguments:

```
# `sum()` lambda function
sum = lambda x, y: x + y;
# Call the `sum()` anonymous function
sum(4,5)
# "Translate" to a UDF
def sum(x, y):
return x+y
```

You utilize anonymous functions when you require an anonymous function for a brief period of time and that is made at runtime. Specific contexts in which this would be significant is the point at which you're working with filter(), map() reduce():

```
from functools import reduce
my_list = [1,2,3,4,5,6,7,8,9,10]
# Use lambda function with `filter()`
filtered_list = list(filter(lambda x: (x*2 > 10), my_list))
# Use lambda function with `map()`
mapped_list = list(map(lambda x: x*2, my_list))
# Use lambda function with `reduce()`
reduced_list = reduce(lambda x, y: x+y, my_list)
print(filtered_list) print(mapped_list) print(reduced_list)
```

The filter() function filters, as the name recommends, the original input list my_list on the basis of a criterion >10. With map(), then again, you apply a function to all items of the list my_list. For this situation, you increase all elements with 2.

Note that the **reduce()** function is part of the functools library. You utilize this function in cumulatively to the items of the my_list list, from left to right and decrease the sequence to a single value, 55, for this situation.

Using main( ) as a Function:

In the event that you have any involvement with other programming languages, for example, Java, you'll realize that a main function is required in order to execute functions. As you have found in the examples above, this isn't really required for Python. In any case, including a main() function in your Python program can be handy to structure your code in a logical way - the majority of the most important components are contained within this main() function.

You can easily define a main() function and call it simply like you have finished with all of the other functions above:

```
# Define `main()` function
def main():
hello()
print("This is a main function")
main()
```

However, as it stands now, the code of your main() function will be called when you import it as a module. To ensure this doesn't occur, you call the main() function when name == 'main'.

That implies that the code of the above code chunk moves toward becoming:

```
# Define `main()` function def main():
hello()
print("This is a main function")
# Execute `main()` function if_name_== '_main_':
main()
```

Note that other than the_main_function, you additionally have a init_function that initializes an instance of a class or an object. Essentially expressed, it goes about as a constructor or initializer and is consequently called when you create another instance of a class. With that function, the recently made object is assigned out to the parameter self, which you saw prior in this tutorial. Take a look at the following example:

```
Class dog:
""""
Requires:
legs - Legs so that the dog can walk.
color - A color of the fur.
"""""
```

```
def init_(self, legs, color):
self.legs = legs
self.color = color
def bark(self):
bark = "bark" * 2
return bark
if name == "_main_":
dog = Dog(4, "brown")
bark = dog.bark()
print(bark)
```

Modules:

A module enables you to legitimately sort out your Python code. Grouping related code into a module makes the code simpler to understand and utilize. A module is a Python object with discretionarily named attributes that you can bind and reference. Basically, a module is a file consisting of Python code. A module can define functions, classes and variables. A module can likewise include runnable code.

Example

The Python code for a module named aname typically resides in a file named aname.py. Here's a example of a basic module, support.py

```
def print_func( par ):
print "Hello: ", par return
```

The import Statement:

You can utilize any Python source document file as a module by executing an import statement in some other Python source file. The import has the following syntax –

```
import module1[, module2[,... moduleN]
```

At the point when the interpreter experiences an import statement, it imports the module if the module is available in the search path. A search path is a list of indexes that the interpreter looks before importing a module. For instance, to import the module support.py, you have to put the following command at the top of the script –

```
#!/usr/bin/python
# Import module support import support
# Now you can call defined function that module as follows
support.print_func("Zara")
```

When the above code is executed, it produces the following outcome –

Hello: Zara

A module is loaded just once, regardless of the number of times it is imported. This keeps the module execution from happening again and again if multiple imports occurs.

The *from...import* Statement

Python's from statement gives you a chance to import explicit attributes from a module into the current namespace. The from... import has the following syntax --

from modname import name1[, name2[,... nameN]]

For instance, to import the function fibonacci from the module fib, utilize the following statement –

from fib import fibonacci

Locating Modules:

When you import a module, the Python interpreter scans for the module in the following sequences –

- The current directory.

- If the module isn't discovered, Python at that point looks through every directory in the shell variable PYTHONPATH.

- If all else fails, Python checks the default path. On UNIX, this default path is normally /usr/local/lib/python/.

The module search path is stored in the system module sys as the sys.path variable. The sys.path variable contains the current directory, PYTHONPATH, and the installation-dependent default.

The *PYTHONPATH* Variable

The PYTHONPATH is a environment variable, consisting of a list of directories. The syntax of PYTHONPATH is equivalent to that of the shell variable PATH.

Here is a typical PYTHONPATH from a Windows system –

set PYTHONPATH = c:\python20\lib;

And here is a typical PYTHONPATH from a UNIX system –

set PYTHONPATH = /usr/local/lib/python

Packages

Introduction

We discovered that modules are files containing Python statements and definitions, similar to function and class definitions. We will learn in this section how to package multiple modules together to frame a package.

A package is essentially a directory with Python files and a file with the name init.py. This implies each directory within the Python way, which contains a file named init.py, will be treated as a package by Python. It's conceivable to put a few modules into a Package.

Packages are a method for organizing Python's module namespace by utilizing "dotted module names". A.B represents a submodule named B in a package named A. Two different packages like P1 and P2 can both have modules with a similar name, suppose A, for instance. The submodule A of the package P1 and the submodule A of the package P2 can be very surprising.

A package is imported like an "normal" module. We will begin this section with a basic model.

We make two basic files a.py and b.py only for filling the package with modules.

> The content of a.py: def bar():
> print("Hello, function 'bar' from module 'a' calling")
> The content of b.py: def foo():
> print("Hello, function 'foo' from module 'b' calling")

We will likewise include an empty file with the name init.py within simple_package directory.

Packages in Python:

A package is a hierarchical file directory structure that characterizes a solitary Python application environment that comprises of modules and subpackages and sub-subpackages, etc.

Consider a file Pots.py accessible in Phone directory. This file has following line of source code

−#!/usr/bin/python def Pots():
print "I'm Pots Phone"

Comparable way, we have another two files having distinctive functions with indistinguishable name from above −

- *Phone/Isdn.py* file having function Isdn()
- *Phone/G3.py* file having function G3()
- Presently, make one more file init.py in Phone directory –
- Phone/ init.py

To make the majority of your functions accessible when you've imported Phone, you have to put express import statements in init.py as pursues –

```
from Pots import Pots
from Isdn import Isdn
from G3 import G3
```

After you add these lines to init.py, you have these classes accessible when you import the Phone package.

```
#!/usr/bin/python
# Now import your Phone Package. Import Phone
Phone.Pots()
Phone.Isdn()
Phone.G3()
```

At the point when the above code is executed, it delivers the accompanying outcome –

```
I'm Pots Phone
I'm 3G Phone
I'm ISDN Phone
```

A More Complex Package:

We will exhibit in the following example how we can make a more complex package. We will utilize the hypothetical sound-Module which is utilized in the official tutorial. (see https://docs.python.org/3/instructional exercise/modules.html)

```
sound
|-- effects
| |-- echo.py
| |--_init.py
| |-- reverse.py
| `-- surround.py
|-- filters
| |-- equalizer.py
| |-- init.py
| |-- karaoke.py
| `-- vocoder.py
|-- formats
| |-- aiffread.py
| |-- aiffwrite.py
| |-- auread.py
| |-- auwrite.py
| |-- init.py
| |-- wavread.py
| `-- wavwrite.py
`--_init._py
```

File Handling

File handling is an important part of any web application. Python has so many functions for creating, reading, updating, and deleting files. The key function for working with files in Python is the open() function.

Open( ):

The open() function takes two parameters; filename, and mode. There are four various techniques (modes) for opening a file:

- "r" - Read - Default value. Opens a file for reading, error if the file does not exist
- "a" - Append - Opens a file for appending, creates the file if it does not exist
- "w" - Write - Opens a file for writing, creates the file if it does not exist
- "x" - Create - Creates the specified file, returns an error if the file exists
- Moreover you can determine if the file ought to be handled as binary or text mode
- "t" - Text - Default value. Text mode
- "b" - Binary - Binary mode (e.g. images)

Syntax

To open a file for reading it is sufficient to indicate the name of the file: f = open("demofile.txt")

The code above is equivalent to: f = open("demofile.txt", "rt")

Because "r" for read, and "t" for text are the default values, you don't have to indicate them. **Note:** Make sure the file exists, or else you will get a error.

File handling in Python requires no importing of modules.

File Object

Instead we can utilize the built-in object "file". That object gives essential functions and methods important to manipulate files by default. Before you can read, append or write to a file, you will initially need to it using Python's built-in open() function. In this post I will depict how to utilize the various methods for the file object.

Open()

The open() function is utilized to open files in our system, the filename is the name of the file to be opened. The mode indicates, how the file will be opened "r" for reading, "w" for writing and "a" for an appending. The open function takes two arguments, the name of the file and the mode for which we might want to open the file. As a matter of course, when just the filename is passed, the open function opens the file in read mode.

Example

This little script, will open the (hello.txt) and print the content. This will store the file information in the file object "filename". filename = "hello.txt"

file = open(filename, "r")for line in file: print line,

Read ()

The read functions contains diverse methods, read(),readline() and readlines()

read() #return one major string
readline() #return one line at any given moment
readlines() #returns a list of lines

Write ()

This method composes an arrangement of strings to the file.

write ()#Used to write a fixed sequence of characters to a file
writelines()#writelines can write a list of strings.

Append ()

The append function is utilized to affix to the file instead of overwriting it. To add to an existing file, basically open the file in append mode ("a"):

Close()

When you're done with a file, use close() to shut it and free down any system resources taken up by the open file.

File Handling Examples:

Let's show some examples

- **To open a text file,**
  use:fh = open("hello.txt", "r")

- **To read a text file,**
  use:fh = open("hello.txt","r")
  print fh.read()

- **To read one line at a time,**
  use:fh = open("hello".txt", "r")
  print fh.readline()

- **To read a list of lines**
  use:fh = open("hello.txt.", "r")
  print fh.readlines()

- **To write to a file,**
  use:fh = open("hello.txt","w")
  write("Hello World")
  fh.close()

- **To write to a file,**
  use:fh = open("hello.txt", "w")
  lines_of_text = ["a line of text", "another line of text", "a third line"]
  fh.writelines(lines_of_text)
  fh.close()

- **To append to file,**
  use:fh = open("Hello.txt", "a")
  write("Hello World again")
  fh.close()

- **To close a file,**
  usefh = open("hello.txt", "r")
  print fh.read()
  fh.close()

Date/Time operations:

In Python, date, time and datetime classes gives various function to manage dates, times and time intervals. Date and datetime are an object in Python, so when you manipulate them, you are really manipulating objects and not string or timestamps. At whatever point you manipulate dates or time, you have to import datetime function.

The datetime classes in Python are 5 classes.

- date – Manipulate simply date (Month, day, year)
- time – Time independent of the day (Hour, minute, second, microsecond)
- datetime – Combination of time and date (Month, day, year, hour, second, microsecond)
- timedelta—A duration of time utilized for manipulating dates
- tzinfo—A abstract class for dealing with time zones

Classes:

Classes give a methods for packaging information and usefulness together. Creating another class makes new type of object, enabling new occurrences of that type to be made. Each class case can have attributes joined to it for keeping up its state. Class instances can likewise have methods (characterized by its class) for modifying its state.

Contrasted and other programming languages, Python's class mechanism includes classes with at least new syntax and semantics. It is a blend of the class mechanisms found in C++ and Modula-3. Python classes give all the standard features of Object Oriented Programming: the class inherent mechanism permits various base classes, a derived class can override any methods for its base class or classes, and a technique can call the method for a base class with a similar name. Articles can contain self-assertive sums and kinds of information. As is valid for modules, classes share of the dynamic idea of Python: they are made at runtime, and can be adjusted further after creation.

In C++ terminology, typically class individuals (counting the data members) are open (aside from see below Private Variables), and all member functions are virtual. As in Modula-3, there are no shorthands for referencing the object's memberss from its methods: the method function is pronounced with an explicit first argument representing the object, which is given certainly by the call. As in Smalltalk, classes themselves are objects. This gives semantics to importing and renaming. Not at all like C++ and Modula-3, can built-in kinds be utilized as base classes for expansion by the user. Likewise, as in C++, most built-in with unique syntax (arithmetic operators, subscripting and so on.) can be redefined for class instances. (Lacking generally accepted terminology to discuss classes, I will make occasional utilization of Smalltalk and C++ terms. I would utilize Modula-3 terms, since its object oriented semantics are nearer to those of Python than C++, yet I expect that few readers have known about it.)

A Word about Names and Objects

Objects have independence, and multiple names (in multiple scopes) can be bound to a same object. This is known as aliasing in different languages. This is normally not appreciated on a first look at Python, and can be securely disregarded when with immutable basic types (numbers, strings, tuples). Notwithstanding, associating has a conceivably amazing impact on the semantics of Python code including variable objects, for example, lists, dictionaries, and most different types. This is normally used to the advantage of the program, since aliases behave like pointers in a few regards. For instance, passing an object is modest since just a pointer is passed by the implementation and if a function alters an object go as an argument, the caller will see the change — this removes the requirement for two distinctive argument passing mechanisms as in Pascal.

Python Scopes and Namespaces

Before presenting classes, need to disclose to you something about Python's scope rules. Class definitions play some perfect traps with namespaces, and you have to know how scopes and namespaces function to completely comprehend what's happening.

We should start with a few definitions.

A namespace is a mapping from names to objects. Most namespaces are as of now implemented as Python dictionaries, yet that is ordinarily not discernible at all (aside from performance), and it might change later on. Examples of namespaces are: the set of built-in names (containing functions such as abs(), and built-in exception names); the global names in a module; and the local names in a function invocation. It could be said the set of characteristics of an object likewise form a namespace.

The important thing to think about namespaces is that there is definitely no connection between names in various namespaces; for example, two different modules may both characterize a function maximize without confusion — users of the modules must prefix it with the module name.

Incidentally, I utilize the word attribute for any name following a dot — for instance, in the expression z.real, realis a property of the object z. Entirely, references to names in modules are attribute references: in the expression modname.funcname, modname is a module object and funcname is an attribute of it. For this situation there happens to be a clear mapping between the module's characteristics and the global names characterized in the module: they share the equivalent namespace! Attributes might be read only or writable. In the last case, assignment to attributes is conceivable. Module attributes are writable: you can write modname.the_answer = 42. Writable characteristics may likewise be erased with the delstatement. For example, del modname.the_answer will remove the object the_answer from the object named by modname.

Namespaces are made at various moments and have different lifetimes. The namespace containing the built-in names is made when the Python interpreter starts up, and is never erased. The global namespace for a module is made when the module definition is read in; typically, module namespaces also last until the interpreter quits. The statements executed by the top-level invocation of the interpreter, either read from a content file or interactively, are considered part of a module called main, so they have their own global namespace. (The built-in names entirely live in a module; this is called built-ins.)

The local namespace for a function is made when the function is called, and erased when the function returns or raises an exception that isn't handled within the function. (As a matter of fact, forgetting would be a superior way to depict what really occurs.) obviously, recursive invocations each have their very own local namespace.

A scope is a textual region of a Python program where a namespace is specifically accessible. "Directly accessible" here implies that an inadequate reference to a name endeavors to find the name in the namespace.

In spite of the fact that scopes are determined statically, they are utilized dynamically. Whenever during execution, there are no less than three nested scopes whose namespaces are specifically accessible:

- the innermost scope, which is searched first, contains the local names

- the scopes of any enclosing functions, which are sought starting with the closest enclosing scope, contains non-local, yet in addition non-global names

- the next-to-last scope contains the present module's global names

- the outermost scope (searched last) is the namespace containing built-in names

If a name is announced global, all references and assignments go straightforwardly to the middle scope containing the module's global names. To rebind variables found outside of the innermost scope, the nonlocal statement can be utilized; if not pronounced nonlocal, those variables are read-only (an attempt to write to such a variable will essentially make a new local variable in the innermost scope, leaving the indistinguishably named external variable unaltered).

Usually, the local scope references the local names of the (textually) current function. Outside functions, the local scope references the equivalent namespace as the global scope: the module's namespace. Class definitions place yet another namespace in the local scope.

Realize that scopes are determined textually: the global scope of a function defined in a module is that module's namespace, regardless of from where or by what assumed name the function is called. On the other hand, the actual search for names is done progressively, at run time — be that as it may, the language definition is evolving towards static name resolution, at "compile" time, so don't depend on powerful name resolution! (In fact, local variables are already determined statically.)

An exceptional quirk of Python is that – if no global statement is in effect – assignments to names dependably go into the innermost scope. Assignments don't duplicate information — they simply bind names to objects. The same is true for deletions: the statement del x removes the binding of x from the namespace referenced by the local scope. Actually, all tasks that introduce new names utilize the local scope: in particular, import statements and function definitions bind the module or function name in the local scope.

The global statement can be utilized to indicate that specific variables live in the global scope and ought to rebound there; the non-local statement indicates that specific variables live in an enclosing scope and ought to be rebound there.

Scopes and Namespaces Example

This is an example demonstrating how to reference the diverse scopes and namespaces, and how global and non-local affect variable binding:

```
def scope_test():
def do_local():
spam = "local spam"
def do_nonlocal():
nonlocal spam
spam = "nonlocal spam"
def do_global():
global spam
spam = "global spam"
spam = "test spam" do_local()
print("After local assignment:", spam) do_nonlocal()
print("After nonlocal assignment:", spam) do_global()
print("After global assignment:", spam)
scope_test()
print("In global scope:", spam
```

The output of the example code is:

```
After local assignment: test spam
After nonlocal assignment: nonlocal spam
After global assignment: nonlocal spam In
```

Note how the local assignment (which is default) didn't change scope_test's binding of spam. The nonlocalassignment changed scope_test's binding of spam, and the global assignment changed the module-level binding.

Classes

Classes introduce a little bit of new syntax, three new object types, and some new semantics.

Class Definition Syntax

The most straightforward type of class definition resembles this: class ClassName:

```
class ClassName:
    <statement-1>
    .
    .
    <statement-N>
```

Class definitions, similar to function definitions (def statements) must be executed before they have any effect. (You could possibly put a class definition in a part of an if statement, or inside a function.) Practically speaking, the statements inside a class definition will usually be function definitions, however different statements are permitted, and some of the time helpful — we'll return to this later. The function definitions inside a class regularly have an unconventional type of argument list, directed by the calling conventions for methods — again, this is explained later.

At the point when a class definition is entered, another namespace is made, and utilized as the local scope — subsequently, all assignments to local variables go into this new namespace. Specifically, function definitions bind the name of the new function here.

At the point when a class definition is left ordinarily (through the end), a class object is made. This is fundamentally a wrapper around the contents of the namespace made by the class definition; we'll learn more about class objects in the following section. The original local scope (the one in effect just before the class definition was entered) is reinstated, and the class object is bound here to the class name given in the class definition header (ClassName in the model).

Class Objects:

Class objects support two kinds of operations: attribute references and instantiation.

Attribute references use the standard syntax utilized for all attribute references in Python: obj.name. Valid attribute names are all the names that were in the class' namespace when the class object was made. Thus, if the class definition resembled this:

```
class MyClass:
"""A simple example class"""
i = 12345
def f(self):
return "hello world"
```

then MyClass.i and MyClass.f are Valid attribute references, returning an integer and a function object, separately. Class attributes can likewise be assigned to, so you can change the value of MyClass.i by assignment. doc is additionally a valid attribute, returning the docstring belonging to the class: "A simple exampleclass".

Class instantiation uses function notation. Simply imagine that the class object is a parameterless function that returns another instance of the class. For instance (assuming the above class):

```
x = MyClass()
```

makes a new instance of the class and assigns this object to the local variable x.

The instantiation operation ("calling" a class object) makes an empty object. Numerous classes like to make objects with instances altered to an explicit initial state. In this manner a class may define a special method named init (), like this:

```
def init_(self): self.data = []
```

234 | A Beginners Guide to Internet of Things

At the point when a class defines an init () method, class instantiation consequently invokes init () for the recently made class instance. So in this example, another, initialized instance can be obtained by:

x = MyClass()

Obviously, the init () method may have arguments for greater flexibility. All things considered, arguments given to the class instantiation operator are passed on to init (). For instance,

```
>>> class Complex:
... def init_(self, realpart, imagpart):
... self.r = realpart
... self.i = imagpart
...
>>> x = Complex(3.0, -4.5)
>>> x.r, x.i (3.0, -4.5)
```

Instance Objects:

Presently what would we be able to do with instance objects? The only operations understood by instance objects are attribute references. There are two sorts of substantial attribute names, data attributes and methods.

Data attributes correspond to "instance variables" in Smalltalk, and to "data members" in C++. Data attributes require not be proclaimed; like local variables, they spring into reality when they are first assigned to. For instance, if x is the example of MyClass created over, the accompanying piece of code will print the value 16, without leaving a trace:

The other kind of instance attribute reference is a method. A method is a function that "belongs to" an object. (In Python, the term method isn't unique to class instances: other object types can have methods too. For instance, list objects have methods called append, insert, remove, sort etc. However, in the accompanying discussion, we'll utilize the term method solely to mean methods of class instance objects, unless explicitly stated otherwise.)

```
x.counter = 1
while x.counter < 10: x.counter = x.counter * 2
print(x.counter)
del x.counter
```

Valid method names of an instance object rely upon its class. By definition, all attributes of a class that are function objects define corresponding methods of its instances. So in our example, x.f is a valid method reference, since MyClass.f is a function, but x.i is not, since MyClass.i is not. But x.f is not a similar thing as MyClass.f —it is a method object, not a function object.

Class and Instance Variables:

As a rule, instance variables are for data unique to each instance and class variables are for attributes and methods shared by all instances of the class:

```
Class Dog:
Kind = 'canine' #class variable shared by all instances
Definit_(self name):
Self.name = self # instance variable unique to each instance
>>>d = dog('Fido')
>>>e = dog('buddy')
>>> d.kind # shared by all dogs
'canine'
```

```
>>>e.kind #shared by all dogs
'canine'
>>>d.name #unique to d
'Fido'
>>>e.name #unique to e
'buddy'
```

As talked about in A Word About Names and Objects, shared data can have astonishing impacts with involving mutable objects, for example, lists and dictionaries. For instance, the tricks list in the accompanying code ought not to be utilized as a class variable because just a single list would be shared by all Dog instances:

```
Class Dog:
#mistaken use of a class variable
Definit_(self,name):
Self.name=name
Def add_trick(self, trick):
Self.tricks.append(trick)
>>>d = dog('Fido')
>>>e = dog('Buddy')
d.add_trick('roll over')
e.add_trick('play dead')
>>>d.tricks['roll over', play dead'] #unexpectedly shared by
                                            all dogs
```

Right design of the class should utilize an instance variable:

```
Class Dog:
#mistaken use of a class variable
Definit_(self,name):
Self.name=name
Self.tricks = [ ] #creates a new empty list for each dog
Def add_trick(self, trick):
Self.tricks.append(trick)
```

```
>>>d = dog('Fido')
>>>e = dog('Buddy')
d.add_trick('roll over')
e.add_trick('play dead')
>>>d.tricks['roll over']
>>>e.tricks['play dead']
```

Inheritance:

Obviously, a language feature would not be deserving of the name "class" without supporting inheritance. The syntax for a determined class definition resembles this:

```
Class DerivedClassName(BaseClassName):
<statement-1>
    .
    .
    .
<statement-N>
```

The name BaseClassName must be defined in a scope containing the derived class definition. Instead of a base class name, other arbitrary expressions are likewise permitted. This can be valuable, for instance, when the base class is defined in another module:

class DerivedClassName(modname.BaseClassName):

Execution of a derived class definition continues equivalent to for a base class. At the point when the class object is developed, the base class is recalled. This is utilized for resolving attribute references: if an requested for attribute isn't found in the class, the search continues to look in the base class. This standard is connected recursively if the base class itself is derived from some different class.

There's nothing extraordinary about instantiation of derived classes: DerivedClassName() makes another instance of the class. Method references are settled as follows: the corresponding class attribute is searched, descending down the chain of base classes if fundamental, and the method reference is valid if this yields a function object.

Derived classes may override methods of their base classes. Since methods have no extraordinary benefits when calling different methods of a similar object, a method of a base class that calls another method defined in a similar base class may end up calling a method of a derived class that overrides it. (For C++ developers: all methods in Python are successfully virtual.)

An overriding method in a derived class may in reality need to extend instead of simply replace the base class method of a similar name. There is a basic method to call the base class method specifically: simply call BaseClassName.methodname(self, arguments). This is once in a while valuable to clients also. (Note this just works if the base class is open as BaseClassName in the global scope.)

Python has two built-in functions that work with inheritance:

- Use isinstance() to check an instance's type: isinstance(obj, int) will be True only if obj. class is int or some class derived from int.

- Use issubclass() to check class inheritance: issubclass(bool, int) is True since bool is a subclass of int. Be that as it may, issubclass(float, int) is False since float isn't a subclass of int.

Multiple Inheritance:

Python supports a type of multiple inheritances too. A class definition with multiple base classes resembles this:

```
classDeivedClassName(Base1, Base2, Base3):
<statement-1>
.
.
<statement-n>
```

For most purposes, in the simplest cases, you can think of the search for attributes inherited from a parent class as profundity first, left-to-right, not searching twice in a similar class where there is an overlap in the hierarchy. In this way, if an attribute isn't found in DerivedClassName, it is scanned for in Base1, at that point (recursively) in the base classes of Base1, and if it was not found there, it was looked for in Base2, and so on.

In fact, it is somewhat more complex than that; the method goal is to order changes progressively to help agreeable calls to super(). This methodology is known in some other multiple-inheritance languages as call-next-method and is more powerful than the super call found in single- inheritance languages.

Dynamic ordering is essential since all instances of multiple inheritance display at least one diamond relationships (where something like one of the parent classes can be accessed through multiple paths from the bottommost class). For instance, all classes inherit from object, so any instance of multiple inheritance gives in excess of one path to achieve object. To keep the base classes from being accessed more than once, the dynamic algorithm linearizes the search order in a way that protects the left-to-right ordering indicated in each class, that calls each parent just once, and that is monotonic (meaning that a class can be subclassed without affecting the precedence order of its parents). Taken together, these properties make it conceivable to design reliable and extensible classes with multiple inheritance. For more detail, seehttps://www.python.org/download/discharges/2.3/mro/.

Exception Handling Python Packages-JSON:

JSON (JavaScript Object Notation), indicated by RFC 7159 (which obsoletes RFC 4627) and by ECMA-404, is a lightweight data interchange format inspired by JavaScript object literal syntax (although it is not a strict subset of JavaScript [1]). json uncovered an API well-known to users of the standard library marshal and pickle modules. Encoding essential Python object hierarchies:

```
>>> print(json.dumps("\"foo\bar")) "\"foo\bar"
>>> print(json.dumps('\u1234')) "\u1234"
>>> print(json.dumps('\\')) "\\"
>>> print(json.dumps({"c": 0, "b": 0, "a": 0},
    sort_keys=True))
{"a": 0, "b": 0, "c": 0}
>>> from io import StringIO
>>> io = StringIO()
>>> json.dump(['streaming API'], io)
>>> io.getvalue() '["streaming API"]'
```

Compact encoding:

```
>>> import json
>>> json.dumps([1, 2, 3, {'4': 5, '6': 7}], separators=(',', ':'))
'[1, 2, 3, {"4": 5, "6": 7}]'
```

Pretty printing:

```
>>> import json
>>> print(json.dumps({'4': 5, '6': 7}, sort_keys=True,
    indent=4))
{
"4": 5,
"6": 7
}
```

Specializing JSON object decoding:

```
>>> import json
>>> def as_complex(dct):
... if '_complex_' in dct:
... return complex(dct['real'], dct['imag'])
... return dct
...
>>> json.loads('{"_complex_": true, "real": 1, "imag": 2}',
... object_hook=as_complex) (1+2j)
>>> import decimal
>>> json.loads('1.1', parse_float=decimal.Decimal)
Decimal('1.1')
```

Extending JSONEncoder:

```
>>> import json
>>> class ComplexEncoder(json.JSONEncoder):
... def default(self, obj):
... if isinstance(obj, complex):
... return [obj.real, obj.imag]
... # Let the base class default method raise the TypeError
... return json.JSONEncoder.default(self, obj)
...
>>> json.dumps(2 + 1j, cls=ComplexEncoder) '[2.0, 1.0]'
>>> ComplexEncoder().encode(2 + 1j) '[2.0, 1.0]'
>>> list(ComplexEncoder().iterencode(2 + 1j))
['[2.0', ', 1.0', ']']
```

Using json.tool from the shell to validate and pretty-print:

```
$ echo '{"json":"obj"}' | python -m json.tool
{
"json": "obj"
}
$ echo '{1.2:3.4}' | python -m json.tool
```

> Expecting property name encoding in double quotes: line 1 column 2(char 1)

> **Note:** JSON is a subset of YAML 1.2. The JSON produced by this module's default settings (in particular, the default *separators* value) is also a subset of YAML 1.0 and 1.1. This module can thus also be utilized as a YAML serializer.

Basic Usage:

json.**dump**(*obj, fp, *, skipkeys = False, ensure_ascii = True, check_circular = True, allow_nan = True, cls = N one, indent = None, separators = None, default = None, sort_keys = False, **kw*)

Serialize *obj* as a JSON formatted stream to *fp* (a.write()-supporting file-like object) using this conversion table.

If *skipkeys* is true (default: False), then dict keys that are not of a basic type (str, int, float, bool, None) will be skipped instead of raising a TypeError.

The json module always produces str objects, not bytes objects. Therefore, fp.write() must support str input.

On the off chance that ensure_ascii is valid (the default), the yield is ensured to have all incoming non-ASCII characters escaped. If ensure_ascii is false, these characters will be yield as-is.

If check_circular is false (default: True), the circular reference check for container types will be skipped and a circular reference will result in an OverflowError (or more awful).

If allow_nan is false (default: True), it will be a ValueError to serialize out of range float values (nan,inf, - inf) in strict compliance of the JSON specification. If allow_nan is valid, their JavaScript equivalents (NaN, Infinity, - Infinity) will be utilized.

If indent is a non-negative integer or string, JSON exhibit components and object individuals will be pretty-printed with that indent level. An indent level of 0, negative, or "" will just embed newlines. None (the default) chooses the most compact representation. Utilizing a positive integer indent values that numerous spaces per level. In the event that indent is a string, (for example, "\t"), that string is utilized to indent each level.

If specified, *separators* should be an (item_separator, key_separator) tuple. The default is (', ', ':') if *indent* is None and (',', ': ') otherwise. To get the most compact JSON representation, you must represent (',', ':') to remove whitespace.

Changed in version 3.4: **Use (',', ': ') as default if *indent* is not None.**

Whenever determined, default ought to be a function that gets called for objects that can't generally be serialized. It should return a JSON encodable variant of the object or raise a TypeError. If not indicated, TypeError is raised.

In the event that sort_keys is valid (default: False), the yield of lexicons will be arranged by key.

To utilize a custom JSONEncoder subclass (e.g. one that overrides the default() method to serialize extra types), determine it with the cls kwarg; generally JSONEncoder is utilized.

Changed in version 3.6: All optional parameters are now keyword-only.

Note: In contrast to pickle and marshal, JSON is definitely not an framed protocol, so endeavoring to serialize various objects with repeated calls to dump() utilizing the equivalent fp will result in an invalid JSON file.

json.**dumps**(*obj*, *, *skipkeys=False*, *ensure_ascii=True*, *check_circular=True*, *allow_nan=True*, *cls=No ne*, *indent=None*, *separators=None*, *default=None*, *sort_keys=False*, ***kw*)

Serialize obj to a JSON formatted str utilizing this conversion table. The arguments have indistinguishable meaning from in dump()

Keys in key/value pairs of JSON are dependably of the sort str. At the point when a dictionary is changed over into JSON, all the keys of the dictionary are pressured to strings. Thus, on the off chance that a dictionary is changed over into JSON and, once again into a dictionary, the dictionary may not equivalent the first one. That is,loads(dumps(x)) != x if x has non-string keys.

json.**load**(*fp*, *, *cls=None*, *object_hook=None*, *parse_float=None*, *parse_int=None*, *parse_constant=Non e*, *object_pairs_hook=None*, ***kw*)

Deserialize fp (a.read()- supporting content file or twofold file containing a JSON report) to a Python object utilizing this conversion table.

object_hook is a optional function that will be called with the consequence of any object strict decoded (a dict). The return value of object_hook will be utilized rather than the dict. This component can be utilized to actualize custom decoders (e.g. JSON-RPC class hinting).

object_pairs_hook is a optional function that will be called with the result of any object strict decoded with an ordered list of sets. The return value of object_pairs_hook will be utilized rather than the dict. This element can be utilized to actualize custom decoders. In the event that object_hook is additionally characterized, the object_pairs_hook takes need.

Changed in version 3.1: Added support for *object_pairs_hook.*

parse_float, whenever determined, will be called with the string of each JSON float to be decoded. Naturally, this is equal to float(num_str). This can be utilized to utilize another datatype or parser for JSON floats (e.g. decimal.Decimal).

parse_int, whenever determined, will be called with the string of each JSON int to be decoded. Of course, this is comparable to int(num_str). This can be utilized to utilize another datatype or parser for JSON integers (e.g. float).

parse_constant, whenever indicated, will be called with one of the accompanying strings: '- Infinity', 'Interminability', 'NaN'. This can be utilized to raise a exception if invalid JSON numbers are experienced.

Changed in version 3.1: parse_constant **doesn't get called on _null', _true', _false' anymore.**

To utilize a custom JSONDecoder subclass, determine it with the cls kwarg; generally JSONDecoder is utilized. Extra keyword arguments will be passed to the constructor of the class.

In the event that the information being deserialized is definitely not a substantial JSON document, a JSONDecodeError will be raised.

Changed in version 3.6: **All optional parameters are now keyword-only.**

Changed in version 3.6: fp **can now be a binary file. The input encoding should be UTF-8, UTF- 16 or UTF-32.**

json.loads(s, *, encoding=None, cls=None, object_hook=None, parse_float=None, parse_int=None, parse_constant=None, object_pairs_hook=None, **kw)

Deserialize s (a str, bytes or bytearray case containing a JSON record) to a Python object utilizing this conversion table.

The other arguments have indistinguishable importance from in load(), aside from encoding which is disregarded and censured.

In the event that the information being deserialized is certainly not a substantial JSON document, a JSONDecodeError will be raised.

Changed in version 3.6: s can now be of type bytes or bytearray. The input encoding should be UTF-8, UTF-16 or UTF-32.

class json.**JSONDecoder**(**, object_hook=None, parse_float=None, parse_int=None, parse_constant= None, strict=True, object_pairs_ hook=None*)

Simple JSON decoder.

Performs the following translations in decoding by default:

JSON	Python
object	Dict
array	List
string	Str
number (int)	Int
number (real)	float
true	True
false	False
null	None

It additionally comprehends NaN, Infinity, and - Infinity as their relating float values, which is outside the JSON spec.

object_hook, whenever indicated, will be called with the result of each JSON object decoded and its return value will be utilized instead of the given dict. This can be utilized to give custom deserializations (e.g. to help JSON-RPC class implying).

object_pairs_hook, whenever indicated will be called with the consequence of each JSON object decoded with an arranged list of sets. The return value of object_pairs_hook will be utilized rather than the dict. This element can be utilized to execute custom decoders. On the off chance that object_hook is likewise characterized, the object_pairs_hook priority.

Changed in version 3.1: **Added support for** *object_pairs_hook.*

parse_float, whenever determined, will be called with the string of each JSON float to be decoded. As a matter of course, this is identical to float(num_str). This can be utilized to utilize another datatype or parser for JSON floats (e.g. decimal.Decimal).

parse_int, whenever determined, will be called with the string of each JSON int to be decoded. As a matter of course, this is proportionate to int(num_str). This can be utilized to utilize another datatype or parser for JSON integers (e.g. float).

parse_constant, whenever determined, will be called with one of the accompanying strings: '- Infinity', 'Infinity', 'NaN'. This can be utilized to raise an exception if invalid JSON numbers are experienced.

On the off chance that strict is false (True is the default), control characters will be permitted inside strings. Control characters in this context are those with character codes in the 0– 31 territory, including '\t' (tab), '\n', '\r' and '\0'.

On the off chance that the information being deserialized is anything but a substantial JSON record, a JSONDecodeError will be raised.

Changed in version 3.6: **All parameters are now keyword-only.**

decode(*s*)

Return the Python representation of *s* (a str instance containing a JSON document).

JSONDecodeError will be raised if the given JSON document is not valid.

raw_decode(*s*)

Decode a JSON document from s (a str starting with a JSON document) and return a 2-tuple of the Python portrayal and the file in s where the document finished.

This can be utilized to decode a JSON document from a string that may have superfluous data toward the end.

class json.**JSONEncoder**(**, skipkeys=False, ensure_ascii=True, check_circular=True, allow_nan=True, sort_keys=False, indent=None, separators=None, default=None*)

Extensible JSON encoder for Python data structures. Supports the following objects and types by default:

Python	JSON
list, tuple	array
Str	string
int, float, int- & float-derived Enums	number
True	true
False	false
None	null

Changed in version 3.4: Added support for int- and float-derived Enum classes.

To stretch out this to perceive different objects, subclass and execute a default() method with another method that returns a serializable object for o if conceivable, else it should call the superclass usage (to raise TypeError).

In the event that skipkeys is false (the default), it is a TypeError to endeavor encoding of keys that are not str, int,float or None. On the off chance that skipkeys is valid, such things are just skipped.

In the event that ensure_ascii is valid (the default), the yield is ensured to have all approaching non-ASCII characters got away. On the off chance that ensure_ascii is false, these characters will be yield as it stands.

On the off chance that check_circular is valid (the default), lists, dicts, and exclusively encoded objects will be checked for circular references amid encoding to keep an endless recursion (which would cause an OverflowError). Something else, no such check happens.

In the event that allow_nan is valid (the default), NaN, Infinity, and - Infinity will be encoded all things considered. This conduct isn't JSON specification agreeable, yet is steady with most JavaScript based encoders and decoders. Else, it will be a ValueError to encode such floats.

In the event that sort_keys is valid (default: False), the yield of dictionaries will be arranged by key; this is valuable for relapse tests to guarantee that JSON serializations can be contrasted on multi day-with day premise.

In the event that indent is a non-negative integer or string, JSON exhibit components and object individuals will be pretty-printed with that indent level. An indent level of 0, negative, or "will just embed newlines. None (the default) chooses the most conservative portrayal. Utilizing a positive integer indent values that numerous spaces per level. On the off chance that indent is a string, (for example, "\t"), that string is utilized to indent each level.

Changed in version 3.2: **Allow strings for** *indent* **in addition to integers.**

If specified, *separators* should be an (item_separator, key_separator) tuple. The default is (', ', ':') if *indent* is None and (',', ': ') otherwise. To get the most compact JSON representation, you should specify (',', ':') to eliminate whitespace.

Changed in version 3.4: **Use (',', ': ') as default if** *indent* **is not None.**

If specified, default ought to be a function that gets called for objects that can't generally be serialized. It should return a JSON encodable version of the object or raise a TypeError. If not indicated, TypeError is raised.

Changed in version 3.6: **All parameters are now keyword-only.** **default(*o*)**

Implement this method in a subclass such that it returns a serializable object for o, or calls the base implementation (to raise a TypeError).

For instance, to help arbitrary iterators, you could implement default this way:

```
def default(self, o):
try:
iterable = iter(o)
except TypeError:
pass else:
return list(iterable)
# Let the base class default method raise the TypeError
return json.JSONEncoder.default(self, o)
```

Exception handling Python packages – HTTPLib

The **httplib** module has been renamed to **http.client** in Python 3.0. The 2to3 tool will automatically adapt imports when converting your sources to 3.0.

This module characterizes classes which actualize the client side of the HTTP and HTTPS protocols. It is ordinarily not utilized straightforwardly — the module urllibuses it to deal with URLs that utilization HTTP and HTTPS.

The public interface for this module changed generously in Python 2.0. The HTTP class is held just for in backward similarity with 1.5.2. It ought not be utilized in new code. Allude to the online docstrings for use.

The module gives the accompanying classes:

class httplib.**HTTPConnection** (host[, port[, strict[, timeout]]])

A HTTPConnection instance speaks to one transaction with a HTTP server. It ought to be instantiated passing it a host and optional port number. On the off chance that no port number is passed, the port is extricated from the host string in the event that it has the frame host:port, else the default HTTP port (80) is utilized. Whenever True, the optional parameter strict causes

BadStatusLine to be raised if the status line can't be parsed as a valid HTTP/1.0 or 1.1 status line. In the event that the discretionary timeout parameter is given, blocking operations (like connection attempts) will timeout after that numerous seconds (in the event that it isn't given, the global default timeout setting is utilized).

For instance, the accompanying calls all make instances that associate with the server at a similar host and port:

```
>>> h1 = httplib.HTTPConnection('www.cwi.nl')>>> h2 =
httplib.HTTPConnection('www.cwi.nl:80')>>> h3 = httplib.
HTTPConnection('www.cwi.nl', 80)>>> h3 = httplib.
HTTPConnection('www.cwi.nl', 80, timeout=10)
```

New in version 2.0.: Changed in version 2.6: timeout was added.

class httplib.**HTTPSConnection**(host[, port[, key_file[, cert_file[, strict[, timeout]]]]]])

A subclass of HTTPConnection that utilizes SSL for communication with secure servers. Default port is 443. key_file is the name of a PEM formatted file that contains your private key. cert_file is a PEM formatted certificate chain file.

Changed in version 2.6: timeout was added.

class httplib.**HTTPResponse**(sock[, debuglevel=0][, strict=0])

Class whose instances are returned upon successful connection. Not instantiated specifically by client.

New in version 2.0.

The following exceptions are raised as appropriate:

exception httplib.**HTTPException**

The base class of other exceptions in this module. It is a subclass of Exception.

New in version 2.0.

exception httplib.**NotConnected**

A subclass of **HTTPException**.

New in version 2.0.

exception httplib.**InvalidURL**

A subclass of HTTPException, raised if a port is given and is either non-numeric or empty.

New in version 2.3.

exception httplib.**UnknownProtocol**

A subclass of **HTTPException**.

New in version 2.0.

exception httplib.**UnknownTransferEncoding**

A subclass of **HTTPException**.

New in version 2.0.

exception httplib.**UnimplementedFileMode**

A subclass of **HTTPException**.

New in version 2.0.

exception httplib.**IncompleteRead**

A subclass of **HTTPException**.

New in version 2.0.

exception httplib.**ImproperConnectionState**

A subclass of **HTTPException**.

New in version 2.0.

exception httplib.**CannotSendRequest**

A subclass of **ImproperConnectionState**.

New in version 2.0.

exception httplib.**CannotSendHeader**

A subclass of **ImproperConnectionState**.

New in version 2.0.

exception httplib.**ResponseNotReady**

A subclass of **ImproperConnectionState**.

New in version 2.0.

exception httplib.**BadStatusLine**

A subclass of HTTPException. Raised if a server reacts with a HTTP status code that we don't get it.

New in version 2.0.

The constants defined in this module are:

httplib.**HTTP_PORT**

The default port for the HTTP protocol (always 80).

httplib.**HTTPS_PORT**

The default port for the HTTPS protocol (always 443). and also the following constants for integer status codes:

Constant	Value	Definition
CONTINUE	100	HTTP/1.1, RFC 2616, Section 10.1.1
SWITCHING_PROTOCOLS	101	HTTP/1.1, RFC 2616, Section 10.1.2
PROCESSING	102	WEBDAV, RFC 2518, Section 10.1
OK	200	HTTP/1.1, RFC 2616, Section 10.2.1
CREATED	201	HTTP/1.1, RFC 2616, Section 10.2.2
ACCEPTED	202	HTTP/1.1, RFC 2616, Section 10.2.3
NON_AUTHORITATIVE_ INFORMATION	203	HTTP/1.1, RFC 2616, Section 10.2.4
NO_CONTENT	204	HTTP/1.1, RFC 2616, Section 10.2.5
RESET_CONTENT	205	HTTP/1.1, RFC 2616, Section 10.2.6
PARTIAL_CONTENT	206	HTTP/1.1, RFC 2616, Section 10.2.7
MULTI_STATUS	207	WEBDAV RFC 2518, Section 10.2
IM_USED	226	Delta encoding in HTTP, RFC 3229, Section 10.4.1
MULTIPLE_CHOICES	300	HTTP/1.1, RFC 2616, Section 10.3.1
MOVED_PERMANENTLY	301	HTTP/1.1, RFC 2616, Section 10.3.2
FOUND	302	HTTP/1.1, RFC 2616, Section 10.3.3
SEE_OTHER	303	HTTP/1.1, RFC 2616, Section 10.3.4
NOT_MODIFIED	304	HTTP/1.1, RFC 2616, Section 10.3.5
USE_PROXY	305	HTTP/1.1, RFC 2616, Section 10.3.6
TEMPORARY_REDIRECT	307	HTTP/1.1, RFC 2616, Section 10.3.8

BAD_REQUEST	400	HTTP/1.1, RFC 2616, Section 10.4.1
UNAUTHORIZED	401	HTTP/1.1, RFC 2616, Section 10.4.2
PAYMENT_REQUIRED	402	HTTP/1.1, RFC 2616, Section 10.4.3
FORBIDDEN	403	HTTP/1.1, RFC 2616, Section 10.4.4
NOT_FOUND	404	HTTP/1.1, RFC 2616, Section 10.4.5
METHOD_NOT_ALLOWED	405	HTTP/1.1, RFC 2616, Section 10.4.6
NOT_ACCEPTABLE	406	HTTP/1.1, RFC 2616, Section 10.4.7
PROXY_ AUTHENTICATION_ REQUIRED	407	HTTP/1.1, RFC 2616, Section 10.4.8
REQUEST_TIMEOUT	408	HTTP/1.1, RFC 2616, Section 10.4.9
CONFLICT	409	HTTP/1.1, RFC 2616, Section 10.4.10
GONE	410	HTTP/1.1, RFC 2616, Section 10.4.11
LENGTH_REQUIRED	411	HTTP/1.1, RFC 2616, Section 10.4.12
PRECONDITION_FAILED	412	HTTP/1.1, RFC 2616, Section 10.4.13
REQUEST_ENTITY_TOO_ LARGE	413	HTTP/1.1, RFC 2616, Section 10.4.14
REQUEST_URI_TOO_ LONG	414	HTTP/1.1, RFC 2616, Section 10.4.15
UNSUPPORTED_MEDIA_ TYPE	415	HTTP/1.1, RFC 2616, Section 10.4.16
REQUESTED_RANGE_ NOT_SATISFIABLE	416	HTTP/1.1, RFC 2616, Section 10.4.17
EXPECTATION_FAILED	417	HTTP/1.1, RFC 2616, Section 10.4.18
UNPROCESSABLE_ENTITY	422	WEBDAV, RFC 2518, Section 10.3

LOCKED	423	WEBDAV RFC 2518, Section 10.4
FAILED_DEPENDENCY	424	WEBDAV, RFC 2518, Section 10.5
UPGRADE_REQUIRED	426	HTTP Upgrade to TLS, RFC 2817, Section 6
INTERNAL_SERVER_ ERROR	500	HTTP/1.1, RFC 2616, Section 10.5.1
NOT_IMPLEMENTED	501	HTTP/1.1, RFC 2616, Section 10.5.2
BAD_GATEWAY	502	HTTP/1.1 RFC 2616, Section 10.5.3
SERVICE_UNAVAILABLE	503	HTTP/1.1, RFC 2616, Section 10.5.4
GATEWAY_TIMEOUT	504	HTTP/1.1 RFC 2616, Section 10.5.5
HTTP_VERSION_NOT_ SUPPORTED	505	HTTP/1.1, RFC 2616, Section 10.5.6
INSUFFICIENT_STORAGE	507	WEBDAV, RFC 2518, Section 10.6
NOT_EXTENDED	510	An HTTP Extension Framework, RFC 2774, Section 7

Exception handling Python Packages –SMTPLib

smtplib — SMTP protocol client

The smtplib module characterizes a SMTP client session object that can be utilized to send lettersmail to any Internet machine with a SMTP or ESMTP listener daemon. For details of SMTP and ESMTP operation, counsel RFC 821 (Simple Mail Transfer Protocol) and RFC 1869 (SMTP Service Extensions).

class smtplib.SMTP(*host=", port=0, local_hostname=None, [timeout,]source_address=None*)

A SMTP instance encapsulates a SMTP connection. It has methods that help a full repertoire of SMTP and ESMTP operations. if the host and port parameters are given, the SMTP connect() method is called with those parameters during initialization. Whenever determined, local_hostname is utilized as the FQDN of the local host in the HELO/EHLO direction. Something else, the local hostname is discovered utilizing socket.getfqdn(). In the event that the connect() call returns something besides a success code, a SMTPConnectError is raised. The optional timeout parameter indicates a timeout in seconds for blocking operations like the connection attempt (if not determined, the global default timeout setting will be utilized). On the off chance that the timeout expires, socket.timeout is raised. The optional source_address parameter enables binding to some explicit source address in a machine with numerous network interfaces, and additionally to some explicit source TCP port. It takes a 2-tuple (host, port), for the socket to bind to as its source address before connecting. If omitted (or if host or port are " or and/or 0 respectively) the OS default conduct behavior will be utilized.

For ordinary utilize, you should just require the initialization/connect, sendmail(), and quit() methods. An example is incorporated as follows.

>>> from smtplib import SMTP

The SMTP class supports with explanation. At the point when utilized this way, the SMTP QUIT command is issued consequently when the statement exits. E.g. Changed in version 3.3: Support for the with statement was included.

Changed in version 3.3: source_address argument was included.

New in version 3.5: The SMTPUTF8 extension (RFC 6531) is currently supported.

class smtplib.SMTP_SSL(*host=", port=0, local_hostname=None, keyfile=None, certfile=None, [timeout,]context=None, source_ address=None*)

A SMTP_SSL instance behaves on precisely equivalent to cases of SMTP. SMTP_SSL ought to be utilized for circumstances where SSL is required from the begining of the connection and utilizing starttls() isn't suitable. On the off chance that have isn't determined, the local host is utilized. On the off chance that port is zero, the standard SMTP-over-SSL port (465) is utilized. The optional arguments local_hostname, timeout and source_address have the same meaning as they do in the SMTP class. context, also optional, can contain a SSLContext and permits configuring different parts of the secure connection. If it's not too much trouble perused Security considerations for best practices.

keyfile and certfile are a legacy alternative to context, and can point to a PEM formatted private key and certificate chain file for the SSL connection.

Changed in version 3.3: context was added.

Changed in version 3.3: source_address argument was added.

Changed in version 3.4: The class now supports hostname check with ssl.SSLContext.check_hostnameand *Server Name Indication* (see ssl.HAS_SNI).

Deprecated since version 3.6: keyfile and *certfile* are deprecated in favor of *context*. Please use ssl.SSLContext.load_cert_chain() instead, or let ssl.create_default_context() select the system's trusted CA certificates for you.

class smtplib.LMTP(*host=",   port=LMTP_PORT,   local_ hostname=None, source_address=None*)

The LMTP protocol, which is fundamentally the same as ESMTP, is intensely founded on the standard SMTP client. It's normal to utilize Unix a sockets for LMTP, so our connect() method must help that and in addition an regular host:port server. The optional arguments local_hostname and source_address have indistinguishable meaning from they do in the SMTP class. To determine a Unix socket, you should utilize an absolute path for host, beginning with a '/'.

Authentication is supported, utilizing the regular SMTP mechanism. When utilizing a Unix socket, LMTP actually don't support or require any authenticationn, yet your mileage may fluctuate.

A nice selection of exceptions is defined as well:

exception smtplib.SMTPException

Subclass of OSError that is the base exception class for the various exceptions given by this module.

Changed in version 3.4: SMTPException became subclass of OSError

exception smtplib.SMTPServerDisconnected

This exception is raised when the server unexpectedly disconnects, or when an endeavor is made to utilize the SMTP instance before connecting it to a server.

exception smtplib.SMTPResponseException

Base class for all exceptions that incorporate a SMTP blunder code. These exceptions are created in a few instances when the

SMTP server returns a error code. The error code is put away in the smtp_code attribute of the error, and the smtp_error attribute is set to the error message.

exception smtplib.SMTPSenderRefused

Sender address refused. Notwithstanding the attributes set by on all SMTPResponseException exceptions, this sets 'sender' to the string that the SMTP server refused.

exception smtplib.SMTPRecipientsRefused

All recipient addresses refused. The errors for every recipient are available through the attribute recipients, which is a dictionary of the very same sort as SMTP.sendmail() returns.

exception smtplib.SMTPDataError

The SMTP server declined to accept the message data.

exception smtplib.SMTPConnectError

Error occurred during establishment of a connection with the server.

exception smtplib.SMTPHeloError

The server declined our HELO message.

exception smtplib.SMTPNotSupportedError The command or alternative endeavored isn't upheld by the server. *New in version 3.5.*

exception smtplib.SMTPAuthenticationError

SMTP authentication went wrong. Most likely the server didn't accept the username/password combination provided.

SMTP Objects

An SMTP instance has the following methods:

SMTP.set_debuglevel(*level*)

Set the debug output level. An value of 1 or True for level outcomes in debug messages for connection and for all messages sent to and got from the server. A value of 2 for level outcomes in these messages being timestamped.

Send a command cmd to the server. The optional argument args is essentially connected to the command, isolated by a space.

This returns a 2-tuple composed of a numeric response code and the genuine response line (multiline responses are joined into one long line.)

In typical operation it ought not be important to call this method unequivocally. It is utilized to actualize different methods and might be helpful for testing private extensions.

On the off chance that the connection with the server is lost while waiting for the reply, SMTPServerDisconnected will be raised.

SMTP.connect(*host='localhost', port=0*)

Connect to a host on a given port. The defaults are to connect to the local host at the standard SMTP port (25). If the hostname ends with a colon (':') followed by a number, that suffix will be stripped off and the number interpreted as the port number to use. This method is automatically invoked by the constructor if a host is specified during instantiation. Returns a 2-tuple of the response code and message sent by the server in its connection response.

SMTP.helo(*name*=' ')

Recognize yourself to the SMTP server utilizing HELO. The hostname argument defaults to the completely qualified domain name of the local host. The message returned by the server is put away as the helo_resp property of the object.

In typical operation it ought not be important to call this method expressly. It will be implicitly called by the sendmail() when necessary.

SMTP.ehlo(*name*=' ')

UNIT - V

Introduction

ZigBee is the most well-known industry remote work organizing standard for interfacing sensors, instrumentation and control frameworks. ZigBee, a determination for correspondence in a remote individual zone organize (WPAN), has been known as the "Web of things." Theoretically, your ZigBee-empowered espresso producer can speak with your ZigBee-empowered toaster. ZigBee is an open, worldwide, bundle based convention intended to give a simple to-utilize design for secure, solid, low power remote networks. ZigBee and IEEE 802.15.4 are low information rate remote networks administration measures that can dispose of the exorbitant and harm inclined wiring in modern control applications. Stream or process control hardware can be put anyplace and still speak with whatever is left of the framework. It can likewise be moved, since the network couldn't care less about the physical area of a sensor, pump or valve.

The ZigBee RF4CE standard improves the IEEE 802.15.4 standard by giving a straightforward networks administration layer and standard application profiles that can be utilized to make interoperable multi-merchant customer electronic arrangements.

The advantages of this innovation go a long ways past, ZigBee applications include:

- Home and office automation Industrialautomation.
- Medical monitoring Low power sensors HVAC control
- Building automation like security, HVAC, AMR, light control and access control.
- Consumer electronics like TV, VCR, remote and DVD/CD.
- Personal healthcare like patient monitoring and fitness monitoring.
- Pc and peripheral control like mouse, keyboard and joystick.
- Residential or light commercial control like lightening control and lawn or irrigation control.
- Industrial control, asset management control, environmental control and energy management control.

ZigBee focuses on the application area of low power, low duty cycle and low information rate necessity devices. Figure below demonstrates the case of a ZigBee arrange.

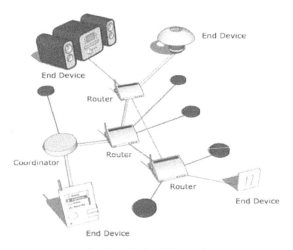

Fig. 5.1. Zigbee Network.

ZigBee is ready to end up the worldwide control/sensor network standard. It has been intended to give the accompanying highlights:

- Low power utilization, simplyimplemented
- Users anticipate that batteries will last numerous months toyears
- Bluetooth has a wide range of modes and states relying on your inertness and power necessities, for example, sniff, stop, hold, dynamic, and so on.; ZigBee/IEEE 802.15.4has dynamic (transmit/get) orrest
- Even mains fueled hardware should be aware of vitality. ZigBee devices will bemore natural than its forerunners sparing megawatts at it fullarrangement.

Low cost (device, installation, maintenance)

Low cost to the clients implies low device cost, low establishment cost and low upkeep. ZigBee devices enable batteries to last up to years utilizing essential cells (low cost) with no chargers (low cost and simple installation). ZigBee's straightforwardness takes into consideration intrinsic arrangement and repetition of network devices gives low maintenance.

High density of nodes per network

ZigBee's utilization of the IEEE 802.15.4 PHY and MAC enables networks to deal with any number of devices. This trait is basic for massive sensor arrays and control networks.

Simple protocol, global implementation

ZigBee's convention code stack is assessed to be around 1/fourth of Bluetooth's or 802.11's. Straightforwardness is fundamental to cost, interoperability, and support. TheIEEE PHY received by ZigBee has been intended for the 868 MHz band in Europe, the 915 MHz band in N America, Australia, and so on; and the 2.4 GHz band is presently perceived to be a worldwide band acknowledged in allnations.

Wireless Communication

All wireless communication networks have the following components:

- Transmitter
- Receiver
- Antenna

Path between the transmitter and the receiver. In short, the transmitter nourishes a flag of encoded information balanced into RF waves into the reception antenna. The receiving wire transmits the flag through the air where it is gotten by the radio wire of the recipient. The collector demodulates the RF waves once more into the encoded information stream sent by the transmitter.

Wireless Network Types

There are various diverse sorts of networks utilized in remote correspondence. Network types are ordinarily characterized by size and area.

WPAN

A remote individual zone organize (WPAN) is intended to traverse a little region, for example, a private home or an individual workspace. It is utilized to convey over a moderately short separation. The detail does not block longer ranges being accomplished with the exchange off of a lower information rate. As opposed to other network types, there is practically zero requirements for foundation with a WPAN. Specially appointed networks administration is one of the key ideas in WPANs. This enables devices to be a piece of the network incidentally; they can join and leave voluntarily. This functions admirably for cell phones like PDAs, PCs andtelephones.

A portion of the conventions utilizing WPAN incorporate Bluetooth, ZigBee, Ultra-wideband (UWB) and IrDA. Each of these is enhanced for specific applications or spaces. ZigBee, with its sleepy, battery-powered end devices, is an ideal fit for remote sensors. Run of the mill ZigBee application spaces include: farming, building and industrial automation, home control, medicinal observing, and security, in case we consider ourselves excessively important, toys, toys and more toys.

WLAN

Wireless local area networks (WLANs) are intended to span a relatively small area, e.g., a house, a building, or a school grounds. WLANs are winding up more pervasive as costs descend and guidelines move forward. A WLAN can be an expansion of a wired neighborhood (LAN), its passage associated with a LAN innovation, for example, Ethernet. A famous convention for WLAN is 802.11, otherwise calledWi-Fi.

WWAN

A wireless wide area network (WAN) is intended to span a large area, for example, a city, state or nation. It makes utilization of phone lines and satellite dishes and radio waves to exchangeinformation.

Wireless Network Topologies

This area talks about the network topologies bolstered by the IEEE 802.15.4 and ZigBee details. The topology of a network describes how the nodes are associated, either physically or rationale.

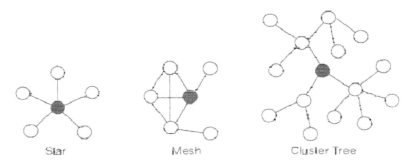

Star   Mesh   Cluster Tree

The physical topology is a geometrical shape coming about because of the physical connections from node to node, as appeared in the figure below. The logical topology maps the stream of information between the nodes.

IEEE 802.15.4 supports star and shared topologies. The ZigBee detail bolsters star and two sorts of shared topologies, work and group tree. ZigBee-agreeable devices are in some cases indicated as supporting point-to-point and point- to-multipoint topologies.

Wireless Standards

The interest for wireless solutions keeps on developing and with it new models have approached and other existing standards have strengthened their situation in the commercial center. This segment thinks about three popular wireless standards being utilized today and records a portion of the plan considerations that separate them.

Comparison of Wireless Standards

Wireless parameter	Bluetooth	Wi-Fi	Zigbee
Frequency Band	2.4 GHz	2.4 GHz	2.4 GHz
Range	9m	75-90m	Indoors: upto 30m Outdoors: upto 100m
Current consumption	60 mA (Tx mode)	400 mA (Tx Mode) 20 mA (stand-by mode)	25-35 mA (Tx Mode) 3 HA (stand-by mode)
Raw data rate	1 mbps	11 mbps	250 Kbps
Protocol stack size	250 KB	1 KB	32 KB 4 KB (for limited function end devices)
Typical network join time	>3sec	Variable, 1 sec typically	30 ms typically
Interference avoidance method	FHSS (frequency hopping spread spectrum)	DSSS (direct sequence spread spectrum)	DSSS (direct sequence spread spectrum)
Minimum quite bandwidth required	15 MHz (dynamic)	22 MHz (static)	3 MHz (static)
Maximum number of nodes per network	7	32 per access points	64k
Number of channels	19	13	16

Every wireless standard tends to the requirements of an alternate market fragment. Picking the best-fit remote standard is a critical advance in the fruitful organization of any remote application. The requirements of your application will determine the wireless standard to pick.

Security in a Wireless Network

This area examines the additional security issues presented by remote networks. The remarkable truth that, signals are going through the air implies that the correspondence is less secure than if they were going through wires. Somebody looking for access to your network require not beat the impediment of taking advantage of physical wires. Anybody in scope of the transmission can possibly tune in on the channel. Remote or not, a network needs a security plan. The primary activity is to choose what dimension of security is suitable for the applications running on your network. For example, money related organization, for example, a bank or credit association offering on the web account access would have considerably unique security worries than would an entrepreneur offering free Internet access at a bistro.

Security Risks

After you have chosen the dimension of security you requirement for your network, survey the potential security chances that exist. Who is in scope of the remote transmissions? Could unapproved clients join the network? What might an unapproved client have the capacity to do on the off chance that they did join? Is delicate information going over the remote channel? Zigbee Network Devices and their Operating Modes Two kinds of devices can take an interest in a LR-WPAN: a full capacity device (FFD) and a decrlowcostd capacity device (RFD).A RFD does not have directing abilities. RFDs can be designed as end nodes as it were. They speak with their parent, which is the node that enabled the RFD to join thenetwork.

A FFD has steering abilities and can be designed as the PAN organizer. In a star organize all nodes speak with the PAN organizer just so it doesn't make a difference on the off chance that they are FFDs or RFDs. In a shared network there is additionally one PAN facilitator, however there are other FFDs which can speak with the PAN organizer, as well as with different FFDs and RFDs. There are three working modes supported by IEEE 802.15.4: PAN organizer, coordinator, and end device. FFDs can be arranged for any of the working modes. In ZigBee wording the PAN organizer is alluded to as just "facilitator." The IEEE expression "organizer" is the ZigBee expression for"switch."

How Zigbee Works?

ZigBee basically uses digital radios to allow devices to speak with each other. A normal ZigBee organize comprises of a few sorts of devices. A network organizer is a device that sets up the network, knows about every one of the nodes inside its network, and oversees both the data about every node and in addition the data that is being transmitted/gotten inside the network. Each ZigBee arrange must contain a network organizer. Other Full Function Devices (FFD's) might be found in the network, and these devices bolster the majority of the 802.15.4 capacities. They can fill in as network organizers, arrange switches, or as devices that interface with the physical world. The last device found in these networks is the Reduced Function Device (RFD), which normally just fill in as devices that communicate with the physical world. As referenced over a few topologies are bolstered by ZigBee, including star, work, and bunch tree. As can be seen in above figure 3, star topology is most helpful when a few end devices are found near one another so they can speak with a solitary switch node. That node would then be able to be a piece of a bigger work organize that eventually speaks with the network organizer. Work organizing takes into account excess in node joins, so that in the event that one node goes down, devices can locate an elective way to speak with each other.

IEEE 802.15.4 Specification:

This chapter is an overview of the IEEE 802.15.4 detail. 802.15.4 Characterizes a standard for a low-rate WPAN (LR-WPAN).

Scope of 802.15.4:

802.15.4 is a bundle based radio convention. It tends to the correspondence needs of remote applications that have low information rates and low power utilization requirements. It is the foundation on which ZigBee is built. Figure 4 demonstrates a disentangled ZigBee stack,which incorporates the two layers indicated by 802.15.4: the physical (PHY) and MAC layers.

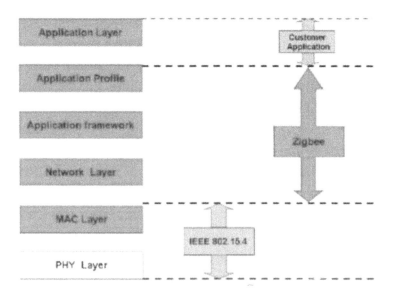

PHY Layer:

The PHY layer characterizes the physical and electrical attributes of the network. The essential assignment of the PHY layer is information transmission and gathering. At the physical/electrical dimension, this includes tweak and spreading procedures that delineate of data so as to enable them to go through the air. Details for beneficiary affectability and transmit yield control are in the PHY layer. The PHY layer is likewise in charge of the accompanying undertakings: Empower/debilitate the radio handset interface quality sign (LQI) forgot bundles vitality discovery (ED) inside the current station clear station appraisal (CCA).

MACLayer:

The MAC layer characterizes how different 802.15.4 radios working in a similar region will share the wireless transmissions. This incorporates organizing handset access to the mutual radio connection and the booking and steering of information outlines. There are organize affiliation and disassociation capacities installed in the MAC layer. These capacities bolster the self-arrangement and distributed correspondence highlights of a ZigBee organize. The MAC layer is in charge of the accompanying assignments:signal age if device is an organizer executing transporter sense different access with crash shirking (CSMA-CA) taking care of ensured schedule vacancy (GTS) network information exchange administrations for upper layers.

Property Description		Prescribed Values	
		915 MHz	2.4 GHz
Raw data bit rate		40 kbps	250 kbps
Transmitter output power		1 mW = 0 dBm	
Receiver (<1% packet error rate)	Sensitivity	-92 dBm	-85 dBm
Transmission range		Indoors: up to 30 m; Outdoors: up to 100 m	
Latency		15 ms	
Channels		10 channels	16 channels
Channel numbering		1 to 10	11 to 26
Channel access		CSMA-CA and slotted CSMA-CA	
Modulation scheme		BPSK	O-QPSK

Transmitter and Receiver:

The power yield of the transmitter and the affectability of the beneficiary are deciding elements of the flag quality and its range. Different variables incorporate any impediments in the correspondence way that reason obstruction with the flag. The higher the transmitter's yield control, the more drawn out the scope of its flag. On the opposite side, the beneficiary's affectability decides the base power required for the radio to dependably get the flag. These qualities are depicted utilizing dBm, a relative estimation that contrasts two signs and 1 milli watt utilized as the reference flag. An expansive negative dBm number means higher recipient affectability.

Channels:

Of the three ISM recurrence groups just the 2.4 GHz band works around the world. The 868 MHz band just works in the EU and the 915 MHz band is just for North and South America. Nonetheless, if worldwide interoperability isn't a prerequisite, the general void of the 915 MHz band in non-European nations may be leverage for a few applications. For the 2.4 GHz band, IEEE 802.15.4 indicates correspondence ought to happen in 5 MHz channels extending from 2.405 to 2.480 GHz.

Network Topologies:

As per the IEEE 802.15.4 particular, the LR-WPAN may work in one of two network topologies: star or shared. IEEE 802.15.4 is intended for networks with low information rates, which is the reason the abbreviation "LR" (for "low rate") is prepended to "WPAN."

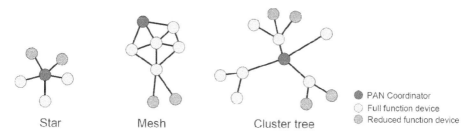

Figure: Network Topologies Supported by IEEE 802.15.4

As appeared in figure 5 over, the star topology has a focal node with every other node discussing just with the focal one. The distributed topology enables companions to discuss straightforwardly with each other. This element is fundamental in supporting lattice networks.

Addressing Modes Supported by 802.15.4

IEEE 802.15.4 supports both short (16-bit) and expanded (64-bit) tending to. An all-encompassing location is allocated to each RF module that conforms to the 802.15.4 determination. At the point when a device partners with a WPAN it can get a 16-bit address from its parent node that is novel in that arrange?

PANID

Each WPAN has a 16-bit number that is utilized as a network identifier. It is known as the PAN ID. The PAN organizer appoints the PAN ID when it makes the network. A device can attempt and join any network or it can restrict itself to a network with a specific PAN ID. ZigBee PRO characterizes an all-inclusive PAN ID. It is a 64-bit number that is utilized as a network identifier instead of its 16-bit antecedent.

ZigBee Specification

ZigBee, its particular and advancement, is a result of the ZigBee Alliance. The Alliance is a relationship of organizations cooperating to guarantee the accomplishment of this open worldwide standard. ZigBee is based over the IEEE 802.15.4 standard. ZigBee gives directing and multi-jump capacities to the bundle based radioconvention.

Logical Device Types

The ZigBee stack dwells on a ZigBee consistent device. There are three coherent device types:

1) Organizer Router

2) End device

It is at the network layer that the distinctions in usefulness among the devices are resolved. It is normal that in a ZigBee organize the organizer and the switches will be mains-fueled and that the end devices can be battery-controlled.

In a ZigBee organize there is one and just a single organizer for each network. The quantity of switches as well as end devices relies upon the application requirements and the states of the physicalsite.

Inside networks that help resting end devices, the facilitator or one of the switches must be assigned as a Primary Discovery Cache Device. These reserve devices give server administrations to transfer and store revelation data, and additionally react to disclosure demands, for the benefit of the dozing end devices.

ZigBee Stack Layers

The stack layers characterized by the ZigBee particular are the network and application structure layers. The ZigBee stack is inexactly founded on the OSI 7-layer show. It executes just the usefulness that is required in the proposed markets.

Network (NWK) Layer

The network layer guarantees the correct activity of the hidden MAC layer and gives an interface to the application layer. The network layer underpins star, tree and work topologies. In addition to other things, this is where networks are begun, joined, left and found. At the point when an organizer endeavors to build up a ZigBee arrange, it completes a vitality output to locate the best RF channel for its new network. At the point when a channel has been picked, the facilitator allots the coherent network identifier, otherwise called the PAN ID, which will be connected to all devices that join the network.

A node can join the network either straightforwardly or through affiliation. To join specifically, the framework originator should by one way or another include a node's all- inclusive location into the neighbor table of a device. The immediate joining device will issue a vagrant output, and the node with the coordinating broadened address (in its neighbor table) will react, enabling the device to join. To join by affiliation, a node conveys a signal demand on a channel, rehashing the reference point ask for on different channels until the point that it finds a worthy network to join. The network layer gives security to the network, guaranteeing both realness and classification of a transmission.

Application (APL)Layer

The APL layer is comprised of a few sublayers. The parts of the APL layer are appeared in figure 7 and examined below. The ovals symbolize the interface, called benefit passageways (SAP), between various sublayer substances.

Application Support Sublayer(APS)

The APS sublayer is responsible for:

- bindingtables
- message forwarding between bounddevices
- group address definition and management
- address mapping from 64-bit extended addresses to 16-bit NWKaddresses
- fragmentation and reassembly ofpackets
- reliable datatransport

The way to interfacing devices at the need/benefit level is the idea of official. Restricting tables are kept by the facilitator and all switches in the network. The coupling table maps a source deliver and source endpoint to at least one goal locations and endpoints. The group ID for a bound arrangement of devices will be the equivalent.

Application Framework

The application network is an execution domain for application items to send and get information. Application objects are characterized by the maker of the ZigBee-empowered device. As characterized by ZigBee, an application question is at the highest point of the application layer and is controlled by the device maker. An application question really actualizes the application; it very well may be a light, a light switch, a LED, an I/O line, and so on. The application profile is controlled by the application objects. Every applicationprotest is tended to through its relating endpoint. Endpoint numbers go from 1 to 240. Endpoint 0 is the location of the ZigBee Device Object (ZDO). Endpoint 255 is the communicated location, i.e., messages are sent to the majority of the endpoints on a specific node. Endpoints 241 through 254 are held for sometime later.

ZigBee characterizes work natives, not an application programming interface (API).

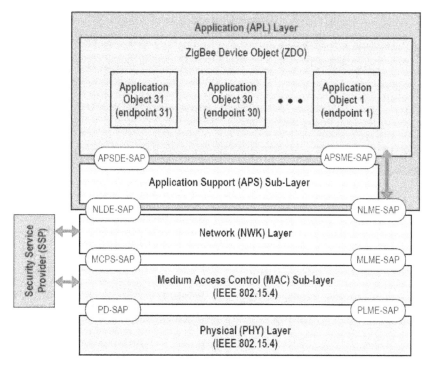

Figure: ZigBee-Defined Part of Stack

ZigBee Device Object (ZDO)

The ZDO is in charge of by and large device the board, explicitly it is in charge of:

- bindingtables
- message forwarding between bounddevices
- group address definition and management
- address mapping from 64-bit extended addresses to 16-bit NWKaddresses
- fragmentation and reassembly ofpackets
- reliable datatransport

Device revelation can be started by any ZigBee device. In light of a device disclosure request end devices send their very own IEEE or NWK address (contingent upon the demand). An organizer or switch will send their own IEEE or NWK address in addition to the majority of the NWK locations of the devices related with it. (A device is related with an organizer or switch in the event that it is a kid node of the facilitator or switch.). Device revelation takes into account a specially appointed network. It likewise takes into consideration a self-mending network. Administration disclosure is a procedure of discovering what application administrations are accessible on every node. This data is then utilized in restricting tables to relate a device offering an administration with a device that needs thatbenefit.

ZigBee Addressing

Before joining a ZigBee arrange, a device with an IEEE 802.15 consistent radio has a 64-bit address. This is a universally remarkable number comprised of an Organizationally Unique Identifier (OUI) in addition to 40 bits doled out by the producer of the radio module. OUIs are gotten from IEEE to guarantee worldwide uniqueness. At the point when the device joins a Zigbee arrange, it gets a 16-bit address called the NWK address. Both of these addresses, the 64-bit expanded location or the NWK address, can be utilized inside the PAN to speak with a device. The organizer of a ZigBee arranges dependably has a NWK address of "0." ZigBee gives an approach to address the individual parts on the device of a node using endpoint addresses. Amid the procedure of administration revelation the node makes accessible its endpoint numbers and the bunch IDs related with the endpoint numbers. In the event that a bunch ID has in excess of one trait, the direction is utilized to pass the quality identifier.

ZigBee Messaging

After a device has joined the ZigBee arrange, it can send directions to different devices on a similar network. There are two different ways to address a device inside the ZigBee organize: coordinate tending to and aberrant tending to.

Guide tending to requires the sending device to know three sorts of data with respect to the accepting device:

- Address
- Endpoint Number
- ClusterID

Roundabout tending to necessitates that the over three kinds of data be focused on a coupling table. The sending device just has to know its own location, endpoint number and group ID. The coupling table passage supplies the goal address(es) in view of the data about the source address. The coupling table can determine in excess of one goal address/endpoint for a given source address/endpoint mix. At the point when a roundabout transmission happens, the whole restricting table is hunt down any sections where the source address/endpoint and bunch ID coordinates the estimations of the transmission. When a coordinating section is discovered, the parcel is sent to the goal address/endpoint. This is rehashed for every passage where the source endpoint/address and clusterID coordinate the transmission esteems.

Broadcast Addressing

There are two particular dimensions of communicated tends to utilized in a ZigBee organize. One is a communicated bundle with a MAC layer goal address of 0xFFFF. Any handset that is alert will get the parcel. The parcel is re-transmitted multiple times by every device, hence these sorts of communicates should just be utilized when essential.The other communicate address is the utilization of endpoint number 0xFF to make an impression on the majority of the endpoints on the predefineddevice.

Group Addressing

An application can allot different devices and explicit endpoints on those devices to a solitary gathering address. The source node would need to give the group ID, profile ID and source endpoint.

The ZigBee Network Layer

Zigbee support a few network topologies; in any case, the most ordinarily utilized setups are star, work and group tree topologies. Any topology comprises of at least one organizer. In a star topology, the network comprises of one organizer which is in charge of starting and dealing with the devices over the network. Every other device are called end devices that straightforwardly speak with organizer. This is utilized in ventures where all the end point devices are expected to speak with the focal controller, and this topology is basic and simple to convey.

In work and tree topologies, the Zigbee organize is stretched out with a few switches where organizer is in charge of gazing them. These structures enable any device to speak with some other adjoining node for giving repetition to the information. On the off chance that any node falls flat, the data is steered naturally to other device by these topologies. As the excess is the primary factor in businesses, consequently work topology is for the most part utilized. In a bunch tree arrange, each group comprises of a facilitator with leaf nodes, and these organizers are associated with parent facilitator which starts the whole network. Because of the upsides of Zigbee innovation like low cost and low power working modes and its topologies, this short range correspondence innovation is most appropriate for a few applications contrasted with other restrictive interchanges, for example, Bluetooth,

Wi-Fi, and so forth a portion of these examinations, for example, scope of Zigbee, principles, and so forth., are given below.

	ZigBee	Sub–GHz	Wi-Fi	Bluetooth
Physical Layer Standard	802.15.4	Proprietary / 802.15.4g	802.11	802.15.1
Application Focus	Monitoring & control	Monitoring & control	Web, email, video	Cable replacement
Battery Life (days)	100 – 1,000+	1,000+	0.5 - 5	1 - 7
Network Size	100s to 1,000s	10s to 100s	32	7
Bandwidth (Kbits/s)	20 - 250	0.5 – 1,000	11,000+	720
Range (meters)	1 – 100+	1 – 7,000+	1 – 30+	1 – 10+
Network Architecture	Mesh	Point-to-point, star	Star	Star
Optimized For	Reliability, low power, low cost, scalability	Long range, low power, low cost	Speed	Low cost, convenience
Silicon Labs Products	Ember® ZigBee® EM35x Series	EZRadio®, EZRadioPRO®, Si10xx wireless MCUs	N/A	N/A

Fig. 5.4 Comparison Table of Zigbee

ZigBee Application Support Sublayer (APS)

The application support sublayer (APS) provides services to the application layer and the network layer through the application support data entity (APSDE) and application support management entity (APSME).

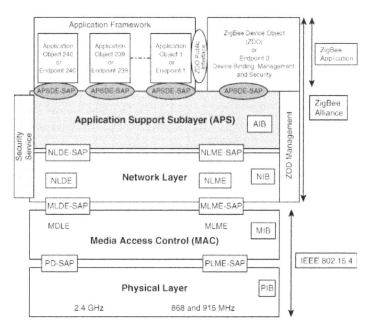

Application Support Sublayer, or APS, sits over the NWK layer, and is the layer in ZigBee which comprehends applications. The APS outline over-the-air incorporates endpoints, bunches, profile IDs, and even gatherings.

- APS is in charge of the accompanying exercises:
- Sifting through parcels for non-enlisted endpoints, or profiles that don't coordinate
- Creating end-to-end acknowlegment with retries
- Keeping up the nearby restricting table
- Keeping up the nearby gatherings table
- Keeping up the residential location

APS has the activity of filtering through bundles for endpoints that don't exist in the node. APS channels bundles that don't coordinate profile IDs. APS additionally channels copy parcels, which can occur in a network that bolsters programmed retries.

It's the activity of APS to perform programmed retries, if acknowlegment is asked for by the sender, to most extreme the shot of fruitful transmission and to educate the sender regardless of whether the bundle was conveyed.

APS additionally keeps up an assortment of utilization level tables. Restricting is tied in with interfacing an endpoint on this node to at least one endpoints on different nodes. Gatherings are around a subjective accumulation of utilizations dwelling on a self- assertive arrangement of nodes all through the network. The location outline a 64-bit MAC address with a ZigBee 16-bit NwkAddr.

APS and the Application Framework (AF) together shape the ZigBee interface utilized by applications (see Figure 4.26). Lower layers are not called upon straightforwardly, but rather are utilized by APS and ZDO The Application Framework does not have an over-the-airframe of its own, yet rather is the arrangement of schedules, or API, that the ZigBee stack merchant has decided for applications to communicate with ZigBee. This incorporates how endpoints are actualized, and how information demands, affirms, and signs are executed for that specific seller. In the Freescale arrangement, you've just observed the Application Framework at work with the capacities:

AF_DataRequest() BeeAppDataConfirm()
BeeAppDataIndication()
Furthermore, with the endPointList found in EndPointConfig.c.

While the MAC layer gives per-jump acknowledgment, the APS layer is the thing that gives end-to-end affirmations, additionally called ACKs.

To illustrate, investigate Figure 4.27. Assume a switch (the ZED) needs to turn on a light (the ZR), and it needs to check that the light got the direction. The switch utilizes the discretionary ACK include in the AF_DataRequest() txOptions field.

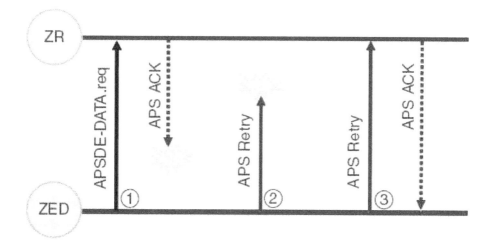

The separation between the nodes is insignificant. They could be neighbors, or 10 bounces away. The impact is the equivalent.

Assume the underlying information ask for broke through to the ZR. It at that point forms that order instantly, maybe flipping the light. In any case, the APS ACK did not make it back, for reasons unknown. So APS will consequently retry after the time-out period (which defaults to 1.5 seconds). Be that as it may, this retry, named (2), doesn't endure. APS attempts once more, and this time it succeeds. At exactly that point does APS advise the sender that the outcomes were fruitful?

Incidentally, this situation is to a great degree improbable. It is utilized only as a delineation. ZigBee utilizes something like three MAC ACKs per bounce, so except if the channel is noisy to the point that correspondence is incomprehensible, or the way is broken in light of the fact that one node has dropped off the network, or the physical condition has transformed (one of the switches along the course can never again hear its neighbors), APS ACKs are seldom called into play.

APS is sufficiently brilliant not to send the bundle up to the application twice. In Figure 4.27, both (1) and (3) endure, but since the information ask for was at that point heard at (1), the duplicate at (3) will be dropped by the APS layer after it sends the ACK to the sender. Your application doesn't must have any unique rationale to deal with copies.

ZigBee does it for you.

APS Binding

Authoritative in ZigBee enables an endpoint on one node to be associated, or "bound" to at least one endpoints on another node.

Think about a switch controlling a light, or a temperature sensor sending its information to an indoor regulator. The sender (switch or temperature sensor) is "bound" to the accepting device(light or indoor regulator).

Restricting is unidirectional, in that the change is bound to the light, however the light isn't bound to the switch.

Ties are put away locally by the sending node(the switch or temperature sensor). Each coupling table passage stores the accompanying data:

Source endpoint

Goal NwkAddr and endpoint or goal gathering Group ID

The coupling table size defaults to five sections in BeeStack, and can be set by changing gMaximumApsBindingTableEntries_c in BeeStackConfiguration.h.

In the event that numerous passages from a similar source endpoint exist in the table, different goals will be sent moreover.

say the binding table contains the entries shown in Table 4.12.

Table 4.12: ZigBee Binding Table

Src EP	Destination Addr	Addr/Grp	Dst EP	Cluster ID
5	0x1234	A	12	0x0006
6	0x796F	A	240	0x0006
5	0x9999	G	-	0x0006
5	0x5678	A	44	0x0006

On the off chance that the application, issues an AF_DataRequest() from endpoint 5 with location mode gZbAddrModeIndirect_c, at that point three information solicitations will be sent over the air, one to node 0x1234 endpoint 12, one communicate to bunch 0x9999, and one to node 0x5678 endpoint 44 in a specific order:

```
afAddrInfo_t addrInfo;
addrInfo.dstAddrMode = gZbAddrModeIndirect_c; addrInfo.
srcEndPoint = 5;
addrInfo.txOptions = gApsTxOptionDefault_c;
addrInfo.radiusCounter = afDefaultRadius_c;
Set2Bytes(addrInfo.aClusterId, 0x0006); (void)AF_
DataRequest(&addrInfo, 10, "ToggleLed2", NULL);
```

Is it beginning to wind up clear exactly how incredible restricting is?

Except if compelled by too little memory, there is no reason not to incorporate authoritative in all ZigBee devices. Authoritative, combined with the over-the-air ZDP restricting directions, enables any endpoint on any node to be associated effortlessly with any endpoint on some other node. Authoritative (or figuring out which nodes in the network talk together) is one of the basic advances when setting up a ZigBee arrange. Restricting makes it simply that a lot less demanding.

Nearby restricting directions are upheld by the APS layer. Over-the-air restricting directions are upheld by the ZigBee Device Profile (ZDP). The nearby (APSME) restricting calls (appeared in Table 4.13) return promptly in the Freescale arrangement. All things considered, they simply control in-memory tables. The over-the-air (ZDP) restricting considers issue a callback, yet I'll depict that in detail in Chapter 5, "ZigBee, ZDO, and ZDP. "

Table 4.13: ZigBee Binding Commands

ZigBee Name	Freescale Prototype
APSME-BIND.request	zbStatus_t APSME_BindRequest(zbApsmeBind Req_t *pUnbindReq);
APSME-UNBIND.request	zbStatus_t APSME_UnbindRequest(zbApsme UnbindReq_t *pUnbindReq);

ZDP.B ind_req	void
	APP_ZDP_BindUnbindRequest
	(
	    zbCounter_t* pSequenceNumber,
	    zbNwkAddr_taD estAddress,
	    zbMsgId_tB indUnbind,
	    zbBindUnbindRequest_t
	*pBindUnBindRequest
	);

ZDP.Unbind_req	void
	APP_ZDP_BindUnbindRequest
	(
	    zbCounter_t* pSequenceNumber,
	    zbNwkAddr_taD estAddress,
	    zbMsgId_tB indUnbind,
	    zbBindUnbindRequest_t
	*pBindUnBindRequest
	);

Restricting isn't required, at any rate not in Manufacturer Specific Profiles. Don't hesitate to send specifically to singular nodes, gatherings, or to utilize a communicate mode, however restricting makes the appointing procedure simpler and more adaptable. As clarified beforehand, bunches give a channel to information signs. In the event that an endpoint doesn't have a place with the gathering, it doesn't get the approaching over-the- air message. Notwithstanding coordinating the gathering ID, APS additionally coordinates the profile ID for that endpoint. On the off chance that the two IDs coordinate, the message is sent through to the endpoint. If not, the parcel is dropped. While investigating, in the event that you see a bundle going over-the-air, however the parcel isn't gotten at the information sign, check both these fields first. Having the wrong gathering or profile ID has caused me troubleshooting pain various occasions.

BeeStack monitors groups in a little table, the size of which is characterized by the BeeKit property gApsMaxGroups_c found in BeeStackConfiguration.h.

Table 4.14: APS Group Management Commands

ZigBee Name	Freescale Equivalent Function
APSME-ADD-GROUP.request	zbStatus_tA psmeAddGroup(zbApsmeAddGroupReq_t* pRequest);
APSME-REMOVE-GROUP.request	zbStatus_tA psmeRemoveGroup(zbApsmeRemoveGroupReq_t* pRequest);
APSME-REMOVE-ALL-GROUPS.request	zbStatus_tApsmeRemoveAllGroups(zbApsmeRemoveAllGroupsReq_t *pRequest);
(none)	bool_tApsGroupIsMemberOfEndpoint(zbGroupId_taGroupId,z bEndPoint_te ndPoint);

These directions are entirely simple. The ApsmeAddGroup() work adds a gathering to an endpoint. ApsmeRemoveGroup() work expels a gathering from an endpoint. ApsmeRemoveAllGroups() work expels all gatherings from an endpoint. The ApsGroupIsMemberOfEndpoint() verifies whether an endpoint is an individual from a specific gathering. Notwithstanding the APS neighborhood bunch the executives capacities, there are over-the-air directions aggregate administration works as a major aspect of the ZigBee Cluster Library. These directions incorporate AddGroup, RemoveGroup, RemoveAllGroups, AddGroupIfIdentifying and others," The ZigBee Cluster Library."

The ZigBee Device Object (ZDO) and the ZigBee Device Profile (ZDP)

The ZigBee Device Object (ZDO) is an application protest in charge of introducing the Application Support Sublayer (APS), Network Layer (NWK), and Security Service Provider (SSP). It keeps running on the saved endpoint 0 in each ZigBee device.

ZDO is normally required when building up a ZigBee item that will interoperate in an open profile, for example, Home Automation or Smart Energy, or when speaking with ZigBee devices from different sellers. The ZDO can likewise be utilized to play out a few administration capacities, for example, recurrence deftness, finding courses and neighbors, and overseeing device network.

The application profile characterized for ZDO is the ZigBee Device Profile (ZDP), which has an application profile identifier of 0x0000. ZDP is an administration and revelation benefit layer upheld on all ZigBee devices. Like every single other profile, it characterizes an arrangement of administrations that can be utilized to play out an assortment of cutting edge organize the board and device and administration revelation choices.

ZDP administrations incorporate the accompanying highlights:

- View the neighbor table on any device in the network
- View the directing table on any device in the network
- View the end device offspring of any device in the network
- Get a rundown of upheld endpoints on any device in the network
- Power a device to leave the network
- Empower or cripple the allow joining quality on at least one devices

Each administration has a relegated bunch ID, and most administration demands have a related reaction. In those cases, the customer device makes a demand, and afterward the server devicesends the reaction back to the customer device. The group ID for the reaction is actually equivalent to the bunch ID for the demand, however with the high piece set. For instance, the Network Address Request is bunch 0x0000, and the Network Address Response is 0x8000.

The following table describes some ZDP services:

Cluster Name	Cluster ID	Description
Network Address Request	0x0000	Request a 16-bit address of the radio with a matching 64-bit address
Network Address Response	0x8000	Response that includes the 16-bit address of a device
LQI Request	0x0031	Request data from a neighbor table of a remote device
LQI Response	0x8031	Response that includes neighbor table data from a remote device
Routing Table Request	0x0032	Request to retrieve routing table entries from a remote device
Routing Table Response	0x8032	Response that includes routing table entry data from a remote device
Active Endpoints Request	0x0005	Request a list of endpoints from a remote device
Active Endpoints Response	0x8005	Response that includes a list of endpoints from a remote device

Zigbee Security

Introduction

Web of Things (IoT) has turned out to be progressively prominent in the previous couple of years. In this manner, the security of the IoT devices ends up vital, particularly numerous devices approach exceedingly close to home ized and touchy information. Zigbee is a standout amongst the most broadly utilized gauges for remote correspondence between di erent IoT devices and has been embraced by many significant organizations, as Samsung and Philips. Zigbee is an open standard for low- control, minimal effort remote individual territory arranges that in-terconnect devices essentially for individual employments. The standard intends to give a two-way and solid correspondence convention for applications with a short range, normally 10-100 meters. Zigbee is im-plemented with di erent application standards utilized in an assortment of use territories, including home computerization, brilliant vitality, remote control and social insurance.Despite the fact that Zigbee was structured in view of the significance of security, there have been exchange o s made to keep the devices minimal effort, low-vitality and very good. A few sections of the standard's security controls are inadequately executed, which unavoidably prompt security dangers. This paper features the primary security dangers and aftereffects of endeavored assaults on a couple IoT devices actualized with Zigbee standard.

Responsible Disclosure

With the end goal to perform security examination on Zigbee convention, we acquired the Samsung SmartThings Node v2, the Smart Outlet, and the Iris Contact Sensor. As per the Digital Millennium Copyright Act (DMCA) security investigate exception for purchaser devices, which was in e ect since October 28, 2016, and goes on for a long time, we are legitimately directing this security examination of Zigbee convention by testing on these bought Zigbee devices. In more points of interest, the exclusion "approved security analysts who are acting in accordance with some basic honesty to direct controlled research on shopper devices in as much as the examination does not damage other laws."[1] Our venture satis es this depiction in light of the fact that rst, we have just been utilizing publicly rellowcostd projects as apparatuses to test Zigbee devices and the devices are legitimately gained. At that point, we are playing out the examination and "hacking" with great confidence since we plan to inspect the vulnerabilities of Zigbee convention as a nal venture for 6.857. This paper will likewise be distributed on 6.857 course site as extra proof for "good-confidence." Lastly, the Zigbee devices we picked are incorporated into the exception since they are intended for use by individual purchasers, rather than industry.

Security Policy

5.6.2.1 Principals

First, we introduce the ve principals in Zigbee's security policy. A graph is included to illustrate the technical components of a Zigbee network.

Owner

The proprietor of Zigbee devices buy the devices and need to build up the network with the coor-dinator and include different switches and end devices to the network. The proprietor can likewise remotely control the devices.

Other Users

Other users in the household are also a principal in the policy. They can remotely control the devices and might be able to control the network by the permission of the owner.

Coordinator

Each Zigbee organize must have one facilitator that deals with the general network. A facilitator generally works as the trust focus that gives security control of the network. The facilitator is in charge of building up the network. In that procedure, it picks the direct that is utilized in the network for the devices to impart. At that point the facilitator offers authorization to different devices to join or leave the network and monitors all the end devices and switches. Likewise, it con gures devices and empowers end-to-end security between devices. All the more imperatively, the facilitator stores and appropriates the network keys. In a Zigbee organize, the organizer can't rest and should be constantly powered.

Router

Switches in a Zigbee organize go about as middle of the road nodes between the organizer and the end devices. Switches need to join the network rst by the authorization of the organizer. At that point they can switch c between end devices and the organizer, and transmit and get information. A switch likewise ready to permit different switches and end devices to join the network. Like the facilitator, switches likewise can't rest as long as the network is established.

End Device

A Zigbee end device is the most straightforward sort of device on a Zigbee network, and usually low-power or battery-control. End devices are what the clients are more acquainted with, similar to movement sensors, contact sensors, and smartlights. The end devices likewise should join the network rst to speak with different devices. In any case, in contrast to the organizer and the switches, the end devices don't course any tra c and can't enable different devices to join the network. Because of the powerlessness to hand-off messages from different devices, the end devices can just impart inside the network through their parent nodes, regularly switches. Additionally not quite the same as the other two kinds of devices, the end devices can enter low power mode and rest to ration power. This component makes battery control feasible for end devices.

Security Measures

Zigbee cases to give best in class security instruments permitting its part organizations to make the absolute most secure IOT remote devices. Its security depends on symmetric-key cryptography, in which two gatherings must have the equivalent keys to impart. Zigbee utilizes the very secure 128-piece AES-based encryption framework. Zigbee convention is based on the IEEE 802.15.4

remote standard, which has two layers, the physical layer (PHY) and the medium access control layer (MAC). Zigbee constructs the network layer (NWK) and the application layer (APL) over PHY and MAC. As an lowcost convention, Zigbee expect an 'open trust' show where the convention stack layers trust one another. Henceforth, cryptographic insurance just exists between devices, however not between di erent layers in a device. This permits keys reusing among layers of a similar device. For straightforwardness of the interoperability of devices, Zigbee utilizes a similar security level for all devices on a given network and all layers of a device. Moreover, it sets up the rule 'the layer that starts a casing is in charge of at first securing it'.

Furthermore, Zigbee direction incorporates a casing counter to stop replay assaults (in which an assailant could record and replay an order message). The accepting endpoint dependably checks the edge counter and disregards copy messages. Zigbee additionally underpins recurrence spryness, in which its network is moved if there should be an occurrence of a sticking assault.

Security Model

To fulfill an extensive variety of utilizations while keeping up minimal effort and power, Zigbee cases to o er two network designs and relating security models: conveyed and concentrated. They di er by they way they concede new devices into the network and how they secure messages on the network. [6] A circulated security display gives a less-anchored and less complex framework. It has two devices types: switches and end devices. Here, a switch can shape a disseminated security arrange when it can't nd any current network. Every switch can issue organize keys. As more switches and devices join the network, the past switches on the network send the key. To partake in dispersed security arranges, all switch and end devices must be pre-con gured with a connection key that is utilized to encode the network key when passing it from a switch parent to a recently joined node. Every one of the devices in the network encrypt messages with a similar network key.

A concentrated security demonstrate gives higher security. It is likewise more confounded as it incorporates a third device type, the Trust Center (TC), which is typically additionally the network facilitator. The Trust Center structures an incorporated network, con gures and confirms switches and devices to join a network. The TC sets up a one of a kind TC Link Key for every device on the network as they join and connection keys for each match of devices as asked. The TC additionally decides the network key. To take an interest in a concentrated security arrange display, all substances must be pre-con gured with a connection key that is utilized to scramble the network key when passing it from the TC to a recently joined element.

Security Keys

Zigbee network and devices utilize a network key and connection keys to impart. The beneficiary party dependably realizes which keys are utilized in ensuring the messages.

A network key is a 128-bit key shared by all devices in the network, which is utilized for broadcasting correspondences. There are two kinds of network keys: standard and high-security. The sort typically controls how a network key is circulated as the network key must itself be secured by encryption when it is passed to the joining node. For this encryption, a pre-con gured connect key is utilized; this key is known by both the Trust Center and the joining device for brought together security; this key is known by all nodes in appropriated security.

A connection key is a 128-bit key shared by two devices. There are two kinds of connection keys: worldwide and one of a kind. The sort decides how the device handles different TC messages

(APS directions). In an incorporated security organize, there are three sorts of connection keys: 1) worldwide connection key utilized by the TC and all nodes in the network, 2) one of a kind connection key utilized for a coordinated connection among TC and a node, later supplanted by the Trust Center connection key, and 3) application interface key, that is utilized between a couple of devices. Here, interface keys related with the TC are typically pre-con gured utilizing an out-of-band technique, for example, QR code in the bundling, while connect keys between substances are frequently produced by the Trust Center and scrambled with the network key. In a circulated security arrange, interface keys just exist between a couple of devices.

When arrange level security is set up, application-level security can be set up for more secure correspondence. The keys for the application layer are as per the following:

- Pre-arranged worldwide connection key, as clarified previously. This key is utilized for correspondence between the TC and every single other node.

- Pre-designed one of a kind connection key, as clarified previously. This key is utilized for correspondence between the TC and one other node.

Trust Center Link Key (TCLK), which is utilized between the TC and one other node. This 128-piece key is gotten from the pre-con gured one of a kind connection key utilizing Matyas-Meyer-Oseas (MMO) hash work or haphazardly created by the TC. [6,13] This key is passed from the TC to the important node with encryption utilizing the network key and (if exists) the pre-con gured one of a kind connection key for the node. This Trust Center Link Key at that point is utilized to encode all ensuing correspondence between the TC and the significant node, supplanting the pre-con gured remarkable connection key. In any case, the node still keeps the pre-con gured interface enter on the off chance that it needs to rejoin later on.

Application Link Key, which is utilized between a couple of nodes (without the TC) to commu-nicate. This key is asked for to the TC by one of the two end devices, at that point created by the TC with relationship with the IEEE/MAC locations of the two nodes. The TC scrambles this key with the network key and, if exists, the pre- designed interesting connection key for every node to transport this key to every node. The keys utilized by a brought together security model of Zigbee convention be summarized in Figure 5.7.3.3.1.

Security Key	Description	
Network-level Security		
Network key	• Essential key used to encrypt communications between all nodes of the network • Randomly generated by the Trust Centre • Distributed to joining nodes, encrypted with a pre-configured link key (see below)	
Application-level Security		
Global link key (pre-configured)	• Used between the Trust Centre and all other nodes • Pre-configured in all nodes (unless a unique link key is pre-configured - see below) • Also used in joining to encrypt network key transported from Trust Centre to joining node • If ZigBee-defined, allows nodes from all manufacturers to join the network • If manufacturer-defined, allows only nodes from one manufacturer to join the network • Touchlink Pre-configured Link Key is a key of this type • Distributed Security Global Link Key is a key of this type	
Unique link key	Optional key used to encrypt communications between a pair of nodes - may be one of:	
	Pre-configured unique link key	• Used between the Trust Centre and one other node • Pre-configured in Trust Centre and relevant node • Also used in joining to encrypt network key transported from Trust Centre to joining node • Install Code-derived Pre-configured Link Key is a key of this type
	Trust Centre Link Key (TCLK)	• Used between the Trust Centre and one other node • Randomly generated by the Trust Centre • Distributed to node encrypted with network key and pre-configured link key (if any) • Replaces pre-configured link key (if any) but application must retain the pre-configured key in case it needs to be reinstated
	Application link key	• Used between a pair of nodes, not including the Trust Centre • Randomly generated by the Trust Centre • Distributed to each node encrypted with network key and pre-configured link key (if any)

Figure 5.7.3.3.1: Zigbee Security Key Summary for Centralized Model

Distributed Security Model

The keys used for the network and application layer in the distributed security model are as follows:

Network key, as described above. Distributed d Security Global Link Key, which is utilized to encode the correspondence between the Router parent and a joining node. This key is processing plant modified into all nodes. Pre-designed Link Key, which is additionally used to scramble the correspondence between the Router parent and a joining node. This key is additionally plant modified into all nodes utilizing authorizing apparatus. There are three kinds of this key: { Development key, which is utilized amid improvement before Zigbee accreditation. {Master key, which is utilized after fruitful Zigbee accreditation. {Certification key, which is utilized amid Zigbee confirmation testing. Toward the end, the connection key utilized ought to be the master key that demonstrates an effective Zigbee certification.

Security Architecture

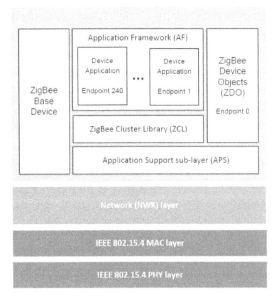

Figure 5.7.4: Outline of the Zigbee Stack Architecture

As referenced previously, Zigbee manufactures NWK and APL layers over the IEEE 802.15.4

PHY and MAC layers. The APL layer incorporates Application Support (APS) sublayer, the Zigbee Device Object (ZDO), and applications. The ZDO is in charge of dealing with the security arrangements and the secu-rity conguration of a device. The APS layer gives an establishment to adjusting ZDO and Zigbee applications.

The architecture includes security mechanisms at three layers of the protocol stack: the MAC, NWK, and APS layers.

MAC Layer Security

The MAC layer security depends on the security of IEEE 802.15.4 (in view of its specication) aug-mented with CCM. CCM is an improved counter with CBC-MAC mode task encryption plot, while CCM will be CCM with encryption-just and respectability just abilities. The MAC layer utilizes a single key for all CCM security levels (CCM all through the MAC, NWK, and APS layers). As a major aspect of the open trust demonstrates, the MAC layer is in charge of its own security preparing, yet the upper layers figure out which keys or security levels to utilize. The upper layer sets the MAC layer default key to correspond with the dynamic network key and the MAC layer connect keys to match with any connection keys from the upper layer. [5] MAC layer interface keys (which are set by the upper layer are favored. The accompanying gure demonstrates an active MAC outline in Zigbee convention with its security handling.

NWK (Network) Layer Security

The NWK layer is in charge of the handling steps expected to transmit active edges and safely get approaching casings safely.

Like the MAC layer, upper layers set up the proper keys and edge counter and build up which security level to utilize.

The NWK layer here and there communicate course ask for messages and process got course answer messages. In doing as such, the NWK layer utilizes connect keys if accessible; else, it utilizes its dynamic network key. Here, the casing position expressly demonstrates the key used to secure the edge. The accompanying gure demonstrates a case of a encrypted network layer.

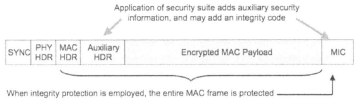

Figure 5.7.4.2.1: Zigbee frame with security at the MAC layer

key. Here, the frame format explicitly indicates the key used to protect the frame. The following gure shows an example of an encrypted network layer.

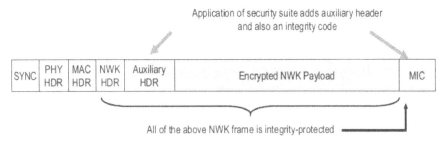

Figure 5.7.4.2.2: Zigbee frame with security at the NWK layer

5.7.4.2.3 Application (APL) Layer Security

All the security related with the APL layers is dealt with by the APS (application bolster) sublayer. The APS layer is in charge of the preparing steps expected to safely transmit active edges, safely get approaching casings, and safely set up and oversee cryptographic keys. Upper layers control the security level or the administration of cryptographic keys by issuing natives to the APS layer. The accompanying gure demonstrates a case of encoded APS layer.

In Zigbee 3.0, Zigbee convention can likewise make an application-level secure connection between a couple of devices in the network by building up an exceptional arrangement of AES-128 encryption keys between a couple of devices. This supportss the virtual private connections between a couple of devices which needs higher security. A precedent is in an utilitarian network of home territory arrange that associates numerous devices (lights, indoor regulators,occupancy sensors, entryway locks, window sensors, and carport entryway openers), an additional layer of security quali cation is built up between entryway bolts and carport entryway openers to restrain the capacity of an assailant gaining the network key to infuse messages that would open the entryway bolt; for this situation the aggressor would likewise require the connection scratch between entryway bolts and carport entryway openers.

Updates on Zigbee 3.0

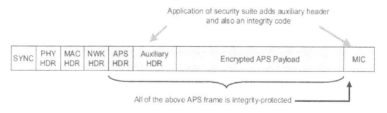

Figure 5.7.5: Zigbee frame with security at the APS layer

There is a structured "snapshot of weakness" in the Zigbee HA 1.2 specification that utilizes an outstanding symmetric encryption key known as the Trust Center Link Key to circulate a one of a kind network key when a device rst joins the network. This is a tradeo that the Zigbee Alliance made among security and effortlessness - with a moderated effect given that an aggressor would need to catch Zigbee arrange trac while another device is being joined to the network.

This strategy has been expelled from the forthcoming Zigbee 3.0 specification and supplanted with a procedure that requires a for every device establishment code that is utilized to create an interesting joining key, which is then used to procure the Zigbee organize key. The introduce code might be imprinted on the device, be a 2D standardized identification that is checked by a camera, or some other out-of-band strategy for passing the code from the end-device to the Zigbee Coordinator device (for our situation, the SmartThings Node, for example, NFC or Bluetooth Smart. Not withstanding, our devices did not support the out-of-band key foundation and rather used the Trust Center Link Key portrayed previously.

Previous Work

There have been a few undertakings done in the previous couple of years on misusing Zigbee vulnerabilities. Huge numbers of the hacks are performed on speci c Zigbee devices since di erent equipment and programming setups can confine the kinds of assaults programmers can perform. Here we give three instances of past work with Zigbee.

Killerbee

Killerbee is a Python-based network used to abuse the security of the devices actualized with Zigbee standard. Killerbee gives offices to sni ng the keys, infusing network tra c, disentangling the parcels caught, and bundle control. Killerbee was rst grown with the goal that different clients can expand the structure and construct different instruments and perform different sorts of attacks[8]. Killerbee is effectively extendable on the grounds that it has negligible library conditions. We have utilized the Killerbee network when our group assaulted the Zigbee standard with the devices we bought.A portion of the prominent apparatuses incorporated into Killerbee network include: 1) zbassoc ood, used to crash the device from too many associated stations; 2) zbdsni, used to catch Zigbee tra c and restore the key whenever discovered; 3) zbstumbler, a functioning network disclosure device that sends signal demand outlines out and returns the client data on found devices.

Security Analysis

For our Zigbee IoT setup, we obtained a few shrewd devices to actualize a Zigbee Coordinator, Router, and End Device. We additionally utilize an arrangement of devices including both equipment and programming to have the capacity to listen in on Zigbee's 802.15.4 network. These tools give us aloof listening usefulness, as well as enable us to perform parcel ooding, replay, and spoo ng assaults.

Security Analysis

For our Zigbee IoT setup, we acquired a few smart devices to execute a Zigbee Coordinator, Router, and End Device. We likewise utilize an arrangement of tools including both equipment and programming to have the capacity to listen stealthily on Zigbee's 802.15.4 network. These instruments give us aloof listening usefulness, as well as enable us to perform parcel ooding, replay, and spoo ng assaults.

Key Sniffing

Our essential assault centered us around catching a key transport from our Zigbee arrange which could possibly be utilized to decode messages and send directions to devices. Initially, we associated our RZUSB with our custom killerbee rmware to a Ubuntu Virtual Machine. We at that point called zbdump on channel 19 and yield the parcel catch information to a libpcap le. With the RZUSB sni ng for bundles, we opened the SmartThings iOS application to put the Node into matching mode.

We at that point found both the Iris Contact Sensor and the Centralite Smart Outlet and spared them to the Node's network. After the affiliation was finished, we clowcostd sni ng and ported the bundle catch information to WireShark. The results are displayed in the figure below:

9	2.999943	0x0000		ZigBee	28	Beacon, Src: 0x0000, EPID: 42:9d:ab…
10	2.999937	00:0d:6f:00:0d:ed:…	0x0000	IEEE …	21	Association Request
11	2.999937			IEEE …	5	Ack
12	2.999939	00:0d:6f:00:0d:ed:…	0x0000	IEEE …	18	Data Request
13	2.999939			IEEE …	5	Ack
14	2.999939	24:fd:5b:00:00:01:…	00:0d:6f:00:0d:ed:…	IEEE …	27	Association Response, PAN: 0xd75f A…
15	2.999976			IEEE …	5	Ack
16	2.999976	0xe6ca	0x0000	IEEE …	12	Data Request
17	2.999976			IEEE …	5	Ack
18	2.999977	0x0000	0xe6ca	ZigBee	65	APS: Command
19	2.999977			IEEE …	5	Ack
20	2.999979	0xe6ca	Broadcast	ZigBee	54	Data, Dst: Broadcast, Src: 0xe6ca

```
Counter: 110
▼ ZigBee Security Header
  ▼ Security Control Field: 0x10, Key Id: Key-Transport Key
      ...1 0... = Key Id: Key-Transport Key (0x2)
      ..0. .... = Extended Nonce: False
    Frame Counter: 24581
    Message Integrity Code: 36d88e5e
  ▼ [Expert Info (Warning/Undecoded): Encrypted Payload]
      [Encrypted Payload]
      [Severity level: Warning]
0000  61 88 ad 5f d7 ca e6 00  00 08 00 ca e6 00 00 1e   a.._....  ........
0010  d7 21 6e 10 05 60 00 00  2b 80 b3 12 5c 15 c5 78   .!n..`..  +...\..x
0020  f2 0f b0 67 29 1e 56 e6  5b 45 91 b7 f7 19 ce f5   ...g).V.  [E......
0030  ce 20 a7 67 a6 8b fc ad  66 71 6b 36 d8 8e 5e ba   . .g....  fqk6..^.
0040  c8                                                  .
```

A few things are of enthusiasm here. For the rst 9 bundles, we watch straightforward communicate messages by the Node searching for devices to include. Parcel 10 shows an Association Request by a device with just a MAC Address. After Acknowledgments and an effective Association Response in which the device is allocated another PANID, we touch base at Packet 18 which is portrayed as an APS: Command from the Node organizer to the recently included device.

Digging further into the Command bundle demonstrates to us that it is encoded with a Key-Transport Key. As indicated by the Zigbee Speci cation, a Key-Transport Key is a "key used to secure key transport messages." at the end of the day, this message spoke to a vehicle of the mutual Network Key to the recently included device, scrambled with a Key-Transport Key. After further research, we found that this Key-Transport Key is otherwise called the Trust Center Default Link Key. This Default TC Link Key is openly known to be the hex encoding of the string ZigbeeAlliance09.

With the encrypted hex key:

0xcc 0x60 0x47 0x4c 0x93 0x42 0xe2 0xf7 0x7f 0x78 0x1b 0xfb 0x26 0xe1 0xbb 0x0f 0xa1 0x15 0x79 0x13 0x64 0x92 0xde 0x6b 0xda 0x7c 0x0d 0xe2 0xd5 0xc5 0xc0 0x57 0x78 0xc4 0xa5

And the hex encoding of the Default TC Link Key:

0x5a 0x69 0x67 0x42 0x65 0x65 0x41 0x6c 0x6c 0x69 0x61 0x6e 0x63 0x65 0x30 0x39 We could decrypt the Network Key by passing it to an Advanced Encryption Standard (AES)

decrypter with the Link Key to get a plaintext Zigbee Network Key:

ef bf bd ef bf bd ef bf bd 7d 11 29 23 ef bf bd 3b 44 ef bf bd 0c ef bf bd 45 ef bf bd 79 ef bf bd 70 30 ef bf bd 1b ef bf bd 3f 44 ef bf bd ef bf bd 5e 49 ef bf bd ef bf bd ef bf bd e5 bc a3 ef bf bd 1c ef bf bd ef bf bd ef bf bd ef bf bd ef bf bd 75 5f 65 0a

This Network Key would now be able to be utilized to decode any tra c on the network including necrypted sensor readings from the Iris Contact Sensor, directions to turn the Centralite Smart Outlet On/O by the Node, or on the off chance that we had other well known IoT devices, we could even perform more evil assaults like opening entryways or changing indoor regulator temperatures. From a director point of view, access to the Network Key gives an enemy add up to control of the network. Self- assertive devices can be joined or expelled from the network including possibly vindictive ones. Subjective directions can be given to singular smart devices and the network can be disbanded voluntarily.

The way that we could find this Key ought to be extremely troubling for IoT organize proprietors. Obviously, this worry is made light of by the Zigbee Alliance in view of the short window of oppor-tunity that enemies need to sni a Key Transport. Our next assaults demonstrate that this window can really be self-assertively opened by enemies.

Association Flooding

Since we can effectively sni keys from a Zigbee organize, our next bearing of assault was to have the capacity to induce an encoded Network Key transport without requiring the proprietor to include another device. Our rst thought was to send a blast of Association Requests to devices on the network trying to make the device crash from too many associated stations. We used the following code utilizing tools from the KillerBee Python API to accomplish this:

- Association Request Frame in list form, split where we need to modify assocreqp = ["\x23\xc8",
  "", # Seq num
  "", # Dest PANID
  "\x00\x00", # Destination (coordinator)
  "\xff\xff", # Source PAN (broadcast) "", # Address field
  "\x01\x8e\x67" # Command Frame payload/assoc req
  ]
  assocreqinj = ".join(assocreqp)
  try:

- Send the associate request frame kb.inject(assocreqinj)
  time.sleep(0.05) # Delay between assoc and data requests

- Send the data request frame kb.inject(datareqinj)
  except Exception, e:
  print "ERROR: Unable to inject packet" print e
  sys.exit(-1)

After this, we would likewise tune in for an affirmation and reaction from the objective device. Utilizing the SmartThings designer web-based interface, we could decide the PANIDs for every one of the devices on our network. We then ooded every one of these device PANIDs thusly with many Association Requests (one each 10 milliseconds).

While we played out our Association Flooding assault, we attempted to get to usefulness from the SmartThings iOS application by turning on and o the Centralite Outlet and endeavoring to get to readings from the Iris Contact Sensor.

We found that in spite of the high volume of Association Requests that we were transmitting to every device, usefulness was not debilitated and we could get to and use the network as expected. There are a few conceivable clarifications for why this assault did not work. On the off chance that we had approached another RZUSB stick, we could have sni ed arrange tra c as we were ooding a Zigbee device to decide if the device was really reacting to our solicitations. In the event that we had the equipment to troubleshoot this assault, we could utilize it to crash the Zigbee Node and initiate the network proprietor to setup the network once again by re-matching all devices, giving an enemy the chance to start sni ng for a Network Key Transport.

Replay Attack

We likewise endeavored a replay assault on the Zigbee Network by infusing recently encoded and transmitted messages on the network. To execute this attack, we utilized the accompanying code actualizing KillerBee's API usefulness:

```
while args.count != packetcount: try:
packet = cap.pnext()[1]
```

- We don't want to replay ACK packets from the capture, typically. if not packet_ack(packet):
  packetcount += 1 kb.inject(packet[0:-2]) time.sleep(args. sleep)
  except TypeError: # raised when pnext returns Null (end of capture) break

We found that replaying tra c from les containing directions to turn on/o the Outlet did not initiate the Centralite Outlet to react. We verified that the reason that a replay assault was ine ective was because of the execution of a counter as a component of the encryption and validation framework. In every one of the parcels, WireShark showed a counter eld that incrlowcostd with every bundle. One counter was kept up for every device on the network being spoken with. We could hypothetically have altered these bundles to refresh the counter information to be over the present framework counter. We leave this avenue for future work.

Device Spoofing

For different specialized reasons, neither the Association Flooding nor the Replay Attack appeared to work for us. Because of conceptualizing and investigating our methodology, in any case, we conceived another assault to prompt a Network Key Transport. Our idea was to imitate a Zigbee device with a realized MAC deliver and communicate solicitations to join the network. We found that when a network proprietor needs to match another device to his network, our device will naturally be recognized and related also.

To play out this attack, we basically developed our very own information bundle dependent on a legitimate Association Request from a past parcel catch session extended below:

```
    7 9.999962                          Broadcast          IEEE …    10 Beacon Request
    8 9.999955       0x0000                                ZigBee    28 Beacon, Src: 0x0000, E
    9 9.999976       00:0d:6f:00:05:5b:…  0x0000            IEEE …    21 Association Request
   10 9.999976                                             IEEE …     5 Ack
   11 9.999996       00:0d:6f:00:05:5b:…  0x0000            IEEE …    18 Data Request
   12 0 000006                                             IEEE       5 Ack
 ▶ Frame 9: 21 bytes on wire (168 bits), 21 bytes captured (168 bits)
 ▼ IEEE 802.15.4 Command, Dst: 0x0000, Src: Ember_00:05:5b:70:9c
   ▶ Frame Control Field: 0xc823, Frame Type: Command, Acknowledge Request, Destination Addressing Mode: Sh
     Sequence Number: 64
     Destination PAN: 0x6414
     Destination: 0x0000
     Source PAN: 0xffff
     Extended Source: Ember_00:05:5b:70:9c (00:0d:6f:00:05:5b:70:9c)
     Command Identifier: Association Request (0x01)
   ▶ Association Request
     FCS: 0x25fd (Correct)
0000   23 c8 40 14 64 00 00 ff  ff 9c 70 5b 05 00 6f 0d   #.@.d... ..p[..o.
0010   00 01 8e fd 25                                     ....%
```

Notice that the packet is totally decoded, obviously, and that we essentially needed to alter the Extended Source eld and comparing hex qualities to be the MAC address of our pernicious RZUSB device. Specifically, we just replayed the hex bundle with an altered MAC address:

23 c8 40 14 64 00 00 ff ff 9c 70 5b 05 00 6f 0d 00 01 8e fd 25

When we had developed our fake parcel, we essentially replayed the bundle over the network and tuned in for an Association Response from the SmartThings Node. One issue we experienced here was the especially low latency of the Zigbee arrange. The Response and Network Key Transport were produced under 0.00004 seconds after the underlying Association Request. This didn't give us sufficient time to change the RZUSB from replaying a bundle to sni ng for the Network Key. We would require an extra RZUSB to sni the network while the other RZUSB could discharge the Association Request. Indeed, even in spite of not having the extra equipment, we found that we could effectively instigate a Key-Transport to untrusted equipment taking on the appearance of a Zigbee device.

The ZigBee Cluster Library (ZCL)

The ZigBee Cluster Library (ZCL) is proposed to go about as an archive for group usefulness that is produced by ZigBee and, as an outcome, it will be a working library with ordinary updates as new usefulness is included. A designer building another application profile should utilize the ZCL to discover pertinent group func tionality that can be consolidated into the new profile so as not to "re-invent the wheel". This additionally permits ZigBee profiles to be produced with a greater amount of a question situated style approach.

Client/Server Model

Throughout the ZCL, a client/server model is employed. This model is illustrated in Figure 5.8.1.

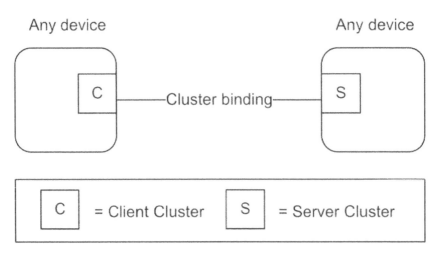

Note: Device names are examples for illustration purposes only

Figure 5.8.1. The ZCL Client Server Model

A group is a related gathering of directions and characteristics, which together characterize an interface to explicit usefulness. Commonly, the substance that stores the properties of a group is referred to as the server of that bunch and an element that effects or controls those credits is alluded to as the customer of that bunch. In any case, whenever required, properties may likewise be available on the customer of a cluster. Directions that enable devices to control qualities, e.g., in this report the read property or compose trait directions are (commonly) sent from a customer device and gotten by the server device. Any reaction to those directions, e.g., in this report the read property reaction or the compose trait reaction, are sent from the server device and gotten by the customer device. On the other hand, the direction that encourages dynamic trait announcing, i.e., the report quality order is (regularly) sent from the server device (as commonly this is the place the characteristic information itself is put away) and sent to the customer device that has been bound to the server device.

The groups supported by an application question inside an application profile are recognized through the basic descriptor (see [Z1]), determined on every dynamic endpoint of a device. In the straightforward descriptor, the application input group list will contain the rundown of server bunches bolstered on the device and the application yield bunch list will contain the rundown of customer bunches upheld on the device.

Functional Domains

The ZCL is partitioned into various utilitarian spaces, every area tending to bunches identifying with explicit usefulness. The utilitarian spaces characterized in the ZCL are recorded in Table 5.8.1

Functional Domain	Cluster ID Range
General	0x0000 – 0x00ff
Closures	0x0100 – 0x01ff
HVAC	0x0200 – 0x02ff
Lighting	0x0300 – 0x03ff
Measurement and sensing	0x0400 – 0x04ff
Security and safety	0x0500 – 0x05ff
Protocol interfaces &commercial building	0x0600 – 0x06ff
Energy	0x0700 – 0x07ff
Security credentials	0x0800 – 0x8ff
Telecom	0x0900 – 0x09ff

Table 5.8.1. Functional Domains Defined in the ZCL

ZigBee Application profiles:

Each data ask for in ZigBee is sent (and got) on an Application Profile.

Application Profile IDs are 16-bit numbers and range from 0x0000 to 0x7fff for open profiles and 0xbf00 to 0xffff for producer explicit profiles. Think about a profile as an area space of related applications and devices. Open profiles are those predetermined by the ZigBee Alliance (instead of private profiles indicated by individual OEMs).

Home Automation is an open application profile which characterizes an extensive variety of ZigBee organized devices proposed for use in the home, including lights and switches, divider outlets, remotes, indoor regulators, forced air networks, and radiators. Another open profile, Commercial Building Automation, characterizes ZigBee devices, for example, propelled lights and switches, and keyless section and security frameworks.

Any number of Application Profiles, both open and maker explicit, may exist in a solitary ZigBee organize. Truth be told, any number of profiles may exist in a solitary node on the network, isolated on various endpoints.

The ZigBee Alliance keeps on dealing with open profiles to guarantee they coordinate the necessities of OEMs delivering items. It is the OEMs in the ZigBee Alliance who characterize the profile in any case. Table demonstrates a short rundown of the ZigBee open profiles.

Table 4.10: ZigBee Public Profile IDs

Profile ID	Profile Name
0101	Industrial Plant Monitoring (IPM)
0104	Home Automation (HA)
0105	Commercial Building Automation (CBA)
0107	Telecom Applications (TA)
0108	Personal Home & Hospital Care (PHHC)
0109	Advanced Metering Initiative (AMI)

Open profiles are structured so items from one producer (X) can work, ideal out-of-the- case, with items from another maker (Y). For instance, an indoor regulator from Honeywell can work with a variable-wind stream valve from Trane, or a light from Philips can work with a change from Leviton.

ZigBee individuals may likewise apply for what is known as a private profile. Private profiles, formally called Manufacturer Specific Profiles (or MSPs), are not characterized by the ZigBee Alliance, but rather are characterized by the OEMs making the items.

Private profiles are utilized for those applications that don't have to communicate with other merchants' items.

Public Profiles

The majority of the devices imagined in Figure 4.22 are a piece of the Home Automation profile. When appointed, every one of these devices play out their fitting activities, essentially and simply.

The light switches (both on/off and dimmer) simply function as light switches should, and the temperature is sent obediently to the indoor regulator once every moment, which controls the warming as well as cooling unit. Lights might be dimmable or not, and might be three-way (flip) or two-way (on/off).

The Freescale arrangement underpins the Home Automation open profile out-of-the-box, including an expansive example of instant HA devices, for example, lights, indoor regulators, and temp sensors. Every one of the devices can be checked by the PC through the ZigBee Environment Demo (ZeD). I'll not portray the ZigBee Environment Demo more here, since the Freescale documentation as of now completes a sufficient activity.

Maker explicit profiles (MSPs) enable the OEM to characterize any arrangement of bunches, endpoints, and devices. ZigBee puts no limitations on what sort of information is transmitted, other than asking for that the information rate stay sensible, so the application doesn't flood the channel. The ZigBee Alliance relegates MSP identifiers upon solicitations from part organizations. As clarified previously, San Juan Software has been alloted a MSP that we use for preparing and demo purposes: 0xc035. Don't hesitate to utilize this MSP for your own demos, remembering that it's not appropriate for delivery items. At the season of this composition, there is no charge for a Manufacturer

Specific Profile ID. Essentially join the ZigBee Alliance and demand one.

To characterize groups in a private profile, begin by mapping out the majority of the devices that will exist in the network, and all the data they should impart. Characterize the payloads to be as little as could reasonably be expected. Usually fine and dandy to accept some data on the two sides. For instance, a solitary direction byte may do the trick. The model in this area, Example 5.10 iPod Controller, demonstrates to utilize a producer explicit profile in an application. It sends a solitary direction byte over the air on a specific bunch. That direction byte is converted into a progression of bytes that are sent over the sequential port to control an iPod.You've likely seen the greater part of the precedents in this book are absolutely programming models. That is fitting since this content is extremely about ZigBee, which beside the radio, is about programming. In any case, no inserted book is ever genuinely entire without something like one equipment venture. To make it more fun, this one includes both a ZigBee organize and an Apple iPod.Truly, in the event that you execute this model, do be watchful so you don't harm either your Apple iPod or your Freescale SRB board.

The ZigBee Gateway Specifications for network devices

A ZigBee passage device gives a correspondence course into a ZigBee PAN or PANs utilizing a TCP/IP based host application (IPHA) and the other way around; a network whereby outer applications can cooperate with individual ZigBee nodes to apply command over or to get information from those nodes or then again an instrument whereby the nodes can convey some data to the outside applications. The different dreams of what an entryway ought to be run from, toward one side, a machine that gave paired encoded remote strategy calls to an API that uncovered the majority of the Service Access Procedures (SAPs), as characterized by the ZigBee stack and IEEE

802.15.4 MAC layer detail, over a UDP based transport layer, from one perspective, through to a completely included motor that would give a graphically based portrayal of the PAN and enable the client to cooperate with the majority of the leaf nodes at the device profile level using a customary internet browser, then again. This record speaks to a bargain between those two posts that endeavors to hold the best of every portrayal without enduring either the complexities or the confinements of both of them.

The purchaser advertise portion necessitates that implementers assemble economical ZGDs, along these lines the ZGD determination will guarantee that the base required arrangement of highlights and their calculation intricacy (CPU cycles/memory utilization) is suitable while giving convincing usefulness to most home/buyer applications. An insignificant ZGD execution exchanges unit cost for expanded usage unpredictability of Host Applications.

Conversely, business, modern, and endeavor applications may expect implementers to manufacture highlight rich ZGDs that can be gotten to utilizing conventions run of the mill of those conditions. Along these lines the ZGD detail guarantees that the discretionary arrangement of highlights and capacities gives an arrangement of convincing usefulness that isn't really confined by computional multifaceted nature. A component rich ZGD usage may diminish the execution multifaceted nature of Host Applications and will permit operational modes unrealistic in an insignificant execution.

With the end goal to meet these criteria and the various requirements mulled over by the individuals from the gathering and the union, by and large, an arrangement of regular highlights dependent on the center usefulness of the ZigBee stack and the necessity of uncovering the ZigBee Cluster Library (ZCL) usefulness was characterized. This set speaks to an insignificant portal instantiation and incorporates:

- ZCL tasks to peruse and compose properties, and arrange and report occasions;
- ZDO and large scale tasks for network and administration disclosure;
- Endpoint the executives;
- Access to a ZGD's AIB, NIB, and PIB traits;
- Flexible start-up and organize join activities;
- Ability to control ZigBee security material and activity;
- Bi-directional correspondence components between a ZGD and IPHA;

Inside a ZGD these activities and capacities frame an almost indistinguishable mapping to the basic ZigBee SAPs and all things considered a ZGD demonstrations a medium through which API calls are performed. Various exemptions exist to this plan as supposed large scale works that involve totals of explicit stack capacities. These incorporate, explicitly, the network and administration revelation capacities. This kind of conglomeration, for instance, enables the host applications to find the majority of the individuals from a PAN with a solitary demand without wasting time with the hidden points of interest of crossing the whole PAN.

Various techniques are thought about with the end goal to meet the differing correspondence needs of the capacities containing the center ZGD. ZGDs and IPHAs will speak with one another by summoning remote capacities on one another; generally both ZGD and IPHA will go about as customers and servers, at the same time. Every connection pursues the standard demand reaction arrange with a discretionary timeout parameter. Through this technique each, ZGD or IPHA, will have the capacity to send messages to their partners at whatever point required. An extra specialized technique, as a get back to handler, has been incorporated to permit portals to deal with messages that begin from inside the ZigBee PAN that should be sent to the IPHA. These callback handlers give adaptability to deal with a wide scope of circumstances anyway their accepted utilize is to forward messages important to an IPHA.

The introduction of the usefulness of a door and the orderly ZigBee network to the TCP/IP based application is typified in three variations. These incorporate two web administrations introduction ties, in view of on SOAP (Simple Object Access Protocol) and REST (Representational State Transfer), both broadly embraced networks for exhibiting organized information to a host or customer application utilizing XML based reports. The third introduction official, the Gateway Remote Interface Protocol (GRIP) rides over an expansion of the ZIPT convention conceived by this gathering for ZigBee connect devices that takes into consideration educationally thick paired messages to be traded over potential secure UDP channels utilizing an ASN.1 encoding plan (the journey from the standard IETF conventions was managed by the way that no protected simply UDP based convention existed).

The expansiveness of the introduction ties gives engineers of ZigBee doors and the offices that will support and interface to ZigBee portals without any difficulty, framework cost, arrange limit, message inactivity and so on along these lines giving them the capacity to advance their expenses. The heavier web administrations based ties give generally speedy improvement ways to the detriment of heavier foundation costs rather than the paired ZIPT introduction which will require higher advancement costs however offer conceivably bring down framework and network costs.

A ZGD permits profile explicit rationale to be externalized to an IPHA by giving an arrangement of profile impartial tasks and abilities. The desire is that IPHAs might be confirmed consistent, as required, with a specific standard profile. In like manner merchant esteem include profile explicit usefulness the ZGD requires accreditation and testing like some other device.

To address different applications in an effective way, an agreeable entryway doesn't have to execute all the RPC ties; it is sufficient to actualize just a single of them, or conceivably more than one, whenever wanted. Application explicit portals that expand on the general ZigBee door detail can demonstrate which restricting must be executed, contingent upon the explicit utilize case as well as the run of the mill situation. Thusly, a profile could order one of the ties for explicit utilize cases or simply leave free the merchant to choose which authoritative to actualize (or characterize a fourth restricting not portrayed in the detail).

- ZigBee Behavior

   The activity example of a ZigBee organize containing at least one ZGDs rely upon the IPHAs associated with them. In this way IPHAs should deal with holding fast to the rules determined by [R1] for the job they are covering.

   In the regular case an IPHA performs information accumulation, at that point it will influence the ZGD to act as a concentrator. In that capacity, every one of the principles indicated in area 3.6.3.5 of [R1] ought to be connected; specifically, either the IPHA (through the PerformRouteDiscovery network), or the ZGD (through some design, whenever bolstered by the usage) ought to publicize the nearness of a concentrator by sending periodical (ordinarily one at a moment) MTORR outlines.

This ought to be finished by setting DstAddrMode parameter to zero, DstAddr parameter to 0xfffc. Span ought to be set to a sensible esteem that relies upon the measure of the network and the nearness of different concentrators, and NoRouteCache to the measure of RAM of the ZGD w.r.t. the span of the network.

- Compatibility

  The ZGD must help both ZigBee and IP conventions and usefulness, to that end it must be good with the two spaces.

- ZigBee

  A ZigBee passage will be perfect with the form of the ZigBee stack that it was intended to benefit.

- Commisioning Cluster

  A ZGD shall support the ZigBee Commissioing Cluster, as defined in [R4].

- IP

  The determination is quiet as for the points of interest of the IP stack that entryway sellers may utilize; thus a door will be good with IPv4 and conceivably IPv6 however not really both.

- Architecture

  At the dimension of the application the accompanying figure indicates theoretically how a ZigBee IP entryway could be utilized in an IPHA driven application. Through the different introduction ties (GRIP, SOAP or REST) the IPHA or the Gateway speak with one another through the execution of remote network calls (RPC) over the

IP organize. The message trades are generally of the demand reaction design, with either device being fit for creating the demand and accepting the reactions. The ask for coordinated to the door from the IPHA can be directions that are executed explicitly on the portal itself or are sent to the tended to ZigBee end node through the entryways radio interface for execution on the remote node. Alternately, asks for guided by the entryway to the IPHA would be overhauled by the IPHA as would messages starting toward the end nodes that are diverted by the door through its callback capacity and being sent to the IPHA.

The following figure provides a conceptual view of the gateway architecture:

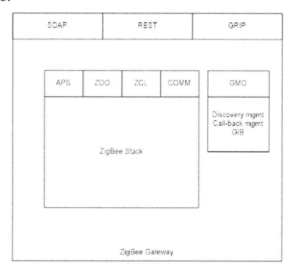

Generic Gateway

Figure 5.10.2: Conceptual Gateway Architecture

With the introduction restricting spoke to at the highest point of the figure giving the interfaces to the IP Network. Below that the Gateway application gives interfaces to Application (APS), ZigBee

326 | A Beginners Guide to Internet of Things

Device Object (ZDO), ZigBee Cluster Library (ZCL) and other Communication (COMM) layers, for example, the Network and MAC layers, and also the Gateway Management Object (GMO). These layers give access to the ZigBee stack inhabitant on the door and exercise elements of the stack.

www.ingramcontent.com/pod-product-compliance
Lightning Source LLC
Chambersburg PA
CBHW051045050326
40690CB00006B/602